48, 52, 75, 94, 97, 98,

 **W9-BAF-520**

Roelof J. Stroeker
Johan F. Kaashoek

with the assistance of L.F. Hoogerheide

Discovering Mathematics with Maple

An interactive exploration for mathematicians, engineers and econometricians

Birkhäuser Verlag
Basel · Boston · Berlin

Authors:

Roelof J. Stroeker
Johan F. Kaashoek
Econometric Institute
Erasmus University Rotterdam
P.O.Box 1738
3000 DR Rotterdam
The Netherlands

1991 Mathematics Subject Classification 00-01, 62P20, 68U99

A CIP catalogue record for this book is available from the Library of Congress, Washington D.C., USA

Deutsche Bibliothek Cataloging-in-Publication Data
Stroeker, Roelof J.:
Discovering mathematics with maple : an interactive exploration for
mathematicians, engineers and econometricians / Roelof J. Stroeker ;
Johan F. Kaashoek. With the assistance of L. F. Hoogerheide. - Basel ;
Boston ; Berlin : Birkhäuser, 1999
   ISBN 3-7643-6091-7 (Basel...)
   ISBN 0-8176-6091-7 (Boston)

The software and hardware terms referred to in this book are in most cases also registered trade-
marks and as such come under the same legal restrictions. The text, illustrations and programs have
been carefully prepared. However, the publisher and the authors accept no responsibility for errors
or their consequences.

© 1999 Birkhäuser Verlag, P.O. Box 133, CH-4010 Basel, Switzerland
Cover design: Micha Lotrovsky, Therwil, Switzerland
Printed on acid-free paper produced of chlorine-free pulp. TCF ∞
Printed in Germany
ISBN 3-7643-6091-7
ISBN 0-8176-6091-7

9 8 7 6 5 4 3 2 1

To Jean
for her unfailing support

To Ging and Arjana
for many stolen hours

Contents

List of Figures

Preface

T his book grew out of the wish to let students of econometrics get acquainted with the powerful techniques of computer algebra at an early stage in their curriculum. As no textbook available at the time met our requirements as to content and presentation, we had no other choice than to write our own course material. The try-out on a group of 80 first year students was not without success, and after adding some necessary modifications, the same material was presented to a new group of students of similar size the year after. Some more adjustments were made, and the final result now lies before you.

Working with computer algebra packages like Derive, Mathematica, and Maple over many years convinced us of the favourable prospects of computer algebra as a means of improving the student's understanding of the difficult concepts on which mathematical techniques are often based. Moreover, advanced mathematical education, be it for mathematics itself or for mathematical statistics, operations research and other branches of applied mathematics, can greatly profit from the large amount of non-trivial mathematical knowledge that is stored in a computer algebra system. Admittedly, the fact remains that many a tough mathematical problem, such as solving a complicated non-linear system or obtaining a finite expression for a multiple parameter integral, can not easily be handled by computer algebra either, if at all. However, the large quantity of immediately accessible and detailed information on many fields of mathematics, together with its fabulous computational power make a computer algebra system an indispensable tool for the future student of advanced mathematics.

One of the major reasons for our choice of the Maple package is the almost obvious way in which input lines and procedures may be written in the Maple language. In this respect we feel that Maple better fits in with higher programming languages like Pascal and C than for instance Mathematica does. The lack of serious programming capabilities make the present version of Derive an unlikely contender for Maple, at least for those users who want more than a black (computing) box. That brings us to yet another important reason for adopting the Maple system:

it is completely open. In addition to the user's own Maple lines, almost all standard library procedures can be viewed on the screen in minute detail. We firmly believe that extensive programming possibilities and versatility of the language are essential ingredients for the practical usefulness of a computer algebra system, especially for experimental purposes. It is also of some importance that a user, whose main interest lies not with the specific peculiarities of the programming language itself, can get familiar with it quickly, without having to acquire much unnecessary know-how. There is no doubt in our minds that the average user belongs to this group.

The central theme of the book is one of interaction and mutual inspiration: Maple inspires the use of otherwise unforseen or hidden mathematics and mathematical ideas inspire the often experimental way in which the Maple tool is applied to complex problems. But, of the two, mathematics comes first. This point of view is illustrated by the selection of non-trivial applications, which forms the core of the book. A natural consequence is that we are mainly concerned with mathematics and only secondarily with the specific properties of the Maple system, so that Maple's vast set of procedures is not fully covered. Our primary goal is to illustrate the practical use of a computer algebra system in the fields of Mathematical Analysis, Linear Algebra, Discrete Probability Theory and Discrete Mathematics, and in what way such a system may enrich the working environment of the practitioner of mathematics. Therefore, this book should be of interest to all students of mathematics, and not exclusively to econometricians.

Of the literature that has greatly contributed to our present knowledge of Maple, we should mention the works of Corless [6] and Heck [11]; most likely their influence will not go unnoticed. Further Engel in his book [7] definitely influenced our choice of problems by which Maple techniques are demonstrated; for instance, the application in 2.3 is adopted from this work (see [7, p. 8]). The subject of the Maple session in 3.3 is an adaptation of [8, Chapter 9].

Finally we wish to thank our colleagues Fons van Engelen, Henk Hoogland and Philip Thijsse for their valuable remarks. Special thanks go to our assistant Lennart Hoogerheide for scrupulously checking all Maple instructions, and for supplying a most useful Quick Guide to Selected Maple Commands (see page 203). It goes without saying that only the authors are fully responsible for any remaining error.

Rotterdam, January 1999

Plan of this Book

E xperience shows that demonstrations and lists of references are often insufficient for students and staff alike to appreciate the fact that computer algebra could be a useful instrument for themselves in their individual professional endeavors. There comes a moment when the prospective user has to sit down at the computer in order to convince himself of the usefulness of such a system—or of the opposite. 'Do it yourself' is an indispensable incitement in this case, and the course material at hand has been devised with this in mind. The structure of the book is that of a course on Maple applications within Mathematics itself. To emphasize this, we shall occasionally use the words 'course' and 'student'.

One should realize however that a computer algebra system can be done justice only at the hands of someone with a reasonable understanding and knowledge of mathematics. Therefore, a beginning student who is still struggling with the basic principles of mathematics, needs careful guidance when introduced to a computer algebra system. One of the objectives is to help the student deepen his understanding of difficult mathematical concepts and to teach him at the same time to put these in the correct perspective. It is our firm belief that computer algebra can be of help in our attempt to achieve this.

The Book

These main reasons made us choose for the worksheet form as the one most fitting our plans. After careful reading of the text, the student should work his way through several worksheets interactively, two for each chapter. Each one of the twelve worksheets contains Maple instructions which should be acted upon one by one in the order in which they are presented. The results and output thus obtained are explained and clarified in text regions inserted between the input groups. Conscientiously working through a worksheet, which includes the scrutiny of the occasional help screen, should take no more than one hour on average. Next, the student should complete a few assignments linked to each worksheet and presented in a separate worksheet of a similar name. These 24 worksheets together with 6 special Maple sessions are available as Maple files and can be found on the CD-ROM. As Maple V Release 5 has been available for some time now, we have chosen for the worksheet standard set by Release 5. For those still working with Release 4 though, a complete set of Release 4 files can be found on the CD-ROM as well.

The software has been developed on a PC with Intel Pentium chip, running Maple V under Windows 95. However, much of the book is system independent. In particular, all Maple worksheets are completely cross-platform compatible.

Apart from the worksheets—the complete text of which is included in the book—each chapter contains a few exercises, some easy and others quite hard. Finally, at the end of each chapter an overview is given of selected Maple expressions and commands introduced and applied in the chapter in question.

Appendix A contains three 'exercises in experimentation', a name for extended assignments with an experimental flavour. Two of these were presented as final assignments to the trial groups of students partaking in the course in 1996 and 1997. In Appendix B hints are given to help the reader with the exercises; full answers are also provided, and sometimes complete solutions are included. Appendix C was compiled by Lennart F. Hoogerheide. It should prove useful especially to those who wish to find the most frequently used Maple commands corresponding to a given mathematical concept without having to experience too many frustrating or fruitless searches.

Maple Software on the CD-ROM

The Maple V Release 5 standard is used throughout the book. But—we mention it again—a complete set of Release 4 files is also available. The directory structure on the CD-ROM is as follows: the root directory has three subdirectories, Demo, Trial and Book. The former contains a demo version of Maple V Release 4 to be used under Windows 3.1, Windows 95/98 or Windows NT. The Readme.txt file explains how to install this demo version. It requires about 5MB of disk space. Not all of Maple's functions are available, and therefore it is impossible to get the full benefit of the (Release 4) book files. However, many files will run uninterruptedly.

The subdirectory Trial contains a single self extracting file with a trial version of Maple V Release 5 for the Windows platform; it can be used for a limited period only. This trial version occupies approximately 32 MB of disk space. All book files will run smoothly under it.

The Book directory has two subdirectories, R4 and R5, one for Maple V Release 4 and one for Release 5. The structure of these subdirectories is identical. Both contain six subdirectories, one for each chapter. The directory \Book\R5\Chapter1\ contains five worksheets: a Maple session TourS1.mws (the second section of Chapter 1 in the book), two worksheets TourW1a.mws and TourW1b.mws and two assignment sheets TourA1a.mws and TourA1b.mws. All subdirectories of chapter type are similar, but some contain more than the five standard files. The extra files serve a special purpose that is explained in the corresponding session or in one of the worksheets.

In the chapters to follow, we shall assume that you have copied a complete set of book files to your hard disk in the directory c:\Maple\Book\, using exactly the same directory structure.

1

A Tour of Maple V

n this chapter you will learn by example how to get on with the Maple computer algebra system (CA system or CAS for short). In getting to know Maple, we shall discover how to deal with basic concepts and techniques such as giving instructions to the computer, correcting errors in input lines, reading input and writing output files, and we shall get acquainted with first principles of Maple's programming language. For the time being we shall merely focus on getting familiar with the computer and the Maple CA system, and not on mathematics as yet. Later, in the chapters to follow, this practical knowledge will be supplemented in order to let Maple play an active role in helping you to improve your understanding of difficult mathematical concepts, and to generally enhance your overall knowledge of mathematics. These chapters introduce the use of the Maple system in branches of mathematics such as Mathematical Analysis, Linear Algebra, Probability Theory, and Discrete Mathematics. Also, in passing, we shall briefly pay attention to the graphical possibilities a CA system has to offer.

1.1 Introduction

Maple is around now for nearly two decades and since it all began around 1980 it has been under constant development by the Symbolic Computation Group of the University of Waterloo at Ontario, Canada. With Maple, complicated computations can be carried out without any trouble and without delay. But beware, you should not make the mistake of thinking that for this reason Maple falls into the category of powerful pocket calculators. Far from it. If you have any experience with computers—and who does not have this at the present time—then you most likely have worked with programming languages like BASIC, Pascal or C. In that case you will know that calculator computation is limited to the manipulation of numbers. A CA system can do much more. CA systems could be characterized by the fact that they are capable of performing calculations not only with numbers, but with symbols as well. You will undoubtedly know that in mathematics one usually manipulates all sorts of objects that do not resemble ordinary numbers; think of vector addition and matrix multiplication, and also functions, polynomials, limits, and integrals can be subjected to suitable arithmetic operations. CA systems can serve us very well in this respect. Further, a CAS can calculate limits, differentiate functions, solve (linear) systems of equations, do definite and indefinite integration and much more. All this uniquely qualifies any CAS, and Maple in particular, to assist the user in his mathematical training and help him in getting to grips with hard mathematical concepts and problems. The symbolic calculations taking part in these undertakings differ in a number of ways from the ordinary computations with numbers. Often the necessary calculations are sufficiently complicated to warrant the breaking down of their execution into several steps. Therefore, modern CA systems are interactive, so that one can wait for the result of each individual step in the calculation in order to decide what the next step should be. This interactive aspect of CA systems is very useful for experimental purposes. For instance, when a relationship is expected between several known quantities, Maple can be of great help in the discovery of a yet unknown formula. What is more, a CAS can calculate much faster and much more accurately than we can ever hope to do on our own, which makes it feasible to assess by experimentation the implications of large and complicated alternative computing processes. This could also increase our understanding of rather intricate problems.

Beside all these positive aspects of the use of Maple, a warning should also be given. First of all, one should realize that no CAS is perfect, Maple included. Perfection is impossible, as will be apparent more than once in the chapters to come. This means that answers given by the Maple system have to be treated with care and checked were possible. Furthermore, it is equally important to appreciate that the mathematical information hidden in the Maple library exceeds by far the knowledge of any individual, so that we could be in for a few surprises. Such surprises are often caused by unexpected extensions of the definitions of the relevant quantities, as illustrated by the following example.

For $n \in \mathbb{N}$, the function $f_n(x) = \cos(n \arccos x)$ is, strictly speaking, only defined for x-values in the interval $[-1, 1]$. The reason is that $\arccos x$, as the inverse function of $\cos x$, is not defined outside this interval. Nevertheless, the functions $f_n(x)$ do have meaningful—and natural—extensions outside $[-1, 1]$. You only need to recognize that, as a matter of fact, $f_n(x)$ is a polynomial of degree n in the unknown x with integer coefficients. Some simple calculations—Maple can do them quite easily—show that $f_0(x) = 1$, $f_1(x) = x$, $f_2(x) = 2x^2 - 1$, and so on.

These are the Chebyshev polynomials of the first kind. In the original definition of $f_n(x)$ given above, the special properties of the cosine function are applied in order to introduce these polynomials quickly and without having to bring in new concepts which might complicate matters unnecessarily.

With such instances in mind—that is when Maple produces an unexpected or incomprehensible result—it is good advise to consult Maple's extensive help facility. In that way, information on the definitions and characteristics of all mathematical concepts and functions known to Maple will be shown on demand, and most help windows offer a number of illuminating examples. Finally, one should not be led to believe that Maple can manage all mathematical problems known to be solvable (within reason of course). Maple can not work miracles. It can even be said that Maple does not act without explicit instruction, in other words, Maple always requires meaningful guidance. A well-considered use of any CAS always relies on the evenly balanced teamwork of user and system.

Over the years many books on Maple have been published. A number of recent works are listed in the bibliography. Also the newest official Maple reference guides are included. A useful reference guide with a nice format is Blachman & Mossinghoff [1], but only Release 3 commands are covered. Also Redfern [16] has a pleasant format to work with.

1.2   Maple's User Interface

We shall be very brief about Maple's User interface. Under all platforms, Maple's interface is essentially the same. Therefore there is some justification for restricting our discussion to Maple's MS-Windows interface. We assume the reader possesses some proficiency with one of Microsoft's Window interfaces for the PC, to wit MS-Windows 3.1 under DOS, Windows 95/98, or Windows NT.

The way in which Maple operates and behaves under these operating systems does not differ in any significant way from that of most other Windows applications. Activating a Maple command, joining input groups, handling text regions, and other practicalities are almost always obvious to anyone having a basic familiarity with Windows. Moreover, typical Maple information is clearly documented and can be found under the help menu.

In figure 1.1 below a worksheet is shown of Maple V Release 5 under Windows95 with some of the Chebyshev polynomials referred to in the preceding section.

At this point we wish to give a brief word of advise. When getting familiar with a new Windows application it is good practice to quickly run through all major menu options just once. Make a note of those options you feel uncomfortable with at first. When an opportunity presents itself, look up the required information on these not quite obvious tools in Maple's help system. Acting in this way could save you a considerable amount of time, and what is even more desirable, it could avoid unnecessary frustration. For problems, typical to the Maple system, the official printed documentation like [10] and [15] can be quite helpful.

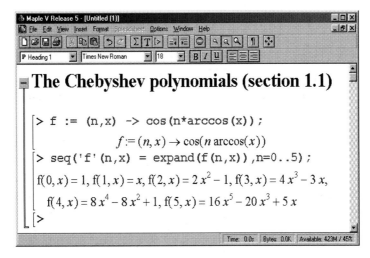

Figure 1.1: Maple worksheet with Chebyshev polynomials

1.3   Just a Maple Session

Under Windows the Maple system is activated by clicking the left mouse button on the Maple icon. An empty worksheet opens with the name Untitled(1) as in figure 1.1 and a Maple prompt ($>$) appears on the first line. More than one worksheet can be open at the same time.The Maple system incorporates a very comprehensive help facility, which can be called upon by typing a question mark after the prompt. If you happen to know the precise Maple expression you need to be helped with, then ?keyword will get you a help window with lots of information on keyword. If help is requested for a word unknown to Maple, an error window appears with the message that help is not available on this word. If uncertain about the correctness of a Maple command, it is advisable to browse the Maple help system. It allows you to explore Maple's commands and features in different ways.

In this session we shall run through a number of examples in order to show the use of Maple as a calculator. But we shall not attempt to give a complete picture of the Maple commands we use. The details will be left to the introductory worksheets TourW1a.mws and TourW1b.mws. This session is merely meant to provide an overall view of the possibilities, without giving much attention to individual commands and all their special features. So, immediate and complete understanding is unlikely and not strictly required. In the worksheets that follow this session, more attention is paid to the details.

1.3.1 Numerical Calculations

We shall adopt the usual convention that Maple commands, constants and variables are recognizable by the font and the style. In the text, a Maple command, a variable, expression or parameter is usually printed in typewriter font, like `expression`. Maple input lines are preceded by a Maple prompt (>) and the Maple instructions are always given in the typewriter font. Finally, Maple variables in an output region are printed in italics, like *variable*.

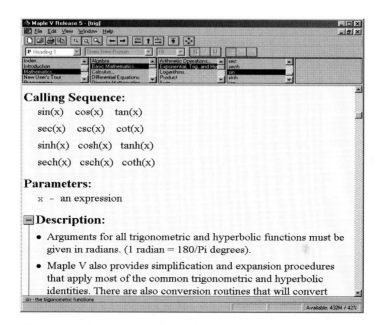

Figure 1.2: Part of Maple's help window for trigonometric functions

After starting a new worksheet, the cursor (|) blinks directly to the right of the Maple prompt. This means that Maple waits for an instruction to be given at this position. We might try `?trig` in order to find out what Maple knows about the trigonometric functions. To indicate that we have finished typing an instruction and wait for Maple to act on it, we hit the <Enter> key.

> ?trig

A help page opens with information on the trigonometric functions (see figure 1.2). From this information we learn that the Maple command sin pertains to the ordinary sine function. Verification of a few values may convince you.

> sin(0),sin(Pi/6), sin(Pi/4), sin(Pi/3),sin(Pi/2), sin(Pi);

$$0, \frac{1}{2}, \frac{1}{2}\sqrt{2}, \frac{1}{2}\sqrt{3}, 1, 0$$

Yes, we recognize the correct values corresponding to the familiar arguments of the sine function. The commas are used to separate the Maple answers and place them in a single row instead of each on an output row of its own. This Maple output row of sine values is made into a so-called 'list' by putting square brackets around it.

> whattype([%]);

$$list$$

Every complete Maple instruction must end in a semicolon (;) or colon (:). The semicolon causes the result of the instruction to appear as output on the screen. This output is suppressed when the colon is used. When the closing symbol (; or :) is omitted, nothing happens after hitting the <Enter> key, simply because Maple is waiting for the instruction to be completed. Newcomers to the Maple system often make the mistake of repeating the instruction in such a situation, with the most likely result of an error message (syntax error) being issued, because Maple tries to read the double instruction as a single one. The best advise is to type a ; in a new input region and hit <Enter> when Maple appears to be waiting.

The ditto-symbol or percentage sign %[1] refers to the last instruction processed by Maple. This symbol should be repeated once (%%) or twice (%%%) if you wish to refer to the one but last Maple instruction or the one before that, respectively. To go back any further requires Maple's history command; see Exercise 1 of section 1.5.

Further, in the previous lines, the use of constants like π (= Pi) catches the eye, and also the fact that $\sqrt{2}$ and $\sqrt{3}$ remain unevaluated. Apparently, Maple does not automatically replace such constants by approximating decimal fractions, but instead keeps working with the symbolic (and thus exact) representations like π, $\sqrt{2}$ and $\sqrt{3}$. Consider the following symbolic expression:

> symbolic_expression := 19*Pi^2 - ln(3)/(1+sqrt(2));

---

[1]In earlier releases of Maple V, the symbol " was used instead of % with the same function.

$$symbolic\_expression := 19\,\pi^2 - \frac{\ln(3)}{1 + \sqrt{2}}$$

If we happen to need a numerical value for this expression, Maple obliges on request by evaluating it to any precision required, that is to say, rounded to as many decimals as we wish.

```
>  evalf(%,50);
```

$$187.06742351094173700132102039271385066814689038057$$

The instruction `evalf(%,50)`—this means: <u>f</u>loating point <u>eval</u>uation; a floating point number, 'float' briefly, is a real number represented by a decimal fraction with a fixed but freely chosen number of digits—produces a numerical value for the quantity `symbolic_expression` rounded to 50 decimal digits. The same result can be achieved by clicking the right mouse button on the Maple output of `symbolic_expression` and selecting `Approximate` in the menu that pops up.

In general clicking the right mouse button on an expression in the Maple output produces a menu of procedures that can be applied to the expression.

The instruction `evalf(%,50)` has no effect on the exact value of the variable `symbolic_expression`.

```
>  symbolic_expression;
```

$$19\,\pi^2 - \frac{\ln(3)}{1 + \sqrt{2}}$$

Maple knows a few mathematical constants, like π and γ, the Euler constant. The names of these constants are protected, so that it is impossible to accidently assign new values to them.

```
>  Pi := 3.14159;
```

```
Error, attempting to assign to 'Pi' which is protected
```

You may assign new values or expressions to such protected names but only after using Maple's command `unprotect`; this is not really recommended.
Another well-known constant is e, the base of the natural logarithm `ln`. This constant is not a Maple constant. In fact, Maple knows the mathematical constant e as `exp(1)`. To avoid having to type the full expression `exp(1)` every time we wish to use e, we could define `e` to have this value throughout the Maple session. But beware, `e` is not a protected constant: we can redefine it if we like.

```
>  e := exp(1);
```

$$e := e$$

```
>  evalf(e), ln(e);
```

$$2.718281828, 1$$

```
>  e := 2.718; ln(e);
```

$$e := 2.718$$

$$.9998963157$$

It is possible to protect a newly defined expression in the following way:

```
>  e := exp(1):  protect('e');
>  e := 2.718;
```

```
Error, attempting to assign to 'e' which is protected
>  ln(e);
```

$$1$$

Without doubt you remember that the mathematical constant e is also equal to the limit value of the sequence $((1 + 1/n)^n)$ as n tends to infinity. Let us check to see if this is known to Maple. Note that **infinity** is also a Maple constant. As you will see below, we first use the **Limit** command with capital L. Use of a capital letter is not accidental but an indication of the so-called 'inert' form of a Maple command, which is returned unevaluated, or rather, evaluated to its name. The use of the lower case command causes the value (in this case of the limit) to appear as output. We shall return to this later.

```
>  Limit((1+1/n)^n,n=infinity) = limit((1+1/n)^n,n=infinity);
```

$$\lim_{n\to\infty} (1 + \frac{1}{n})^n = e$$

```
>  rhs(%) - e; # rhs means right-hand side
```

$$0$$

```
>  evalb(rhs(%%) - exp(1) = 0);
```

$$true$$

This confirms that Maple knows about this limit.
We repeat that Maple distinguishes between lower case and upper case, but not only in Maple commands, also in general. Therefore, e and E are totally different names with possibly totally different meanings. In fact, E is a new name, so that any value can be assigned to it, whereas e = exp(1) is still protected.

```
>  E := 2.178;
```

$$E := 2.178$$

In one of the preceding input lines we used the `evalb` command. The letter `b` comes from the name Boole, so that with `evalb` Boolean expressions are evaluated with two possible outcomes: `true` and `false`. Both are Maple constants. The sharp (`#`) is used by Maple to add comments to an input line. Text following `#` is ignored by Maple. In the current worksheet environment this option is not as useful as it used to be in previous Maple releases, because since Release 4 plain text can be put in text regions anywhere we wish.

You may have noticed that there is a difference between the equality sign $(=)$ and the assignment symbol $(:=)$. This is no surprise for those who are familiar with Pascal. The symbol $:=$ is used to assign a value (or a name) to an arbitrary string of symbols, but remember, no interspacing. The assigned value faces the side of the equality sign. It is this feature that allows Maple (and any other CA system for that matter) to do calculations with symbols, where purely numerical packages can only handle numbers. This distinguishing feature is an essential characteristic of a CAS and that is why it will run through all the forthcoming discussions.

1.3.2 Symbolic Calculations

We continue our tour with examples in which symbols are manipulated like numbers. Apart from numbers, other objects like functions, polynomials and matrices can take part in these computations.

```
>  expand((x+y)^4);
```

$$x^4 + 4\,x^3\,y + 6\,x^2\,y^2 + 4\,x\,y^3 + y^4$$

This is a familiar result; you recognize Newton's Binomium, don't you? If the exponent 4 is increased to 100, precisely 101 terms will be printed to the screen instead of a mere five. This is rather a lot, acknowledging that we most likely are not really interested in every individual coefficient. Therefore, it seems best to suppress the output.

```
>  expand((x+y)^100):
>  coeff(%,x,31);
```

$$663246383068663423796047200\,y^{69}$$

It is good practice not to accept any result face value, so we checked a more or less random coefficient, say number 31. Realizing that we are dealing with binomial coefficients, the outcome should be—apart from the y-power of course—the binomial coefficient $\binom{100}{31}$.
Let us verify this.

```
>  evalb(binomial(100,31) = %/y^69);
```

$$true$$

This is rather convincing. Also

```
>  100!/31!/69!;
```

$$66324638306863423796047200$$

should give the same result, again neglecting the y-power. Factorizing this large integer into prime numbers gives:

```
>  ifactor(%);
```

$$(2)^5 (3)^2 (5)^2 (7)^2 (11) (19) (37) (41) (43) (47) (71) (73) (79) (83) (89) (97)$$

Clearly, there are exactly five factors 2 occurring in this decomposition. Did Maple do a good job? We may gain confidence by counting the number of factors 2 occurring in the binomial coefficient $\binom{100}{31}$ in a different way, and comparing the two results.

```
>  Sum(floor(100/2^i),i=1..6) = sum(floor(100/2^i),i=1..6);
```

$$\sum_{i=1}^{6} \text{floor}\left(\frac{100}{2^i}\right) = 97$$

What does the answer mean? According to Maple, 97 is the precise number of factors 2 occurring in 100! (100 factorial). Recall that floor(x) is the largest integer $\leq x$. Hence, floor($100/m$) is the number of m-multiples ≤ 100. As $2^6 < 100 < 2^7$, which implies that floor($100/2^i$) = 0 for all $i \geq 7$, the summation index i does not need to run beyond 6. As a result, the number of factors 2 occurring in $\binom{100}{31}$ is

```
>  Sum(floor(100/2^i) - floor(31/2^i) - floor(69/2^i),i=1..6) =
>  sum(floor(100/2^i) - floor(31/2^i) - floor(69/2^i),i=1..6);
```

$$\sum_{i=1}^{6}\left(\text{floor}\left(\frac{100}{2^i}\right) - \text{floor}\left(\frac{31}{2^i}\right) - \text{floor}\left(\frac{69}{2^i}\right)\right) = 5$$

Like in **Limit** before, we used the inert form of the Maple command (capital first letter) in the left-hand side of the equality to enhance the readability. As a consequence, evaluation takes place to the name, so that the command's full name is printed to the screen. You probably won't be surprised to learn that Maple is able to differentiate and integrate. Let us choose a differentiable function (any will do), and let us instruct Maple to calculate its derivative and second order derivative.

```
>   f := exp(x*ln(1+x^2) - x);
```

$$f := e^{(x\ln(1+x^2)-x)}$$

```
>   'f' := diff(f,x);
```

$$f' := \left(\ln(1+x^2) + 2\,\frac{x^2}{1+x^2} - 1\right) e^{(x\ln(1+x^2)-x)}$$

```
>   'f''' := diff(f,x$2);
```

$$f'' := \left(6\,\frac{x}{1+x^2} - 4\,\frac{x^3}{(1+x^2)^2}\right) e^{(x\ln(1+x^2)-x)}$$

$$+ \left(\ln(1+x^2) + 2\,\frac{x^2}{1+x^2} - 1\right)^2 e^{(x\ln(1+x^2)-x)}$$

Clearly, the form of the second order derivative is rather involved. Maple does not have any trouble plotting such complicated functions. In Figure 1.3 below the graphs of the function f and its derivative f' are plotted on the interval $[-3, 1]$ and displayed together in a single picture.

Note that those names which have to be taken literally should be surrounded by left quotes as in 'f'' and 'f'''. This is necessary here, because, as we shall see, the single quote ' has a special meaning in the Maple language—this is also the case for the double quote " in Release 4. So, if we wish to use quotes as part of a name (or string), we have to put left quotes around this string.

```
>   plot({f,'f'},x=-3..1,color=black);
```

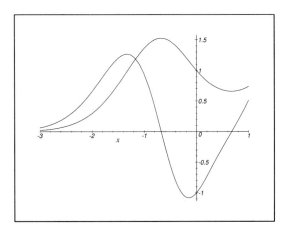

Figure 1.3: A function and its derivative

It is not so difficult to distinguish the two graphs, because f has positive values only and its derivative f' has positive and negative values. Judging by the graphs, the function f has a local maximum and a local minimum on the interval $[-3, 1]$. Indeed, the derivative vanishes at two different points which are positioned symmetrically with respect to the origin. This symmetry is obvious from the analytical form of the derivative: $f'(x)/f(x)$ is a function of x^2.

```
> fsolve('f'' = 0,x=-3..1);
```

$$-.6743390969$$

We see that `fsolve`(the letter f again comes from 'float') finds only one of the two zeros of f'. This is not a mistake in the Maple program as you might think, but an unavoidable consequence of the numerical process of calculating roots of equations. At a later stage we shall try to clarify this point.

```
> minimum, maximum =
> evalf(subs(x=-%,f)),evalf(subs(x=%,f));
```

$$minimum,\ maximum = .6560084484,\ 1.524370612$$

To verify Maple's computation of the derivative, we could try to reverse the process and calculate the indefinite integral by giving the following instruction:

```
> Int('f'',x) = int('f'',x);
```

$$\int \left(\ln(1 + x^2) + 2\,\frac{x^2}{1 + x^2} - 1 \right) e^{(x \ln(1+x^2) - x)}\, dx = e^{(x\,(\ln(1+x^2) - 1))}$$

Apparently, this is quite easy, as Maple recovers the original function very quickly. Indefinite integration—or finding a primitive—of the function f itself may prove much harder, if not impossible.

```
> int(f,x);
```

$$\int e^{(x \ln(1+x^2) - x)}\, dx$$

As was to be expected, Maple is unable to find a primitive function for f and shows this by echoing the integration formula. Note that the first letter of `int` is lower case. Therefore, the failure to produce a result can not be attributed to an inert command. In fact, Maple's lack of success does not come as a surprise, because it is impossible to express a primitive for this function f in terms of elementary functions or other special functions. On the other hand, Maple is able to calculate the definite integral of f over the interval $[-3, 1]$ without difficulty, if instructed to proceed numerically.

```
>   Int(f,x=-3..1) = evalf(Int(f,x=-3..1));
```

$$\int_{-3}^{1} e^{(x \ln(1+x^2)-x)} \, dx = 3.009051623$$

The capital letter I of Int in the right-hand side of the last input line prevents Maple from first trying to integrate symbolically before finally turning to numerical integration methods. This makes sense, because we already know that Maple is unable to integrate this function symbolically. The procedure evalf/int from the Maple library has the same objective. It is not available at startup, but has to be read from the library by

```
>   readlib('evalf/int');
```

$$\mathbf{proc}(f, e, \textit{digits}, \textit{flag}) \ldots \mathbf{end}$$

Again, note the back quotes; here the forward slash (/) is not the symbol for 'division', but merely a simple connector for joining the two commands evalf and int. In other words, it is part of the name of the procedure. The actual advantage of this procedure over the sequence of the individual commands int and evalf is that it gives more control over the precision and the numerical integration procedure we wish Maple to use. In fact Maple automatically calls evalf/int when we apply evalf after Int (with a capital I).

To complete this Maple session we give a few examples of the use of matrices under Maple. With this in mind, we first load the linalg package of linear algebra procedures. A Maple package is just a collection of Maple procedures written for a common type of application. In order to avoid making the Maple system top-heavy by including too many instantly available procedures in the default Maple library, a selection was made of generally applicable routines, that is to say, of procedures that are useful in more than one specific situation. Procedures of a less general nature are grouped in special packages. The Maple command with(), in which the name of the particular package is put between the parentheses, is used to load all procedures of this package simultaneously. During the active session all procedures of the package thus loaded into the Maple library remain instantly available.

```
>   with(linalg):
```

```
Warning, new definition for norm
Warning, new definition for trace
```

These warnings mean that the norm and trace procedures which are part of the standard Maple library are replaced by the special linalg routines of the same name.

```
>   A := matrix([[1,2,3],[2,3,5],[3,4,6]]);
```

$$A := \begin{bmatrix} 1 & 2 & 3 \\ 2 & 3 & 5 \\ 3 & 4 & 6 \end{bmatrix}$$

Let us compute the determinant of the matrix A, its trace, and its characteristic polynomial.

```
>  'determinant of A' := det(A);
>  'trace of A' := trace(A);
>  'characteristic polynomial of A' := charpoly(A,lambda);
```

$$determinant \ of \ A := 1$$

$$trace \ of \ A := 10$$

$$characteristic \ polynomial \ of \ A := \lambda^3 - 10\,\lambda^2 - 6\,\lambda - 1$$

The values of the determinant and the trace agree with the coefficients of the characteristic polynomial in as much as $-1 = -\det(A)$ and the coefficient of λ^2 is $-10 = -\mathrm{trace}(A)$. With the Maple command fsolve we can compute all zeros of the characteristic polynomial of A, including the complex ones.

```
>  fsolve('characteristic polynomial of A',lambda,complex);
```

$$-.2881244360 - .1074047995\,I, \ -.2881244360 + .1074047995\,I, \ 10.57624887$$

It is clear that A has one real and one pair of complex conjugate eigenvalues. Be warned that the Maple constant I is not used as the standard notation for the general identity matrix, but instead denotes the complex number $i = \sqrt{-1}$.

The matrix A is invertible, because its determinant does not vanish, and hence A is non-singular. Let us verify that Maple computes the inverse correctly.

```
>  evalm(A)*inverse(A) = multiply(A,inverse(A));
```

$$\begin{bmatrix} 1 & 2 & 3 \\ 2 & 3 & 5 \\ 3 & 4 & 6 \end{bmatrix} \begin{bmatrix} -2 & 0 & 1 \\ 3 & -3 & 1 \\ -1 & 2 & -1 \end{bmatrix} = \begin{bmatrix} 1 & 0 & 0 \\ 0 & 1 & 0 \\ 0 & 0 & 1 \end{bmatrix}$$

There is no doubt about the correctness of this result. By using evalm(A) (matrix-evaluation) the matrix and all its elements are printed on the screen; the input A; echoes only the name A and thus hides the matrix elements. The asterisk * is the symbol for multiplication. However, it can not be used for matrix multiplication, for which the composite symbol &* is reserved. Here we have applied the equivalent procedure multiply.

We close by mentioning that a Maple session can be ended with either one of the instructions `quit`, `done`, or `stop`. A closing semicolon or colon is not needed. Of course, a Maple session can also be ended through the E<u>x</u>it option in the <u>F</u>ile menu.

We have come to the end of this Maple session. We hope that this introductory Maple session has whetted your appetite. You can now work through the worksheets TourW1a.mws and TourW1b.mws, and try your hand at the corresponding assignments in worksheets TourA1a.mws and TourA1b.mws.

1.4 Worksheets and Assignments

1.4.1 Worksheet 1a. Numbers

It is a well-known saying that the practical side of a subject can not be fully mastered by merely reading about it or listening to experts, one needs to be actively involved. It is certainly true that in order to get some proficiency with the Maple system you need to sit down in front of the computer, switch on and start learning by doing.

• Information about this Computer Algebra Course

But before you start, you should know a thing or two about the worksheets that are part of this Computer Algebra course. The main subdirectory Book\R5 itself has six subdirectories, each corresponding to a chapter. These subdirectories contain one session, two worksheets and two assignment worksheets.

The Maple sessions are aimed at demonstrating the many possibilities Maple has to offer. Apart from the first session—this is the one we have just gone through in the preceding section—each of the remaining five Maple sessions focuses on a specific field of application. All sessions with their input groups, output, and text regions are reproduced entirely in printed form.

The worksheets can be recognized by the chapter's name: TourW1a.mws is the first worksheet associated with the session TourS1.mws and Chapter 1: A tour of Maple V. The printed form of these twelve worksheets does not include the full output, and a few input lines are left out as well. You are expected to conscientiously work through the worksheets, with close attention to the remarks and instructions.

Likewise, there are twelve assignment worksheets with similar names; for instance TourA1b.mws is the second assignment worksheet associated with the first chapter. It goes without saying that the assignments are text only.

In the present worksheet (TourW1a.mws), the first of twelve, we shall get acquainted with Maple on a very basic level. We shall see how instructions and commands should be given (input), how input errors can be discovered and removed, and learn about the way in which Maple deals with integers, rational numbers, and reals.

In the worksheet TourW1b.mws we shall pay attention to computations with variables. In Chapter 2 we will use Maple to examine functions and sequences. Chapter 3 is about matrices and vectors. In Chapter 4 attention will be paid to summation and to Maple's random generator. In Chapter 5 we will look at derivatives and integrals. Finally in Chapter 6 we will consider linear transformations, eigenvalues and eigenvectors.

- **Giving Instructions to Maple**

Usually, it will be clearly indicated which instruction should be given, but occasionally you will have to decide for yourself. The different regions or groups, composed of lines of input, output, or text are clearly distinguishable by the differences in colour and type of font. In the printed form these differences are less pronounced.

Let us start by making the active worksheet as large as possible. Next, place the cursor on the first input line, immediately after the prompt. This can be achieved by clicking the left mouse button on this position, or by using the arrow keys. Now type the following Maple instruction, and make sure to include spaces and the semicolon. Then hit the <Enter> key.

```
>   5*(17 + 21);
```

Observe that Maple immediately produces the correct answer to this most simple of exercises (5 times the sum of 17 and 21) in a newly created output region.

Also note that the cursor jumps to the next input line where it waits for your next instruction. In order to prevent the cursor from jumping too far ahead, which might make it difficult for you to read the suddenly disappearing text block in between these successive input regions, we have inserted a dummy input line following each regular input group. In print this dummy line is not reproduced. As soon as you have finished reading the text, you can move the cursor with the mouse or with the arrow keys (use the scroll bar) to the next input line following the text block. A mistake in the input can be easily corrected by moving the cursor to the relevant position in the input line after which you can remove the error with either <Del> or <BackSpace> keys.

The output of a Maple instruction cannot be edited, only copied or removed, if so required. Just place the cursor somewhere inside the output region and press the <Del> key to remove the entire output. Selecting a (large) part of the worksheet can be done by moving the cursor to the beginning of the selection and clicking the left mouse button right at the end of the selected part while keeping the <Shift> key pressed down.

Now move the cursor to the previous input line, replace the plus sign by a minus sign, and press the <Enter> key. Maple adjusts the answer by replacing old output by new.

Maple does not act on an instruction until the <Enter> key is pressed. Even then, if the instruction is not closed off by a semicolon or colon, still nothing happens. Or so it seems. In fact Maple is waiting until the input instruction is properly terminated by semicolon or colon, indicating that the input instruction is complete. Let us try and see.

Type the next instruction *without* closing symbol (; or :) and hit <Enter>.

```
>  2*(175 - 16)
```

The cursor jumps to the next input line and a warning message is issued which speaks for itself. Completing the instruction or closing it off with a semicolon (in the present case) is sufficient to force Maple into action.

Maple ignores spaces, a feature we can use to enhance the readability of the instructions, not for the benefit of Maple, but for ourselves. Only within numbers or names of commands no spaces must occur.

Next we shall find out how Maple treats numbers and in what way Maple works with the ordinary arithmetic operations of addition (+), subtraction (-), multiplication (*), division (/), and exponentiation (^). In reverse order this is the usual order of operation: multiplication before addition and exponentiation before multiplication. In case of equal priority, the execution order is from left to right. There is only one exception to this rule. Two successive exponential operations, like in 2^3^4, is not allowed. If in doubt, use parentheses or some other kind of bracketing, because operations of bracketed expressions are always executed first.

Let Maple evaluate the following nine expressions. Observe that they are separated by commas. In this way a sequence of instructions is created, which will produce a similar sequence of output results.

```
>  2 - 3 + 4, 2 - (3 + 4), 2/(3/4), 2/3/4, (2 + 5/3)*3^2,
>  2 + 5/3*3^2, 2 + 5/(3*3)^2, 2^(3^2), (2^3)^2 ;
```

Inspect the resulting output and make sure you agree with the outcome of each instruction. Observe with care the placing of the parentheses. Now give the following instruction:

```
>  2^3^4;
```

and consider the error message that Maple returns.

You probably noticed that fractions appearing in Maple output are not replaced by approximate numerical values. But Maple does write fractions in lowest terms.

Let us consider a large integer: 2 to the power one thousand will do nicely. Give the Maple code for this number, hit the <Enter> key and see what happens.

The backslash (\) marks the place where the output is broken off, to continue on the next line without interruption. Maple uses the backslash in output that is too long for one line.

Next let Maple calculate 1000!, which is, as you know, the product of all positive integers up to and including 1000.

Before we continue our tour of Maple, it makes sense to remove from the screen the very large output caused by these numbers. This can be done in several ways. First, select the relevant output region and then press the <Del> key. Alternatively, replace the closing semicolon of the corresponding Maple instruction by a colon, and hit <Enter>. Output is now suppressed, because new output replaces old.

At this point you can try and complete **assignment 1** of worksheet **TourA1a.mws** (see page 21).

In order to find out how far we can go, let us try a huge integer next. What about 2 to the power ten million?

```
>  2^10000000:
```

Apparently, even for Maple this is too large an object. Dropping the exponent to one million leaves a power of 2 that is not too large for Maple's taste; even so, one should not instruct Maple to expand this huge number, because it would take a very long time indeed. Moreover, once the calculation of this large number has started, it can not be interrupted. In other words, Maple does not react to clicking the <STOP> button on the icon bar. The only way out is the brute force way of halting the Maple program by pressing simultaneously the <Ctrl>, <Alt>, and <Del> keys (followed by End Task under Windows95), which will cause the loss of unsaved information. Generally, a computational process consists of a sequence of so-called primary calculations. A primary calculation can not be interrupted, but has to run its full course. The computational process can only be interrupted or stopped (by clicking the <STOP> button) when one primary calculation is completed and before the next one is started.

Maple is able to keep track of the time needed to complete a calculation. This can be done by means of the Maple procedure `time()`, a procedure that calculates the computing time (in seconds) elapsed since the start of the Maple session. The total amount of time Maple has used for computations can also be found in the `Time` window on the status bar.

```
>  now := time():  2^100000:  computime := time() - now;
```

Assignment 2 of worksheet TourA1a.mws (see page 21) asks for the determination of the computing time of a similar computation.

• Numerical Computations

We have established that Maple performs exact computation on integers and rational numbers, provided the integers in question are not outrageously large. These number types have in common that they can be expressed uniquely with only finitely many digits. Let us call any finite expression, exclusively built from finitely many rational numbers and the four standard arithmetic symbols (+,-,*,/), a finite representation. Irrational numbers do not have such finite representations. For instance, the number π (the ratio of the circumference of a circle and its diameter), the number e (the base of the natural logarithm), and $\sqrt{2}$ have no finite representation in this sense. In spite of this, we often like to know the approximate size of these numbers too, that is to say, how large they are compared with the unit of measurement, the number 1. We know that all real numbers can be written as infinite decimal fractions in essentially one way only. For instance, in

$$\pi = 3.141592653...$$

the first ten digits of the number π are given. But how does this decimal expansion continue? Nobody knows for sure what the billionth decimal digit of π is. Nevertheless, it is not a matter of choice, there is only one such digit. Not knowing it is of no great importance, but is does mean that in order to include π in our calculations we are forced to make do with only finitely many digits and thus with a inexact, approximate value for π. On request, Maple will transform exact values into approximate values, and what is more, we may even choose the number of digits precision Maple should use in its calculations.

Now give the following instruction:

```
>  evalf(Pi,48);
```

This gives the floating point representation of π rounded to 48 digits. Because of rounding, only the final digit may be wrong, all other digits are correct. Check this, by comparing `evalf(Pi,48)` with `evalf(Pi,50)`. With the Maple command `Digits` we can change the number of digits precision for internal computations with floats.

```
>  Digits := 50; evalf(Pi);
```

Setting `Digits` to 50 forces Maple to carry out all subsequent floating point calculations in 50 digit arithmetic with rounding.
Now reset `Digits` to 10, its default value.

As we mentioned before, exact or symbolic expressions like π, $\sqrt{2}$, $\ln 3$ and so on, can also be shown as floats. Naturally, this does not change their actual exact values; asking Maple to show 48 digits of π does not alter the value of π for future calculations! Further, floats are 'contagious' in the following sense. If an expression contains floats next to (exact) rational numbers then it automatically evaluates to a float.
Try this out by giving the following instructions:

```
>  (1/2 + 1/3)*2, evalf((1/2 + 1/3)*2), (1/2 + 1/3)*2.0;
```

In this way it is easy to calculate (approximate) values of well-known functions such as `ln` and `sin` without having to use Maple's `evalf` command.

```
>  sqrt(3), evalf(sqrt(3)) = sqrt(3.0);
>  sin(11/10), evalf(sin(11/10)) = sin(1.1);
>  evalf(ln(2/5)); ln(0.4); evalb(% = %%);
```

In the third input line we used the command `evalb`. Recall that with `evalb` Boolean expressions are evaluated with two possible outcomes: **true** or **false**.

In the next chapter we shall consider in detail the mathematical functions known to Maple, and the use of functions in general. Here let it suffice to ask Maple for information on the logarithmic function.

```
>  ?ln
```

Carefully read the information on this function; don't skip the examples, much can be learned from them.

Now turn to **assignment 3** of worksheet **TourA1a.mws** (see page 21), in which the logarithmic function should be used to determine the number of digits of the integer $2^{10000000}$.

1.4.2   Assignments 1a. Numbers

The assignments below are closely linked to the topics discussed in the first worksheet. These assignments are collected in worksheet TourA1a.mws. Extra exercises, some easy, some rather difficult, are collected in section 1.5.

1. Divide 3^{175} by 50!. What is the numerator of the resulting (reduced) fraction? How many factors 3 does the factorization of this integer contain? Use Maple's **numer** command to obtain the numerator. Then click the right mouse button on this number, after which you can choose the option **Integer Factors** from the pop-up menu[2].

2. Determine the time Maple needs to compute 5000!. What takes more time, computing 5000! or 5000^{5000}?

3. (a) Compute $\log(x)$ (the logarithm to the base 10) for the numbers $x = 56$, 123, 5120, and 98765. Use Maple's **evalf** command to obtain numerical values.

   (b) Now compute the largest integer smaller than or equal to $\log(x)$ for $x = 56$, 123, 5120, and 98765. Use Maple's **floor** function. The mathematical notation for this function is $\lfloor x \rfloor$.
   What is the relation between $\lfloor \log(x) \rfloor$ and the number of digits of the number x?

   (c) What is the number of digits of the huge integer $2^{10000000}$ (2 to the power ten million)?
   Use Maple's **floor** and **log10** commands and remember that $\log(2^k) = k \log(2)$.

1.4.3   Worksheet 1b. Variables and Names

In this worksheet we shall continue our tour of Maple which was interrupted at the end of Worksheet 1a. There we saw how Maple treats numbers and we learned about the way in which Maple can be used as a sophisticated calculator. The present worksheet is about variables, or rather about Maple's use of variables, and about names for variables and other mathematical objects. An important point is the way in which values are assigned to these objects, and how Maple evaluates them. Further we shall briefly go over the principles of programming in the Maple language. Finally we shall see how we can save our work, or part of it, in a text file, a Maple file or a Maple worksheet.

---

[2]This feature is not available in Release 4; the command **ifactor** has the same effect though.

• Symbolic Computations

So far we learned that, by nature, Maple does its calculations symbolically, and where integers and rational numbers are concerned, Maple performs exact arithmetic; numbers and results of calculations are converted to approximate decimal fractions only on explicit request of the user. Every rational number has a unique representation as an ordered pair of relatively prime integers. Because of uniqueness, one could think of this integer pair as the name of the rational number in question. Many irrational numbers also have 'names', like $\sqrt{2}$, $\ln 3$, or $\sin(\frac{1}{8}\pi)$. When such numbers are involved in computational processes, Maple leaves them unevaluated, in other words, without changing their 'names' into numerical values. As with rational numbers, Maple does exact arithmetic with such numbers. Moreover, Maple arithmetically manipulates these named irrational numbers in more or less the same way as it does ordinary numbers. Now, doing arithmetic with names is called 'symbolic computation'.

Give the following Maple instruction (note the assignment symbol :=):

```
>  irr_number := (sqrt(8) + 2)*sin(Pi/8);
```

By means of the assignment symbol, the expression to the right of this symbol is assigned to the variable named **irr_number**. The value of **irr_number** is more than just the numerical value. The combination of symbols defining the number to the right of := is the value of the variable **irr_number**.

Before going into the way in which Maple evaluates mathematical expressions in any detail, let us see how Maple handles **irr_number** in compound expressions.

```
>  1/(irr_number - 1/irr_number)^2;
```

Apparently, Maple is unwilling to work out the square automatically. Of course Maple can undoubtedly evaluate this expression, but it makes good sense to refrain from actually carrying it out as the expanded form of a power expression might be much more complicated than its original power form. The converse could also be true, and that is the sensible reason for leaving it to us to indicate which expression has our preference.

The following input instructs Maple to expand our square. Note that we use the percentage symbol (%) to refer to the preceding result.

```
>  normal(%);
```

It goes without saying that here the expanded form is much to be preferred over the unexpanded square expression. By the way, it is rather obvious that Maple does know how to handle symbolic expressions like $\sqrt{2}$ in the course of a calculation.

Just to make sure, click the **right mouse button** on the Maple output of the last two instructions and convert these symbolic expressions to their numerical values by choosing **Approximate** in the resulting menu. Verify that the numerical values are the same.

Also try the input:

> `expand((1+x)^136);`

to convince yourself that it may be very useful to leave well alone and let simple power expressions be unexpanded. Leaving this kind of decision to the user is rather judicious.

It makes sense to wipe the huge output from the screen. This can be done quickly by selecting the output and subsequently cutting it, or alternatively, by letting Maple act on the last input line again after replacing the semicolon by a colon.

The procedures **normal**, **simplify** and **expand** are three most important and useful Maple commands. Applying **normal** to a rational expression will give this expression its most natural or normal appearance, or rather, Maple will try to do this. So this command is especially useful for simplifying quotients of complicated expressions. It is however not always obvious what **normal** will do, because it is often unclear what the most natural form of a given expression should be.

In order to see some examples of the use of **normal**, you should give the following instruction:

> `???normal`

The **simplify** command behaves in a similar way. But the difference is that **simplify** also carries out simplifications of different types, like trigonometric or logarithmic simplification.
The **expand** procedure distributes products over sums.

> `???expand`

By the way, the Maple command **factor** has the opposite effect of **expand**, in the sense that **factor** computes the factorization of a polynomial.

● **Name-giving and Assigning Values to Variables**

Maple allows names to be unlimited in size, they may contain letters, digits and most other symbols like the underscore (_), but spaces are not permitted. If for whatever reason spaces or other unusual symbols are required in a name, the entire name must be enclosed by left (or back) quotes ('). Further, a name should never begin with a digit, and some names are reserved by Maple for special purposes, and hence can not be used for anything else. Examples of such reserved and protected words are: `expand`, `if`, `next`, `proc`, `quit`, etc. If you try to use a protected name as a variable, Maple issues an error message.

```
>  given_name.1 := 5;
>  'given name'.2 := sqrt(2);
>  expand := (x+y)^2;
>  proc := 3*t^2;
```

Observe the use of the dot (.) in the first two names. This dot is known as the 'concatenation' operator and is used by Maple to join names (or rather strings of symbols) together.

In the Maple language a name or variable, call it x, does not need to be declared, and hence is never unassigned. If no numerical value or other mathematical expression is assigned to it, its own name serves as its (assigned) value. As soon as another value is assigned to x the old value is abandoned and x takes on the new one. Note that we use the word value in a very broad sense: any number, mathematical expression, or string of symbols could be used for the value of a variable. This assigning process allows us to repeatedly alter the value of x, and in order to empty x of any unwanted value, we reassign its own name to it, which is x again.

Give the following instructions:

```
>  x := 'x'; p := x^3 - 2*x^2 + 3*x - 4;
```

Clearly x has no other value than its own name, and to p a certain cubic polynomial in x is assigned.
Next we give x a different name, say y, and subsequently y is given a numerical value. We then consider the effect these reassignments have on the polynomial p. Finally we let x refer to its own name again, and see what happens to p as a result.

Type after the prompt the following instructions. Don't forget to insert a semicolon between every two instructions, so that the order in which you have typed them is precisely the order in which they will be executed by Maple. Observe the right quotes placed around x in the fifth instruction.

```
>  x := y; p; y := 5; p; x := 'x'; p;
```

A few words of explanation are in order. The variable x first gets the name y, that is to say, x becomes a reference to the variable y, and because Maple usually[3] tries to carry out complete evaluation, the variable p, pointing to a cubic polynomial in x, now points to the same cubic polynomial in y. Next y

---

[3]No evaluation is done in the case of arrays (vectors or matrices).

gets the value 5 and the effect of complete evaluation $(x \to y \to 5)$ is that p becomes a reference to the cubic polynomial in which the variable y is replaced by 5, hence to $5^3 - 2 \cdot 5^2 + 3 \cdot 5 - 4 = 86$, to be precise. Finally, x is given back its own name and consequently p shows its true form again as a cubic polynomial in x. Right quotes enclosing an expression, as in 'x', prevent evaluation of that expression.

A mistake easily made is when a variable, say x, is meant to be used as a symbol— as in a polynomial expression—while it has slipped your mind that x still has a numerical value resulting from a previous calculation.

```
>  diff(ln(y),y);
```

Here we try to differentiate $\ln(y)$ as a function of y and instead of the correct answer we get an error message (which incidentally does not deserve a prize for clarity). The reason is that y still has the numerical value 5, its last assigned value. But as soon as we assign to y its own name again, no further obstruction is encountered.

Check this by letting Maple execute the previous instruction once more, after having given its own name back to y. Thus

```
>  y := 'y'; diff(ln(y),y);
```

We should take care not to forget placing right quotes around the name of a variable when giving its own name back to it. Although $y := y$ can do no harm, we have to be very careful with assignments like $y := y + 1$.
Let us try this.

```
>  y := y + 1;
```

A warning appears, because currently y does not have a numerical value and hence y is made to refer to an expression in which the name y itself occurs. This causes an infinite loop. Apart from problems of a strictly logical nature, Maple usually has trouble in coping with such recursive definitions. That a computer language like Pascal accepts assignments like $y := y + 1$ as syntactically correct is due to the fact that in Pascal a declared variable has a numerical value at all times, so that the assignment $y := y + 1$ simply adds 1 to y's current value.

Now we wish to make certain that y has no other value than its own name. This process of emptying a variable is extremely practical and undoubtedly will be useful on many future occasions.

```
>  y := 'y';
```

You can now try your hand at another example of a recursive definition in **assignment 1** of worksheet **TourA1b.mws** (see page 29).

• **Maple's Programming Language**

At first glance Maple's programming language resembles Pascal in a number of ways. The important Pascal requirement of declaring all variables is obviously unnecessary in Maple as every Maple name or variable is automatically assigned its own name on introduction. The Maple language is a procedural language which means that a Maple program essentially is a collection of procedures. Most Maple commands are procedures themselves, which, as you should know by now, can be used interactively, but which can at any time be called from a Maple program as well. The Maple code for almost all Maple commands can be viewed on the screen. Exceptions are the built-in system functions such as `evalf` and some mathematical functions like `diff`.

The following instruction produces the complete Maple code for the `nextprime` procedure:

```
>  interface(verboseproc = 2); print(nextprime);
```

The value 2 for the `interface` parameter `verboseproc` forces the `print` command to print the entire body of the procedure on the screen. When `verboseproc` has its default value of 1 the `print` command only shows the abbreviation: `proc() ... end`, including the relevant procedure parameters.
A close look at the code reveals a number of control structures familiar to the Pascal adept, but slightly different from the Pascal format.

Give the following instructions:

```
>  for i from 1 to 5 do print(i^2) od;

>  n := 1:
>  while n^3 <= 100 do n:=n+1:   od:
>  'n' = n;

>  p := rand(1..100)():
>  if isprime(p) then p = 'prime' else p = 'composite' fi;
```

The first two control structures are examples of repetitions, and the third is an example of a choice structure. The first input group contains a for-loop which prints five squares (numbers, not square boxes) on the screen. Further, the structure of the second group is a while-loop which determines the smallest positive integer n for which $n^3 > 100$. Finally, the third group chooses a random number between 1 and 100 and decides whether this number is prime or composite.

Now have a go at completing **assignment 2** of worksheet **TourA1b.mws** (see page 29), requiring the use of a for-loop and a choice structure.

• Creating Your Own Procedures

It is very easy to create your own procedures. These remain available until quitting the Maple session.

As an example consider the following procedure which arranges a pair of numbers in increasing order:

```
> smallest_largest := proc(a,b) if a < b then a,b
> else b,a fi end;
> smallest_largest(120,45);
```

Recursive procedures are possible, but should be treated with the utmost care. For instance, it makes good sense to always use the **option remember** in such procedures. This takes care of the storing of values calculated by the procedure in a so-called remember table so that repetitive recalculation of values can be avoided.

An example of a number sequence usually defined recursively is the well-known Fibonacci sequence: $0, 1, 1, 2, 3, 5, 8, 13, 21, \ldots$ and so on.

```
> Fib := proc(n) option remember;
> if n <= 1 then n else Fib(n-1) + Fib(n-2)
> fi end;
> Fib(10); Fib(50); Fib(100); Fib(150);
```

The rapid growth of the sequence's elements is evident. Without the **option remember** Maple would not have been able to compute these large values of the **Fib** procedure.

The following procedure **Fib2** also verifies that its argument has the correct type which is **integer** (type-checking), any other type is not allowed.

```
> Fib2 := proc(n)
> if not type(n,integer) then
> ERROR('Argument is not an integer')
> elif n <= 1 then n else Fib2(n-1) + Fib2(n-2)
> fi end;

> Fib2(1.5);
```

A quicker way to achieve this is by checking the argument's type right away in the heading of the procedure, as in

```
> Fib3 := proc(n::integer)
> if n <= 1 then n else Fib3(n-1) + Fib3(n-2)
> fi end;
```

The 'if-then-else' structure is then superfluous. Check the warning Maple gives when the argument n is not an integer.

```
>  Fib3(2.5);
```

The final **assignment 3** of worksheet TourA1b.mws (see page 29) is about type-checking.

• Saving Your Work to a File

When saving a worksheet to a file, we usually choose the Maple worksheet format (extension .mws). This is the default used by Maple; it is an ASCII file containing input, output, graphics and text regions and it can be opened again at any time. On the other hand we may wish to export the worksheet as a human readable text file (extension .txt), or as a LATEX file (extension .tex). Sometimes we do not want to save the entire Maple session into a file, but only one or two objects such as specific procedures or variables. In that case the **save** command can be used.

Give the following instruction (note the unix-like forward slash /; one can also use double backward slashes \\):

```
>  save irr_number, p, `c:/Maple/Book/R5/Chapter1/testfile.mpl`;
```

The variable **irr_number** and the polynomial p are now saved in the file named testfile.mpl. This file is human readable, but also Maple can read from it. Had we used the extension .m in the file's name, then Maple would have written the file in internal Maple format, which is not readable to us. The advantage of such an .m file is that Maple can read it into a Maple session really fast. Maple's **read** command can be used to read the (values of the) variables **irr_number** and p from testfile.mpl into any future Maple session.

```
>  read `c:/Maple/Book/R5/Chapter1/testfile.mpl`:
```

If no specific variable names but only the file's name is used in the **save** command, then the entire contents of the worksheet is saved into this file, including all procedures read with **with()** or **readlib()**.

Sometimes we prefer to use our own familiar editor or text processor to create an ASCII file of Maple instructions with lines of commentary to be read into a Maple session at a later stage. When reading such a file into a Maple session with the **read** command, Maple immediately executes all input instructions and prints the resulting output to the screen. Observe that Maple can only read proper Maple instructions, i.e. lines beginning with the Maple prompt >, text regions cause read errors. Comments, inserted on an input line and preceded by a sharp (**#**) are ignored. Input lines read by Maple normally remain invisible. If the command

```
>  interface(echo = 2);
```

is given before the reading process is started, then input and comments are also printed to the screen, thus giving the impression that the material read from the file is a regular part of the current Maple session. The `interface` procedure regulates the format of the output, in particular the amount and the shape of output visible on the screen. The default value of the `interface` parameter `echo` is 1.

1.4.4 Assignments 1b. Variables and Names

Below you will find a collection of mostly mathematically oriented assignments covering the topics of Worksheet 1b (TourW1b.mws).

1. First type the following input-line:

   ```
   >  x := 'x'; q := x+1; x = sqrt(q);
   ```

   Next type:

   ```
   >  x := sqrt(q); x;
   ```

   Give an explanation for the warning and the error message that appear after giving the second instruction. Also explain why the first instruction did not cause any problems.

2. Instruct Maple to show all the prime numbers between 25 and 50. Use a for-loop and a choice structure. The `print` command can be useful to print the numbers on the screen.

3. The procedure `Factorial` is given as follows:

   ```
   >  Factorial := proc(n) option remember;
   >  if n = 0 then 1 else n*Factorial(n-1)
   >  fi end;
   ```

   Change the procedure `Factorial` in such a way that it verifies that the argument is an integer.
   Check the error message that appears after the instruction

   ```
   >  Factorial(2.5);
   ```

   Give an explanation for the error message that appears after the instruction

   ```
   >  Factorial(-2);
   ```

   Now change the procedure again so that it also verifies that the argument is non-negative.

1.5 Exercises

1. The Maple procedure `history` makes the percentage symbols %, %% and %%% less useful, if not superfluous. First use Maple's help facility to check on the precise functioning of `history`. Then find out if %, %% and %%% are still working as before.
   Note that the `readlib` procedure has to be used to make `history` available.

2. The first step on the way to understanding the proper use of Maple packages such as `linalg` is the issuing of instructions like `?with` and `?linalg`. Find out how a single package procedure can be used without having to load the entire package.

3. Verify that

$$\sum_{i \geq 1} \text{floor}\left(\frac{n}{2^i}\right)$$

   gives the number of factors 2 occurring in the factorization of $n!$.

4. Experiment with the following combinations of left and right quotes:

   (a) `''expression''`, double right quotes,

   (b) `'`string`'`, left quotes within right quotes,

   (c) `''expression_string'`, right quotes within left quotes.

   What happens in each case? Which of these three combinations could be useful? Under which circumstances? Is any of these combinations meaningless, and if so, why?

5. The worksheet TourW1b.mws contains an example of the 'if-then-else' structure (see also page 26). In this example an arbitrary integer between 1 and 100 is checked for primality. Can you adapt the Maple code such that it checks whether an arbitrary integer between 1 and 1000 belongs to a prime pair? Naturally, in a prime pair $(p, p+2)$ both p and $p+2$ are prime numbers. Examples of prime pairs are $(3, 5)$, $(5, 7)$, $(11, 13)$, $(17, 19)$, $(29, 31)$, $(41, 43)$, etc.
   To date the number of prime pairs is still unknown, but it is generally believed to be infinite.

6. What does the following procedure do?

```
welcome := proc()
  local x;
  x := args;
```

```
    if x = NULL then
       print('No input, give CA system')
    elif x = Maple then
       print('Welcome, Maple user!')
    else
       print('Sorry, wrong CA system?')
    fi
 end:
```

7. Think of a way to make Maple compute the thousandth decimal place of the number π. Please do not count off the decimal places as they would appear on the screen after you have given the obvious Maple instruction

   ```
   >  evalf(Pi,1002);
   ```

   Instead, you should try to find a Maple instruction (or a short sequence of Maple instructions) to print the one required decimal place on the screen and no others. Observe that the first decimal place of π is its second digit. It may help to use the Maple command `frac`. Use Maple's help facility to learn about the properties of this Maple function.

8. In Worksheet 1b a polynomial p was introduced, namely

   ```
   >  p := x^3 - 2*x^2 + 3*x - 4;
   ```

   Verify that x evaluates to its own name. In the same worksheet you were then asked to type the following input line:

   ```
   >  x := y; p; y := 5; p; x := 'x'; p;
   ```

   Also verify that y has not been assigned any value other than its own name. What would happen if you accidently typed a comma instead of a semicolon between the 5 and the p in the input line above? Can you explain the warning that is caused by this?

9. Use a single line of Maple code to produce the largest prime pair $(p, p+2)$ with $p < 10000$. See also Exercises 1.5.5.

1.6   Survey of Used Maple Expressions

Below we give a selected list of Maple expressions and commands that have been used or just named in the present chapter. Some of these only appear in this chapter's worksheets TourW1a.mws and TourW1b.mws (see section 1.4).

expression	brief explanation
^, *, /, +, -	– arithmetic operations in correct order of execution
;, :	– close off Maple instructions
?command	– calls up help for command
%, %%, %%%	– percentage symbols refer to preceding output
:=	– assignment symbol
evalf(x,n);	– gives numerical approximation of the number x in n decimal digits
'expression'	– right quotes prevent evaluation of enclosed expression
`name`	– left quotes ensure that the character string name is taken literally
diff(f(x),x);	– derivative of $f(x)$
plot(f(x),x=a..b);	– graph of $f(x)$ over the interval $[a..b]$
fsolve(f(x)=0);	– numerically approximates the zeros of $f(x)$
subs(x=a,f(x));	– substitutes $x = a$ into expression $f(x)$
with(package);	– loads all procedures in package simultaneously
evalm(A);	– shows elements of the matrix A
ifactor(n);	– integer factorization of n
time();	– computing time (in seconds) elapsed since the start of the Maple session
Digits := n;	– sets the number of digits precision to n
evalb(expr1=expr2);	– evaluates the Boolean expression expr1=expr2; evalb returns true or false.

expression	brief explanation
`normal(expr);`	– simplifies rational expressions
`simplify(expr);`	– simplifies expressions in which quotients, logarithms and trigonometric functions occur
`expand(expr);`	– works out **expr** (distributes products over sums)
`factor(p);`	– factorizes polynomial p
`if ... then ... else ... fi`	– choice (logical structure)
`for ... from ... to ... do ... od`	– repetition (logical structure)
`while ... do ... od`	– repetition (logical structure)
`proc() ... end`	– form of a Maple procedure

The following selected procedures appear in this chapter for the first time (use the index for more information):
`det`, `exp`, `floor`, `interface`, `inverse`, `isprime`, `ln`, `log`, `matrix`, `nextprime`, `print`, `rand`, `read`, `save`, `sin`, `sqrt`, `type`, `whattype`.

2

Functions and Sequences

After the first chapter's tour of Maple, in which you may have gained some insight into the workings of the Maple system, it is time to concentrate on mathematics. Naturally, you won't be an accomplished Maple user just yet, but, provided you carefully read the first chapter and worked through both worksheets, you should have some idea as to how Maple could assist in extending and deepening your knowledge of mathematics. Moreover, in this chapter and the ones to come you will gradually learn a great deal about Maple, so that at the end of this book there is a good chance that you will be a reasonably proficient user of the Maple system with an improved insight in mathematics to boot. Anyhow, that is what we aim for. But before reaching that state of affairs you need quite a bit of practice, so let us continue to explore the Maple avenues without further delay.

2.1 Introduction

Most of this chapter will be devoted to the notion of function as encountered in Mathematical Analysis. We shall learn in what way Maple can help us to unveil the properties of real functions and how we can use Maple to investigate the limit behaviour of sequences of real numbers.

In the next section we shall recall the definitions and properties of a number of those well-known concepts in the field of Mathematical Analysis that play a major role in this chapter. Most, if not all, will be familiar, but in order to avoid misunderstanding, precise definitions and descriptions will be given. This also forecloses the need for repeated consultation of Analysis textbooks which could unnecessarily interrupt the continuity of your Maple explorations. You may decide to first skip the next section, to return to it at the moment you need to be reminded of the precise definition of a mathematical concept.

2.2   Selected Concepts from Analysis

A real function is a prescription f that assigns to every element x of a set $A \subseteq \mathbb{R}$ (the domain of f) a definite element $f(x)$ of a set $B \subseteq \mathbb{R}$ (the codomain of f). The usual notation is: $f : A \to B$ and $f : x \mapsto f(x)$. The graph of f is the set of ordered pairs $\{(x, f(x)) \mid x \in A\}$. Often a sketch can be made of the graph of a real function in the plane. Sometimes useful information can be extracted from the graph of a function about its behaviour, but a graph may also be rather misleading.

In case the domain A happens to coincide with a subset $\{n \in \mathbb{Z} \mid n \geq n_0\}$ of the set of integers $\mathbb{Z}$ for some fixed integer n_0 (usually $n_0 = 0$ or 1), the function f is called a sequence of real numbers and we generally write f_n with a subscript n instead of $f(n)$; the usual sequence notation is $(f_n)_{n=n_0}^{\infty}$ or briefly (f_n). In the Maple language, a (finite) sequence is written as a succession of elements, separated by commas. The following Maple input generates the sequence of function values $(f_n)_{n=0}^{10}$:

```
>  r := NULL: for i from 0 to 10 do r := r,f[i] od:   r;
```

$$f_0, \ f_1, \ f_2, \ f_3, \ f_4, \ f_5, \ f_6, \ f_7, \ f_8, \ f_9, \ f_{10}$$

The output sequence is an example of what Maple calls an expression sequence (exprseq).

```
>  whattype(%);
```

$$exprseq$$

For a given function $f : A \to B$ and $a \in \bar{A}$ (the closure of A), we call ℓ the limit of $f(x)$ for x tends to a—notation: $\lim_{x \to a} f(x) = \ell$—if for every $\varepsilon > 0$ a $\delta > 0$ can be found such that $|f(x) - \ell| < \varepsilon$ for every $x \in A$ with $0 < |x - a| < \delta$. Also $a = \infty$ is permitted, but in that case δ should be replaced by N and $0 < |x - a| < \delta$ by $x > N$ in the definition above. If f relates to a sequence, obviously a cannot be anything else but ∞ and ℓ is named the limit of the sequence, provided this limit exists of course. If $\lim_{n \to \infty} f_n$ exists, the sequence is convergent, otherwise divergent.

A function $f : A \to B$ is continuous at $a \in A$ if and only if $\lim_{x \to a} f(x) = f(a)$, and we say that f is continuous on the interval $J \subseteq A$ if f is continuous at each point a of J. Most functions we shall meet are continuous functions, that is to say, continuous on their entire domain. In the exceptional case of a discontinuous function, the number of discontinuities usually is very limited.

Most sequences we shall encounter are convergent sequences, but occasionally we shall come across a divergent sequence with interesting properties. A concept suitable for investigating such divergent sequences is that of limit point, also called accumulation point. A limit point of a sequence (f_n) is a number ℓ with the property that for any arbitrary $\varepsilon > 0$ infinitely many indices $n \in \mathbb{N}$ exist for which $|f_n - \ell| < \varepsilon$. In other words, a limit point of a sequence is the limit of a convergent subsequence. Accepting ∞ and $-\infty$ as possible limits, both can also act as limit points for suitably chosen sequences. Of course, the definition of limit point should then be adjusted accordingly. If, for instance, for every $N > 0$, infinitely many indices $n \in \mathbb{N}$ can be found with $f_n > N$, then by definition ∞ is a limit point of the sequence (f_n). All sequences unbounded from above have limit point ∞, and $-\infty$ is limit point of all sequences unbounded from below. The largest limit point of a sequence (f_n) (∞ included) is written as $\limsup_{n \to \infty} f_n$, and the smallest limit point ($-\infty$ included) is written as $\liminf_{n \to \infty} f_n$.

Further, a function $f : A \to B$ is monotonically increasing or simply increasing on $I \subseteq A$ if $f(y) \geq f(x)$ for any two $x, y \in I$ with $y > x$. Replacing $f(y) \geq f(x)$ by $f(y) > f(x)$ in the last sentence gives the definition of a strictly (monotonically) increasing function on I. Analogously we define (strictly) (monotonically) decreasing functions by inserting the opposite inequality signs ($\leq$ and $<$) between the two function values. Naturally, the definitions given in this paragraph also cover sequences. It is an important fact that a (monotonically) increasing sequence, bounded from above, always converges to a finite limit.

Finally we remind you of the O-symbol $\mathcal{O}$ (pronounced as: big Oh) named after Edmund Landau. We write

$$f(x) = g(x) + \mathcal{O}(h(x)) \quad (x \to a)$$

to mean

$$|f(x) - g(x)| \leq C\,|h(x)|$$

for all x sufficiently close to a; the constant C is positive and independent of x. For instance,

$$s_n = 1 + \frac{1}{n} + \mathcal{O}(\frac{1}{n^2}) \quad (n \to \infty)$$

implies that the sequence (s_n) converges to 1 at exactly the same speed as the sequence $(1 + \frac{1}{n})$.

2.3   A Tricky Probability Function

One of the objectives of the present Maple session is to show what we can find out
about the mathematical functions known to Maple and their properties. Although
we considered this briefly in the first chapter, here we intend to present a more
systematic approach. Further we shall learn to construct our own functions and
use Maple to extract information from the definitions of these functions.

2.3.1   Mathematical Functions

A rather long list of the initially-known mathematical functions (partly shown in
figure 2.1) is given by the command

> ?inifcns

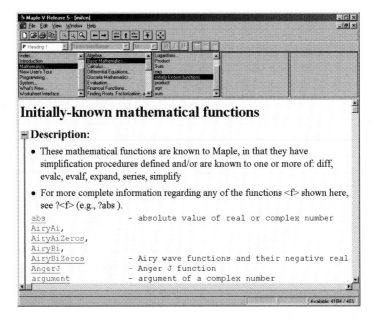

Figure 2.1: An overview of functions known to Maple (partly shown)

You will undoubtedly recognize some of these Maple functions, but others may be
less well-known. The most elementary of mathematical functions, the polynomial
and rational functions, are missing from this list. There is an obvious reason
for this. Indeed, the definition of these functions only involves the standard
arithmetic operations of addition, subtraction, multiplication and division. We
have learned from the first chapter's two worksheets that Maple has a perfect

understanding of these standard operations, even if indeterminate quantities are involved in the arithmetic expressions concerned. Polynomial functions are easy to define, are they not?

```
>  polynomial(x) := x^7 - x^5 + 4;
```

$$\text{polynomial}(x) := x^7 - x^5 + 4$$

```
>  polynomial(t), polynomial(1);
```

$$\text{polynomial}(t), \text{polynomial}(1)$$

Apparently it is not possible to simply substitute values for x in polynomial(x) in the same way we generally use for functions. Let us try another approach.

```
>  polynomial_expression := x^7 - x^5 + 4;
```

$$polynomial\_expression := x^7 - x^5 + 4$$

We wonder whether this truly is a function in the sense of a 'function prescription'. There is no x in the left-hand side, so how can it be a function description? What does Maple have to say about it?

```
>  whattype(polynomial_expression);
```

$$+$$

This output indicates that `polynomial_expression` is an expression sequence of type + (addition). In order to obtain a function (prescription) from an expression like `polynomial_expression`—that is the prescription which assigns to x the expression given by `polynomial_expression`—we have to somehow invert the assigning process. In the usual functional terminology, instead of applying the prescription f to x, we have to extract f from the expression $f(x)$. This inverse process therefore has been given the name `unapply`.

```
>  polynomial := unapply(polynomial_expression,x);
```

$$polynomial := x \rightarrow x^7 - x^5 + 4$$

The form of the output tells us that here we are dealing with a function prescription. Indeed, we immediately recognize the arrow notation generally used for mathematical functions. The verifications

```
>  type(polynomial_expression,procedure);
>  type(polynomial,procedure);
```

$$false$$
$$true$$

confirm that `polynomial_expression` is not and `polynomial` is a procedure. Further, it is clear from the following output that `polynomial` is a traditional mathematical function and `polynomial_expression` is not.

> `polynomial(t);`

$$t^7 - t^5 + 4$$

> `polynomial_expression(t);`

$$\mathrm{x}(t)^7 - \mathrm{x}(t)^5 + 4$$

Observe that in view of the latter, Maple has the impression that x is meant to be dependent on t!

As Maple sees a function merely as a procedure, we can use the procedural form to define a function.

> `f := proc(x) x^7 - x^5 + 4 end;`

$$f := \mathbf{proc}(x)\, x^7 - x^5 + 4\, \mathbf{end}$$

> `evalb(polynomial(t) - f(t) = 0);`

$$\mathit{true}$$

To build complex functions from elementary ones, we normally use addition, multiplication, and composition of the corresponding function prescriptions. So does Maple. A couple of examples should clarify this point. Note the use of parentheses.

> `(sin+log)(t); (sin*log)(t); (sin@log)(t); (f@@3)(t);`

$$\sin(t) + \ln(t)$$

$$\sin(t)\ln(t)$$

$$\sin(\ln(t))$$

$$((t^7 - t^5 + 4)^7 - (t^7 - t^5 + 4)^5 + 4)^7 - ((t^7 - t^5 + 4)^7 - (t^7 - t^5 + 4)^5 + 4)^5 + 4$$

The @ operator is used for function composition. In particular, `(f@@3)(t)` has the same meaning as $f(f(f(t)))$, which is commonly written as $f^3(t)$.

2.3.2   Investigating a Probability Function

In our next example we shall meet a function the behaviour and fundamental properties of which cannot be directly read from its prescription. All the same, this function is not really contrived, on the contrary, the underlying idea is quite a natural one.

Consider the following rather daring betting game. Let x denote our entire present working capital, expressed in some suitable unit ($0 < x < 1$). Our objective is to increase this as quickly as possible to 1. Hence, when $x = 1$ is reached, we have won, and there the game ends. The way we play this game is as follows. If $0 < x \leq \frac{1}{2}$ we stake our entire capital x. In case of a win, we have gained x and so we have $2x$ to bet with in the next round. In case we lose, everything is lost and the game has to stop because there is nothing left to bet with. On the other hand, if $\frac{1}{2} < x < 1$ we stake as much as we need to reach our objective in a single stroke, that is $1 - x$. Now a win gives us $x + (1 - x) = 1$, and a loss leaves us with $x - (1 - x) = 2x - 1 > 0$, which can be used for another bet. Play continues until we reach our objective, or until we have lost our entire capital.

Further, let p be the probability of winning a bet, and suppose the function g expresses the probability of reaching our objective starting with initial capital x. The quantity x is supposed to be the variable and p is an unknown parameter ($0 < p < 1$), which means that for every choice of p there is a function g. We wish to emphasize that so far it is not clear whether these functions g are well-defined for every real x. Who knows whether the process described above will come to an end at all? All the same, let us assume for the moment that the functions g are defined on the entire interval $[0, 1]$. Then clearly, for $x \in [0, 1]$, $g(x)$ belongs to $[0, 1]$ as well. From the function's description we deduce the relations:

$$g(0) = 0, \quad g(1) = 1,$$
$$g(x) = \begin{cases} p\,g(2x) + (1 - p)\,g(0) & \text{if } 0 < x \leq \frac{1}{2}, \\ p\,g(1) + (1 - p)\,g(2x - 1) & \text{if } \frac{1}{2} < x < 1. \end{cases}$$

We would like to find out whether this intriguing function g is continuous on $[0, 1]$, and naturally we have Maple to assist us.

Knowing what we do about the function g, it seems quite natural to use a recursive Maple procedure for its definition; no other information is presently available.

```
>  g := proc(x,p) option remember;
>  if x = 0 or x = 1 then x
>  elif x <= 1/2 then factor(expand(p*g(2*x,p)))
>  else factor(expand(p + (1-p)*g(2*x-1,p)))
>  fi end;
```

$$g := \mathbf{proc}(x, p)$$
$$\quad \mathbf{option}\ \textit{remember};$$
$$\quad\quad \mathbf{if}\ x = 0\ \mathbf{or}\ x = 1\ \mathbf{then}\ x$$
$$\quad\quad \mathbf{elif}\ x \leq 1/2\ \mathbf{then}\ \text{factor}(\text{expand}(p \times \text{g}(2 \times x, p)))$$
$$\quad\quad \mathbf{else}\ \text{factor}(\text{expand}(p + (1 - p) \times \text{g}(2 \times x - 1, p)))$$
$$\quad\quad \mathbf{fi}$$
$$\quad \mathbf{end}$$

The Maple functions `expand` and `factor` are used here to give the g-values a more or less natural appearance.

Calling the function for an arbitrary (hence indeterminate) x causes an error message to appear, and likewise, numerical values for x are not accepted either.

```
>  g(x,p); g(0.2345,p);
```

```
Error, (in g) cannot evaluate boolean
Error, (in g) too many levels of recursion
```

This is not really surprising. The first error is caused by the fact that the indeterminate x can not be compared with the numerical $\frac{1}{2}$ in the inequality $x \leq \frac{1}{2}$, simply because x does not have a numerical value. This error can be prevented by checking the type of x: if x is of type **name**—in which case x has no numerical value—then $g(x, p)$ is returned unevaluated. As in

```
>  if type(x,name) then 'g(x,p)' fi;
```

$$g(x, p)$$

for instance. The second error is more serious. Too many levels of recursion cause a stack overflow, usually as the result of an infinite loop. This is indeed the case here, because the function g is defined in terms of itself (see worksheet TourW1b.mws). Therefore we need to find out for which values of x this recursive process is finite. Clearly, this is so when x has the shape

$$x = \frac{k}{2^n}, \quad \text{where } n \in \mathbb{N} \text{ and } k = 0, 1, \ldots, 2^n.$$

Indeed, starting off with initial x-value of this form, repeatedly applying $2x$ or $2x - 1$ most surely leads to 1 in finitely many steps. For instance,

```
>  g(43/128,p);
```

$$-p^2 \left(-1 - p - p^2 + 5\,p^3 - 4\,p^4 + p^5\right)$$

As the numbers $k/2^n$ for $k = 0, \ldots, 2^n$ are uniformly distributed over the interval $[0, 1]$, a plot of g at these points may give a realistic impression of the overall behaviour of g.

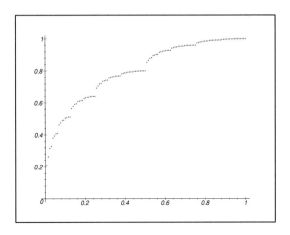

Figure 2.2: The betting function $g(x, 0.8)$

For g to have numerical values, we naturally have to choose a numerical value
for p as well. Let us choose $p = 0.8$, but any other value between 0 and 1 will do
equally well. Next we build a list of points $(x, g(x, p))$ for $x = k/2^7$, $k = 0, \ldots, 2^7$.
It is advisable to suppress the Maple output for such a long list.

```
> p := 0.8:  argumentlist := [seq(k/2^7,k=0..2^7)]:
> pointlist := map(x -> [x,g(x,p)],argumentlist):
```

Here we use the Maple command `seq` for the construction of a list of 129 equidis-
tant points in the interval $[0, 1]$. Next Maple's `map` function is evoked in order to
apply the function $x \mapsto (x, g(x, p))$ to every element of the list `argumentlist`.
This produces a list of points `pointlist` that can be plotted on the screen by
Maple's `plot` command.

```
> plot(pointlist,style=point);
```

We choose the option `style = point` because in the default setting Maple would
otherwise join successive points by little line segments which would obscure possible discontinuities. The plot (see figure 2.2) clearly shows the individual points
$(x, g(x, p))$ well separated. The Maple functions `map` and `seq` are extremely useful, especially when creating datasets as we did above. The former acts on lists,
but also on other objects like arrays and sets. A related function is `zip` by which
two lists (or vectors) can be zipped into a single list of pairs.

```
> dat1 := [1,2,3,4]:  dat2 := [a,b,c,d]:
> zip((x,y) -> (x,y),dat1,dat2);
```

$$[1, a, 2, b, 3, c, 4, d]$$

Returning to the plot (figure 2.2), we observe a reasonably continuous behaviour of g, possibly interrupted by some discontinuities. On the other hand, it might well be that to the immediate right of points like $x = 0$, $\frac{1}{4}$, and $\frac{1}{2}$, the function g is continuous but increases very steeply. The best way to investigate g's continuity is to express its argument x as an infinite binary fraction, i.e.

$$x = b_1 2^{-1} + b_2 2^{-2} + \cdots + b_n 2^{-n} + \ldots, \quad \text{with } b_i \in \{0,1\},$$

abbreviated as $x = (0.b_1 b_2 \ldots)_2$ with $b_i \doteq 0$ or 1. As you probably know, every real number can be expressed in this way, and this representation is also essentially unique. The choice of 2 as base for the representation is inspired by the fact that for numbers of type $x = k/2^n$ the recursive process by which $g(x,p)$ is to be determined, is finite. This is immediately clear from

$$g((0.b_1 b_2 b_3 \ldots)_2, p) = \begin{cases} p\,g((0.b_2 b_3 \ldots)_2, p) & \text{if } b_1 = 0, \\ p + (1-p)\,g((0.b_2 b_3 \ldots)_2, p) & \text{if } b_1 = 1. \end{cases}$$

Summarizing, the recursive definition of g can be used to explicitly calculate $g(x,p)$ for all x with finite or periodic binary expansions. This implies that the g-value of every rational number between 0 and 1 can be explicitly computed in terms of p. An example might be useful at this point. Let $y := g(\frac{1}{5}, p)$. Then

```
>  p := 'p':   y = p*p*(p + (1-p)*(p + (1-p)*y));
```

$$y = p^2 \left(p + (1-p)\left(p + (1-p)\,y \right) \right)$$

because the process of two applications of the $2x$-step followed by two $(2x-1)$-steps returns the original $x = \frac{1}{5}$. This is best understood by considering the binary expansion of $\frac{1}{5}$:

$$\frac{1}{5} = (0.001100110011\ldots)_2,$$

with period 0011.

```
>  'g(1/5,p)' := solve(%,y);
```

$$g(\,1/5, p\,) := \frac{p^3\,(-2+p)}{-1 + p^2 - 2\,p^3 + p^4}$$

It appears that for rational values of x, $g(x,p)$ is a rational function of the parameter p.

This binary expansion also helps us to show that $g(x,p)$ can be defined for every real $x \in [0,1]$ and every indeterminate p. This follows from the inequalities

```
>  abs('g(x,p)' - 'g(y,p)') <= p^i*(1-p)^j;
```

$$|g(x,p) - g(y,p)| \le p^i\,(1-p)^j$$

```
>  k :='k':  p^i*(1-p)^j <= (max(p,1-p))^k;
```

$$p^i\,(1-p)^j \le \max(p,\,1-p)^k$$

for non-negative integers i, j with $i + j = k$, where the first k bits in the binary expansion of x and y coincide. Also the continuity of the function $g(x, p)$ (properly extended to the entire interval $[0, 1]$) as a function of x can be derived from these inequalities. Exercise 1 of section 2.5 considers the continuity and other properties of g; see also Appendix B (page 188) for a detailed discussion.

There is an important conclusion to be drawn from this example. Namely, though very useful in the search for characteristic properties of complicated functions, Maple's proper role is that of a very clever tool that can put us on the right track. But that is all, in the end the user must always supply a rigorous proof by himself.

2.3.3   Investigating a Strange Sequence

Finally we shall give some attention to a diverging sequence of real numbers. We define the following somewhat artificial sequence:

```
>  stranger:= n -> n*log(1+1/n)*(cos(n*Pi/4)+(-1)^(n*(n+1)/2));
```

$$stranger := n \rightarrow n \log(1 + \frac{1}{n})\,(\cos(\frac{1}{4}\,n\,\pi) + (-1)^{(1/2\,n\,(n+1))})$$

Does this sequence perhaps converge to a limit? Let us find out.

```
>  n := 'n':  limit(stranger(n),n=infinity,real);
```

$$-2..2$$

We use the extra argument **real** to coerce Maple into giving a real answer if possible. Maple only gives a numerical range, which means that the value of the limiting expression is known to lie in that range for n sufficiently large. In other words, the limit points are contained in $[-2, 2]$. The command

```
>  ?limit[return]
```

gives information on the meaning of the values returned by Maple's **limit** function (see figure 2.3).

Let us investigate the limit behaviour of this strange sequence by plotting its values for n in the range $[100, 500]$.

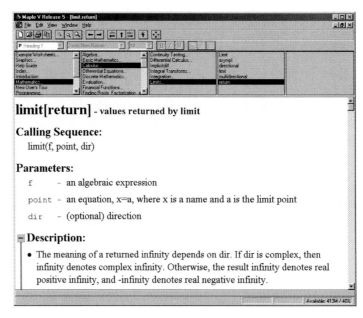

Figure 2.3: Maple's `limit[return]` command

It might improve the picture if we plot these values as functions of $\log(n)$ instead of n. One advantage is that possible accumulations of points (limit points) become more pronounced. As only points with large n-values are considered, we expect to see a few almost horizontal sets of ever more densely packed points. These almost-lines correspond with convergent subsequences and thus with the limit points of the original sequence.

```
> stranger_list := [seq(stranger(n),n=100..500)]:
> logn_list := [seq(log(n),n=100..500)]:
> zip((a,b) -> [a,b],logn_list,stranger_list):
> plot(%,style=point);
```

Figure 2.4 clearly shows that the sequence splits into 7 groups of points, each accumulating around 7 distinct values. Therefore, it seems likely that there are 7 limit points. The limit

```
> n := 'n': Limit(n*log(1+1/n),n=infinity) =
> limit(n*log(1+1/n),n=infinity);
```

$$\lim_{n\to\infty} n\ln(1 + \frac{1}{n}) = 1$$

is easily recognized. Moreover, for $n = 4k + r$ $(r = 0,1,2,3)$ the values of $\cos(\pi n/4)$ and $(-1)^{\frac{1}{2}n(n+1)}$ can be calculated without difficulty. Combining these results and observations confirm that our strange sequence indeed has 7 limit points, namely $2, 0, -1$, and the four points $\pm 1 \pm \frac{1}{2}\sqrt{2}$. In particular, we deduce that $\lim\limits_{n\to\infty}\sup = 2$ and $\lim\limits_{n\to\infty}\inf = -1 - \frac{1}{2}\sqrt{2}$ for this sequence.

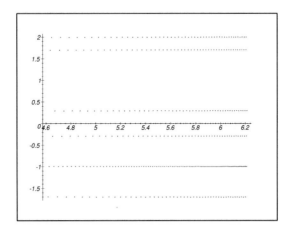

Figure 2.4: A strange sequence with 7 limit points

We have come to the end of this Maple session. The worksheets FuncW2a.mws and FuncW2b.mws offer much exercise material on the Maple commands used in this session, they form a natural sequel to the Maple session we have just ended.

2.4   Worksheets and Assignments

Both worksheets FuncW2a.mws and FuncW2b.mws are integrally reproduced in print. We feel that, going through a worksheet, it often is more comfortable to read the explanatory text from paper than from the computer screen. To a lesser extend this is also true for input and output lines. However, not including the Maple output might stimulate the reader to start the machine (if he has not yet done so) and become a user. We remind the reader of the importance of practice; the objectives and the content of the worksheets can only be fully appreciated by actually seeing Maple at work. Therefore, all output has been deleted. On the other hand, input lines are generally included.

2.4.1   Worksheet 2a. Functions

In this worksheet we shall look at several mathematical functions. First we will
pay attention to a polynomial function, after which rational functions will be
considered. We will then have a look at a periodic function and the worksheet
ends with the investigation of a standard limit.

• Polynomials

We shall begin this worksheet with the most elementary of all mathematical
functions, the polynomial of a single variable. First we stress the difference
between the notions of polynomial *expression* and polynomial *function*. The
former is a finite linear combination of powers of an unknown quantity x, and
the latter stands for the function prescription that assigns to every x a fixed
polynomial expression in x. This subtle difference is important for a thorough
understanding of the Maple command **unapply**, which transforms an expression
into a function prescription.

To clarify this point, please introduce the following polynomial expression p and
polynomial function q, but first give the **restart** command. This wipes the slate
clean, and rids memory of unwanted variables, values or other quantities which
otherwise stay on in the background of the active Maple session.

```
>   restart:
>   p := 4*x^5 + x^4 + 2*x^3 - 5*x^2 - x + 1;
>   q := x -> 4*x^5 + x^4 + 2*x^3 - 5*x^2 - x + 1;
```

Here p is the name of the polynomial expression—as is $q(x)$ actually. However,
the polynomial prescription q is independent of the choice of indeterminate (here
we have chosen x again), while p definitely depends on x.

The unknown x in the expression p can be changed into another indeterminate,
say t, by means of Maple's substitution function **subs**; for q this change is simply
effected by $q(t)$. Verify the equivalence of both expressions with

```
>   subs(x=t,p) = q(t);
```

Instead of q's definition given above, we could have used the **unapply** command
to extract the polynomial prescription from the expression p. Verify this.

The degree and the coefficients of the polynomial (expression) p can be isolated
as follows:

```
>   d := degree(p,x);
>   coeffs(p,x); seq(coeff(p,x,i),i=0..d);
```

Observe the different arrangements of the coefficients: the former instruction gives the coefficients in arbitrary order, while the latter places them in sequential order by terms of increasing degree.

We also point out that the preceding instructions contain the name of the unknown x. This is necessary because a polynomial expression possibly depends on more than one indeterminate. The next polynomial expression can be considered a polynomial in x as well as a polynomial in y.

```
>  pp := expand((x + 2*y)^3 + (3*x - y)^2);
>  collect(pp,y);
>  seq(coeff(%,y,i),i=0..3);
```

The `collect` command gathers all terms of equal degree in the unknown specified (y in this case), so that the expression takes the shape of a polynomial expression in y with coefficients expressed as polynomials in the unknown x. Maple's `expand` function is necessary to first express p in standard form, only then can we justifiably use the word 'coefficient'.

At this point you could interrupt working through this worksheet and try your hand at **assignment 1** of worksheet **FuncA2a.mws** (see page 54), in which a certain binomial polynomial is considered.

In many situations it is important to get information on the location of the zeros of a given function. It is not often though that they can be calculated in exact form. This is generally the case for polynomials of degree 5 and higher. Usually we have no choice but to be content with numerical approximations.

Approximations for the real zeros of the polynomial p can be obtained by means of the Maple command:

```
>  fsolve(p,x);
```

Because p is a polynomial of degree 5, it has at least one and at most five real zeros. Indeed, the Fundamental Theorem of Algebra tells us that a polynomial of degree d with real coefficients has exactly d zeros, real or complex, where the non-real zeros come in complex conjugate pairs. In order to find all zeros, including the complex ones, the parameter `complex` should be added to `fsolve` as in

```
>  fsolve(p,x,complex);
```

Verify that these are indeed good approximations of the zeros of q by giving the following instruction (q is the polynomial function introduced right at the beginning of this worksheet on page 48):

```
>  map(q,[%]);
```

The effect of the `map` command is that the polynomial prescription q is applied to each element of the sequence of zeros `[%]`.

Indeed, all q-values are close to zero. If you wish to increase the number of digits precision, first step up the default value of Maple's `Digits` function and then call the same commands again.

For arbitrary functions, Maple's `fsolve` does not find more than a single real zero, even though others may exist. The reason is, there is no general method by which the exact number of real zeros of a non-polynomial function on a given interval can be determined; how could we then tell at what point in our search process all zeros (if any) have been found? Almost all numerical methods for locating zeros are based on the following iteration scheme: choose an interval containing a zero, start with an educated guess, and try to successively improve this initial approximation until some closeness criterion is met.
In order to restrict the search region, a range `[a..b]` could be added as extra parameter for `fsolve`. Only for polynomial functions Maple tries to produce all zeros at once.

Also the `plot` procedure can be very useful in the process of locating real zeros.

```
> print('The zeros of q in [0,1]' = fsolve(q(x),x,0..1));
> plot(q,0..1);
```

There are many more interesting facts to impart on polynomials, but here we wish to confine ourselves to polynomial functions as the most natural of all mathematical functions.

• Rational Functions

Next in line is the rational function, which is the name given to a quotient of two polynomial functions. We again use the same polynomial q, defined in this worksheet, so that it should still be available.

```
> f := x -> q(x)/(2*x+1);
> simplify(f(x)); f(-1/2);
```

The function f is not defined at $x = -\frac{1}{2}$, clearly on account of the vanishing of the denominator at this point. Maybe the limit of $f(x)$ exists for $x \to -\frac{1}{2}$?

```
> Limit(f(x),x = -1/2) = limit(f(x),x = -1/2);
```

Apparently, the answer is negative. As a matter of fact, left and right limits at this point do exist, they are distinct though. Verify this by giving the following instructions:

```
> Limit(f(x),x=-1/2,left) = limit(f(x),x=-1/2,left);
> Limit(f(x),x=-1/2,right) = limit(f(x),x=-1/2,right);
```

Maple's answers suggest a possible vertical asymptote at $x = -\frac{1}{2}$. A plot of f should confirm this.

```
>  plot(f,-1..2,-1..8);
```

We have truncated the graph by only considering functional values between -1 and 8 as can be seen from the third argument of `plot`; this argument defines the vertical range of the plot. The Maple graph is a collection of small line segments joining neighbouring points. Choosing `style=point` in the plot should make the discontinuity at $x = -\frac{1}{2}$ easier to spot.

The plot also shows two zeros both contained in the interval $[0, 1]$. The command

```
>  fsolve(f(x),x,0..1);
```

only finds the smallest zero; restricting the search interval to exclude this one will give an approximation of the largest zero.

```
>  fsolve(f(x),x,0.5..1);
```

Limits for $x \to \infty$ are no problem for the Maple system. Try for instance:

```
>  Limit(f(x)/x^4,x=infinity) =
>  limit(f(x)/x^4,x=infinity );
```

Earlier on in this worksheet we mentioned the impossibility of the explicit determination of zeros of arbitrary functions including general polynomial functions of degree at least five. This is rather unfortunate, because polynomial zeros have an essential significance for many mathematical problems and processes. Moreover, there is real danger in replacing exact zeros by numerical approximations, because repeated rounding in complex computational processes may cause the accumulation of small errors beyond reasonable bounds, with a substantial loss of significance as a result.

Maple has a feature for the fixation of polynomial zeros in some sort of place holders, which allows further exact computation with polynomial zeros for which no explicit expressions are available. The Maple function with this action has the rather apt name of `RootOf`. The next few lines show how to apply this procedure.

```
>  solve(q(x),x);
>  alias(alpha = RootOf(q(x)));
>  qzeros := allvalues(alpha);
```

In the second line, the 'general' zero of q is given the alias α. The `alias` command is used to replace a complicated, long name by a more manageable one. So $q(\alpha) = 0$, which as a matter of fact is α's defining property. From here on, in all calculations to follow, Maple will use the variable α as the exact 'generic' root of the equation $q(x) = 0$. The third and last instruction checks whether α keeps the correct numerical values.

Another way of verifying that Maple is familiar with α's role as 'root-keeper' is by direct substitution of $x = \alpha$ into $q(x)$.

```
>  q(alpha); evala(%);
```

The a at the end of evala is the first letter of 'algebraic'. Algebraic evaluation is the evaluation of algebraic numbers, and algebraic numbers are, by definition, the roots of polynomial equations with rational coefficients.

Next consider the quotient of $q(x)$ and $x - \alpha$. Because α is a simple zero of q—which can be seen from the list qzeros of α-values—this quotient has a limit for $x \rightarrow \alpha$.

```
>  Limit('q(x)'/(x-alpha),x=alpha) =
>  limit(q(x)/(x-alpha),x=alpha);
```

Result is $q'(\alpha)$

Clearly, Maple simplified the quotient of $q(x)$ and $x - \alpha$ and substituted α for x in the reduced rational expression.
Finally, in the resulting α-expression, replace α by the largest real zero of q, or rather by an approximation of it.

```
>  subs(alpha = qzeros[5],%);
```

rhs(%)

Now you are invited to complete **assignment** 2 of worksheet FuncA2a.mws (see page 54). This assignment considers the limit of a rational function at a rather special point.

• A Periodic Function

Let us next try to define our own function. The following procedure gives a sort of sawtooth function:

better: use "is"

```
>  sawtooth := proc(x) local k;
>  k := floor(x);
>  if type(k,even) then x - k
>  elif type(k,odd) then 1 - x + k
>  else 'sawtooth(x)'
>  fi end;
```

if is(k,even)...
if is(k,odd)...

We remind you of the **floor** function, also called the 'entier' function. By definition $\lfloor x \rfloor$, which is the mathematical way of writing **floor(x)**, returns the largest integer less or equal its argument value x.
Observe that $k = \lfloor x \rfloor$ is indeterminate when x is, so that the parity of k in the **sawtooth** procedure cannot be determined. Therefore, **sawtooth(x)** cannot be evaluated for indeterminate x. That is why the **sawtooth** procedure returns the string **sawtooth(x)** unevaluated in that case. Consequently, the **limit** procedure can not be applied either, for this procedure tries to evaluate **sawtooth(x)** for

indeterminate x. On the other hand it is possible to view the graph of the
`sawtooth` function, because the `plot` procedure uses the function values of only
finitely many explicit points.

```
>   limit(sawtooth(x),x=1);
>   plot(sawtooth,-4.2..5.2);
```

This sawtooth function can be defined in more than one way. Another definition
uses its periodicity. First we define the unique part of sawtooth to be repeated
(the period), for which any interval of length 2 may be chosen, so $[0, 2]$ will do.
Here, sawtooth can be seen as a piecewise function, comprising two parts, namely:
$\text{sawtooth}(x) = x$ on the subinterval $[0, 1]$, and $\text{sawtooth}(x) = 2 - x$ for $x \in [1, 2]$.
Maple has the `piecewise` procedure for just such an occasion.

```
>   sawperiod := x -> piecewise(x <= 1,x,1 < x,2 - x);
```

Please check that the `sawperiod` and `sawtooth` functions coincide on the interval
$[0, 2]$. Next, in the following function prescription, the periodic behaviour is added
by applying the `floor` function.

```
>   sawtooth2 := x -> sawperiod(x - 2*floor(x/2));
```

For this second sawtooth function,

$$\lim_{x \to 2k} \texttt{sawtooth2}(x) = 0 \quad \text{and} \quad \lim_{x \to 2k-1} \texttt{sawtooth2}(x) = 1$$

for any $k \in \mathbb{Z}$.

This is a good place to have a break and try your hand at the final assignment
of worksheet FuncA2a.mws (see page 54). The subject of **assignment 3** of this
worksheet is a continuous, piecewise function.

• Some Standard Limits

Maple knows a large number of elementary functions, amongst which are the
trigonometric functions and their inverse functions, and the logarithmic and exponential functions. Two standard limits are:

```
>   Limit(x*log(x),x=0) = limit(x*log(x),x=0);
>   Limit(x*sin(1/x),x=0) = limit(x*sin(1/x),x=0);
```

To illustrate the latter, it is instructive to have a look at the graph of the function
$x \sin(1/x)$ close to 0. The lines $y = x$ and $y = -x$ are added for clarity.

```
>   plot({x*sin(1/x),x,-x},x=-0.1..0.1,-0.1..0.1);
```

Note that the first argument of the `plot` procedure is a set of three expressions in
the variable x; these are plotted and displayed in one and the same Maple plot.

Finally, consider another rather well-known limit.

```
> assume(a,positive):
> Limit(x^b/exp(a*x),x=infinity) =
> limit(x^b/exp(a*x),x=infinity);
```

Maple's `assume` command is used to indicate that the unknown a is assumed to be positive. It is clear that the limit above can not be evaluated without knowing the sign of a. Note that in Maple's output a tilde is added to a: $a\sim$. This symbol tells us that Maple has some knowledge of a, without knowing its exact numerical value. Also observe that the sign of b is of no consequence.

```
> a;
> about(a);
```

Apparently Maple knows that a belongs to the open interval $(0, \infty)$.

2.4.2   Assignments 2a. Functions

The next assignments are contained in worksheet FuncA2a.mws associated with the worksheet FuncW2a.mws.

1. Determine the polynomial form of the expression

    $$(1 + x)^4$$

    and verify that the coefficient of the monomial x^k is equal to `binomial(4,k)` for each $k = 0, 1, \ldots, 4$; this follows directly from Newton's Binomium. Note that the command `binomial(n,k)` gives the binomial coefficient $\binom{n}{k}$.

2. Use Maple to determine the limit of the function

    ```
    > g := x -> (x^3+5*x^2+8*x+4)/(x+1);
    ```

    for $x \to -1$. To check your answer, take a close look at the graph of $g(x)$ over the interval $[-3, 1]$.

3. We define the function f_3 as follows:

    $$f_3(x) = \begin{cases} a(x - 2)^2 & \text{if } x < 0 \\ \exp(x) & \text{if } x \geq 0 \end{cases}$$

    For what value of $a \in \mathbb{R}$ is f_3 a continuous function?
    For this value of a, create a Maple procedure `f3` using the `piecewise` function. Look at the graph of this function over the interval $[-5, 5]$ and also over its subinterval $[-1, 1]$. Do these graphs suggest that `f3` is differentiable at $x = 0$? Can you decide whether a function is differentiable by only looking at its graph?

2.4.3 Worksheet 2b. Sequences

This worksheet is about sequences of numbers. As you may recall, sequences are merely functions defined on some set of integers including all natural numbers. We have seen in Worksheet 2a (FuncW2a.mws) how functions can be introduced, and this obviously covers sequences as well.

The most important question we can ask about a given sequence is this: does it converge to a limit? Maple knows most standard limits that can be found in an average textbook on Mathematical Analysis. But Maple is also very good at offering help with limits not included in the standard Maple collection, such as inductively defined sequences; by and large these are unknown to Maple.

Summarizing, we shall mainly focus on Maple's standard limits, limit points and limits in general, monotonic sequences, inductively (or recursively) defined sequences and their convergence behaviour.

• A monotonic Sequence

The first sequence we shall consider is very well known to Maple. We begin our session again with a restart.

```
> restart:
> a := n -> (1-1/n)^(n+1):  a[n]=a(n);
> Limit(a[n],n=infinity) = limit(a(n),n=infinity);
```

Maple seems to be familiar with this sequence's limit behaviour. Note that we have used the standard notation for functions $a(n)$, where the n-th term of a (mathematical) sequence usually is denoted by a_n with index n. The notation a[n] is standard Maple notation for the n-th element of the list a. Our a however, as defined above, is not a Maple list, but a function (procedure). A mathematical sequence usually is a sequence of numbers, where a Maple sequence is a finite expression sequence of objects, separated by commas.

```
> b := seq(a(n),n=1..6):
> type(a,procedure); type(a,list);
> whattype(b);
```

Hence b[n]$= a(n)$ for $n = 1, \ldots, 6$.
We can check this with the for-loop

```
> for i from 1 to 6 do b[i] - a(i) od;
```

Returning to our (mathematical) sequence a, we could ask: is this sequence monotonic? To get some idea about its behaviour, let us compute a few numerical values. There is no need for a great deal of precision yet: four significant digits will do for the moment.

```
>  seq(evalf(a(n+1)/a(n),4),n=2..20);
```

We get the impression of dealing with a monotonically increasing sequence, because the quotient of successive elements approaches 1 from above, or so it appears. To confirm this, let us first remove n's present value of 21 by assigning its own name to the variable n.

```
>  n := 'n':   a[n+1]/a[n] = asympt(a(n+1)/a(n),n);
```

The Maple command `asympt` gives the asymptotic expansion of its first argument in terms of powers of its second argument. In other words, $a(n+1)/a(n)$ is expressed as a sum of powers of n so that we can immediately read off its behaviour for $n \to \infty$. In fact we deduce that $a(n+1)/a(n)$ converges to 1 with the same speed as n^{-2}. Although it seems evident that a is monotonically increasing, a cast iron proof of this fact has not yet been given. However, we do know that $a(n+1)/a(n) > 1$ for n sufficiently large. In order to really prove this for all $n \geq 1$, Maple is of limited use. In fact, observe that for all $n > 1$,

$$
\frac{a(n+1)}{a(n)} = \frac{n}{n+1}\left(1 + \frac{1}{n^2 - 1}\right)^{n+1} > \frac{n}{n+1}\left(1 + \frac{n+1}{n^2 - 1}\right) = \frac{n^2}{n^2 - 1} > 1.
$$

• Stirling's Asymptotic Formula

Next we turn to Stirling's asymptotic formula for $n!$. Maple also knows about it. To verify this, use the following `stirling` function:

```
>  stirling := n -> (n/exp(1))^n*sqrt(2*Pi*n);
>  Limit(n!/stirling(n),n=infinity) =
>  limit(n!/stirling(n),n=infinity);
```

More information about the way the stirling expression behaves for large n, such as its convergence speed relative to that of n-powers, can be obtained with

```
>  n!/stirling(n) = asympt(n!/stirling(n),n,3);
```

The third argument of the `asympt` procedure (3 in the present case) controls the number of terms of the asymptotic expansion.

Now turn to **assignment 1** of worksheet FuncA2b.mws (see page 59) and try and answer a few questions about this **stirling** function.

Maple is rather clever at calculating limits, even quite difficult ones, but now and then it gets confused, mostly for obvious reasons. Occasionally Maple is able to surprise us by giving up on a seemingly innocent limit. Consider the following example:

```
>   limit(sqrt(1+(-1)^n)/n,n=infinity);
```

Apparently, Maple is unable to compute this limit! However, a simple application of the sandwich (or pincer) theorem shows that this limit exists and has value 0. Indeed, the expression is bounded by 0 from below and by $\sqrt{2}/n$ from above for all $n \geq 1$.

• Recurrently Defined Sequences

We shall close this worksheet with a brief look at a few recurrently defined sequences, 'recurrences' for short. For instance:

```
>   recurrence := 2*c(n) = c(n-1) + c(n-2);
```

We can use the Maple command `rsolve` (`r` for recurrence) to try and find an explicit expression for $c(k)$.

```
>   'c(k)' = rsolve({recurrence,c(0)=c[0],c(1)=c[1]},c(k));
```

The result speaks for itself. Note that the recurrence relation and the initial conditions together are placed between set braces.

Assignment 2 of worksheet FuncA2b.mws (see page 59) pays attention to the (recurrently defined) Fibonacci numbers.

For the definition of the next recurrent sequence we shall use the following function:

```
>   g := x -> x/2 + 2/x^2;
```

The recurrence we have in mind is given by the iteration

$$x_{n+1} = g(x_n),$$

where (x_n) is initialized by $x_0 = 1.5$.

Now define the following simple Maple procedure:

```
>   x := proc(n::integer) option remember;
>   if n = 0 then 1.5
>   else g(x(n-1))
>   fi end;
```

The first few elements of this sequence are quickly generated by

```
>   seq(x(n),n=0..10);
```

We have deliberately chosen to evaluate the elements of the sequence numerically. Do you know why? If you are not sure about the answer, change 1.5 to $\frac{3}{2}$ in the sequence's defining procedure and try again to evaluate the beginning of the sequence. Be warned though, it may take some time!

Inspection of the values thus obtained suggests the beginning of a convergent process. The values of $x(n)$ for $n = 30, \ldots, 40$ confirm this: there is no visible difference. However, this does not yet prove convergence, at least not rigorously. The Maple file iteratio.mpl contains a simple animation of this iterative process. The following lines instruct Maple to read this file (don't miss the back quotes around the name):

```
>   interface(echo=2):
>   read 'c:/Maple/Book/R5/Chapter2/iteratio.mpl';
```

Click on the graph with your right mouse button, choose the submenu 'animation' from the pop-up menu, and then select the 'play' option. This animation shows clearly that $x(n)$ comes closer to the intersection of the graph of $y = g(x)$ and the line $y = x$ with each increasing n. The limit value of the sequence $(x(n))$ therefore appears to be equal to the real solution of the equation $x = g(x)$.
Manipulating the buttons on the button bar of the animation window you can repeat the animation step by step, or play it in reverse order. The animation speed can also be adjusted.
It also follows that the function g maps the square $D = \{(x, y) \mid 1.45 \le x, y \le 1.75\}$ into itself. Thus $g|D : D \to D$ (the notation $g|D$ is short for the 'restriction of g to D').

Consider $\lim_{n \to \infty} x(n)$. What could its value possibly be? It was suggested that this limit is a root of the equation $x = g(x)$. Let us call this root α. So

```
>   alias(alpha = RootOf(x=g(x),x));
>   allvalues(alpha);
```

Maple gives three possible values for α, only one of which is real. So this must be the limit value we are looking for. Hence, the only real root of $x = g(x)$ is $x = \alpha = 4^{1/3}$. First redefine α.

```
>   alpha := 4^(1/3):
```

Calculating the limit of the quotient

```
>   Limit(('g'(x)-'alpha')/(x-'alpha'),x='alpha') =
>   limit((g(x)-alpha)/(x-alpha),x=alpha);
```

shows that it has a negative value. This explains that successive elements of $(x(n))$ lie on opposite sides of α. Further, the absolute value of this limit is less than 1, therefore $x(n + 1)$ is closer to α than $x(n)$. All this implies that $x(n)$ converges to α when n tends to infinity.

Assignment 3 of worksheet FuncA2b.mws (see page 59) considers a similar recurrently defined sequence associated with a different function g.

2.4.4 Assignments 2b. Sequences

The following assignments are part of worksheet FuncA2b.mws.

1. On page 56 we defined the following `stirling` function:

   ```
   >  stirling := n -> (n/exp(1))^n*sqrt(2*Pi*n);
   ```

   Use the `evalf` procedure to compare the stirling value `stirling(k)` with $k!$ for $k = 3, 4, 5, 6, 7$. Does this `stirling` function give a good approximation?

   Now define the sequence (d_n) by

   $$nd_n := \frac{\texttt{stirling}(n)}{\texttt{stirling}(n-1)}.$$

   Determine the limit of this sequence (d_n). Explain Maple's answer.

2. The Fibonacci numbers are usually introduced by the following recurrent definition:

   $$recur := fib(n) = fib(n-1) + fib(n-2);$$

   Use the `rsolve` procedure to solve the recurrence. Note that $fib(0) = 0$ and $fib(1) = 1$.

   Compute $fib(3)$, $fib(4)$ and $fib(5)$ using Maple's solution. The `subs` procedure can be useful to substitute $n = 3$, $n = 4$ or $n = 5$ into the solution; the `factor` command can be used to give Maple's answer a normal appearance.

3. The sequence (z_n) is defined recurrently by

   $$z_0 = 1, \; z_n = \sqrt{2 + z_{n-1}} \quad \text{for} \quad n = 1, 2, \ldots$$

   Write a procedure of the form

   ```
   >  z := proc(n::integer) option remember; ...  end;
   ```

   and use it to compute the (numerical values of the) first 10 elements of the sequence. The `seq` command can be useful.

   Why does $\lim_{n \to \infty} z_n$ exist, and what is its value L? Note that L has to satisfy the equation $L = \sqrt{2 + L}$, because

   $$L = \lim_{n \to \infty} z_n = \lim_{n \to \infty} z_{n-1}.$$

2.5 Exercises

1. The function $g(x, p)$ investigated in this chapter's Maple session (see page 41) can be defined quite naturally as a continuous function of x on the interval $[0, 1]$ for any $p \in (0, 1)$. Verify this. Further show that this function is strictly monotonically increasing and that $g(x, p) = x$ for all $x \in [0, 1]$ in case $p = \frac{1}{2}$.

   Remark. This exercise is rather difficult. A complete solution is given in Appendix B on page 188.

2. It is claimed that the strange sequence introduced in the Maple session of this chapter by the name of `stranger` (see page 45) has seven limit points. Prove this.

3. For what value(s) of the constant a is the function

$$f(x) = \begin{cases} \dfrac{\log(1 - a^2 + a^2 x)}{x - 1} & \text{if } 0 \le x < 1 \\ \dfrac{1}{1 - ax} & \text{if } x \ge 1 \end{cases}$$

   continuous at each point of the interval $[0, \infty)$?

4. Compute

$$\lim_{n \to \infty} \frac{\left(2n^{1/n} - 1\right)^n}{n^2}.$$

   See also assignment 2 of FuncA2b.mws (page 61).

5. Show that the sequence with general term

$$\left(1 + \frac{1}{n}\right)^{n^2} n^{-(n+\frac{1}{2})} n!$$

   is monotonically decreasing and determine its limit.

6. The recurrent sequence (a_n) given by

$$a_0 = 1, \quad a_n = \sqrt{1 + a_{n-1}} \ \text{ for } n = 1, 2, \ldots$$

   is monotonic and bounded. Prove this. Also compute its limit.

7. It is not very difficult to check that the sequence (x_n), generated by repeated application of the sine function to an initial value $x_0 \in (0, \pi)$, is strictly monotonically decreasing to 0. Thus for $x_0 \in (0, \pi)$ and

$$x_{n+1} = \sin(x_n) \ \text{ for } n = 0, 1, \ldots,$$

we have $0 < x_{n+1} < x_n$ and $\lim_{n\to\infty} x_n = 0$. Prove this. Also calculate the limit

$$\lim_{n\to\infty} \left(\frac{1}{x_{n+1}^2} - \frac{1}{x_n^2} \right).$$

8. Use Maple to get information on the existence of the limit (right and/or left limit if necessary) of the function

$$x^a \ln(|x|) \quad (a \text{ real})$$

as x tends to 0. Observe that for any real non-zero a, the power x^a is only defined for $x > 0$. Use the `assume` function to distinguish between $a = 0$, $a > 0$, and $a < 0$.

9. Write a Maple procedure that, given the input pair (f, x), returns the function value $f(x)$ if $f(x) > 0$ and 0 otherwise. Here f is a general function (hence a procedure) and x is an indeterminate. Name this procedure `Plus`. It may help you to think of Maple's `max` function. Similarly, a procedure `Minus` should be written, returning a negative function value $f(x)$ or 0. Give the Maple code for both procedures.
   There is a relation between `Plus`, `Minus`, and Maple's `abs` function. What is it?

10. It is a well-known fact that the sequence with general term

$$(1 - 1/n)^n, \quad n = 1, 2, \ldots$$

is strictly monotonically increasing. Use Maple to prove this. Clearly, the sequence is bounded and hence convergent. Compute its limit. Apply the technique used in Worksheet 2b (`FuncW2b.mws`).

11. Assume $k > 0$ and constant. Let Maple compute the limit of the sequence with n-th term

$$(2k^{\frac{1}{n}} - 1)^n.$$

The answer may surprise you, it may even make you suspect that it could be wrong. To find out, apply the natural logarithm function to the general term and remember that

$$\lim_{x\to 0} \frac{\log(1 + x)}{x} = 1.$$

It may also be a good idea to first consider the limit

$$\lim_{n\to\infty} n(k^{\frac{1}{n}} - 1).$$

Show in a few lines of Maple code (with corresponding output of course) what you tried and discovered.

12. The purpose of this exercise is to calculate the limit of the following recursively defined sequence:

$$a_0 = 0, \; a_1 = \frac{1}{2}, \quad a_{n+1} = \frac{1}{3}(1 + a_n + a_{n-1}^3) \; \text{ for } n \geq 1.$$

First show that it strictly increases, and that $a_n \in [0, 1)$ for all n. The fact that (a_n) is monotonic and bounded is a direct consequence of the definition (why?); you do not need to use Maple to prove this.

2.6   Survey of Used Maple Expressions

Below you will find once again a list of Maple expressions and commands used in the present chapter.

expression	brief explanation
`?inifcns`	– yields a list of mathematical functions known to Maple
`f := x -> f(x);`	– (arrow) definition of function f
`f := proc() presc end;`	– definition of prescription **presc** for function f
`unapply(expression,x);`	– extracts the prescription for a function from **expression** depending on x
`map(f,L);`	– applies the function prescription f to each element of the list, vector or matrix L.
`limit(f(x),x=a);`	– limit of $f(x)$ for $x \to a$.
`limit(f(x),x=a,left);`	– limit of $f(x)$ for $x \uparrow a$.
`option remember`	– generates remember table for procedure; prevents stack overflow for recursive procedures
`piecewise`	– used for defining piecewise functions
`RootOf`	– placeholder for zeros of polynomials
`NULL`	– the empty expression sequence

The following selected procedures appear in this chapter for the first time (use the index for more information):
abs, alias, allvalues, assume, asympt, coeff, coeffs, collect, degree, max, min, rsolve, seq, solve, zip.

3

Matrices and Vectors

J ust like Mathematical Analysis, Linear Algebra too offers a number of techniques of great importance for many areas of mathematical application. We leave Analysis for the moment; in a later chapter we shall return to it with topics like differentiation and integration of mathematical functions. Although the present chapter is not of an analytic nature, what we have learned so far, especially about functions, will be rather useful to us in this chapter as well.

3.1   Introduction

The designers of the Maple system have opted for bringing together all Maple functions and procedures about vectors, matrices, vector spaces and linear transformations in a single specialized package called `linalg`. As you already know, Maple packages have to be loaded separately, which means that its procedures are not automatically available at start-up. This the user must do by issuing the Maple command:

```
> with(linalg);
```

In this chapter we shall focus our attention on matrices and vectors and naturally we shall require Maple's assistance to reveal their properties. The next section is again reserved for reminding you of certain basic concepts, this time taken from the field of Linear Algebra. We shall also have occasion to preview some advanced principles and methods you possibly have not been exposed to before. However, all concepts and techniques discussed in this chapter can be found in most standard works on Linear Algebra.

3.2   Selected Concepts from Linear Algebra

It may seem a bit overdone to repeat the definitions of objects like matrix and vector. However, there is no harm in reviewing what most of us seem to agree on when talking about these notions.

An $m \times n$ matrix $A = (a_{ij})$ consists of m columns and n rows, and the matrix element a_{ij} is positioned where the i-th row and the j-th column meet. The related matrix $A^t = (a^t_{ij})$, with $a^t_{ij} = a_{ji}$ for all pairs (i, j), is the transpose of A. The matrix A is called square in case the number of its rows coincides with the number of its columns, that is when $m = n$. An $m \times 1$ matrix is also known as a column vector and likewise, a $1 \times n$ matrix is a row vector. Often rows and columns of a matrix are also called row vectors and column vectors respectively. The set of vectors $\{v_1, v_2, \ldots, v_k\}$ is (linearly) independent if

$$c_1 v_1 + c_2 v_2 + \cdots + c_k v_k = 0$$

only when $c_i = 0$ for all $i = 1, 2, \ldots, k$. The rank of a matrix is the largest possible number of independent column vectors (the column rank). This number happens to be equal to the maximum number of independent row vectors (the row rank). Hence rank = column rank = row rank. Therefore, the rank of any $m \times n$ matrix A satisfies the inequality

$$\text{rank}(A) \leq \min\{m, n\}.$$

We say that A is of full or maximal rank if the equality sign applies in the inequality above. The column vectors of a matrix span a vector space, the so-called column space of the matrix. Furthermore, the span of a set of vectors is by definition the collection of all linear combinations of these vectors. The dimension of the column space of a matrix agrees with the (column) rank of the matrix, and any basis of this space comprises just as many vectors.

An $m \times n$ matrix A of rank k can always be written as a product of two matrices of full rank k. Thus, an $m \times k$ matrix B and an $k \times n$ matrix C exist, such that

$$A = BC \quad \text{and} \quad \text{rank}(B) = \text{rank}(C) = k.$$

This so-called rank factorization is not unique.

A square matrix is non-singular if it is of full rank. Otherwise, it is singular. Every non-singular matrix A is invertible, in other words, it has a unique inverse matrix A^{-1}. A matrix A and its inverse A^{-1} are related by: $AA^{-1} = A^{-1}A = I$. Here $I = (\delta_{ij})$ denotes the identity matrix: $\delta_{ij} = 0$ for all pairs (i, j) with $i \neq j$ and $\delta_{ij} = 1$ for all pairs (i, j) with $i = j$. A necessary and sufficient condition for a square matrix A to be singular is the vanishing of its determinant: $\det(A) = 0$.

A straightforward criterion for the solvability of a system of linear equations $Ax = b$, with matrix of coefficients A of size $m \times n$, depends on the rank of the augmented matrix $A_a = (A \mid b)$: the system is solvable just when $\text{rank}(A_a) = \text{rank}(A)$. An overdetermined system of linear equations, that is a system with more equations than unknowns $(m > n)$, generally will not be solvable. On the other hand, if $m < n$, the system usually will have infinitely many solutions. Finally, if A is square and non-singular, the system has the unique solution $x = A^{-1}b$.

The overdetermined case is encountered in practical situations, where many more observations are available than independent parameters. We shall go into this interesting case in more detail now, because in the next Maple session we intend to give an example of a method for finding a vector which could justly be called a 'near' solution to an overdetermined system of linear equations.

As we mentioned before, a system $Ax = b$, with $m \times n$ matrix A and $m > n$, usually admits no solutions. All the same, there is nothing to stop us searching for a vector x that resembles a solution as closely as possible. Therefore, we have to look for an x forcing the residue vector $r = b - Ax$ to be small, or rather, close to the zero vector. The expression 'close to' can be interpreted in a variety of ways. One of the oldest and most prevailing one is known as the least squares approach. This method chooses x to minimize the Euclidean length (or Euclidean norm) $\|r\|_2$ of the residue vector r. This least squares choice vector x is the solution to the system of linear equations

$$A^t A x = A^t b,$$

the so-called normal equations. As this system happens to be solvable for any A and b, such a solution x always exists. When A has full rank, that is when $\text{rank}(A) = n$, this solution is unique and may be written in the form $x = (A^t A)^{-1} A^t b$. Indeed, in that case the $n \times n$ matrix $A^t A$ is non-singular and hence invertible. Then again, for $\text{rank}(A) < n$, the solution to the normal equations is no longer unique. Now we apply rank factorization to A, that is, we write $A = BC$ where B and C have full rank. Let

$$A^{\text{inverse}} = C^t (CC^t)^{-1} (B^t B)^{-1} B^t.$$

Then $x = A^{\text{inverse}} b$ solves the normal equations, which is readily verified by direct substitution. Of all solutions to our least squares problem, this is the one of shortest Euclidean norm. The matrix A^{inverse} is called the generalized inverse or Moore-Penrose inverse of the matrix A. This definition of the generalized inverse is independent of the particular rank factorization of A we choose. Moreover, in case of a non-singular A, the generalized inverse A^{inverse} coincides with the (normal) inverse A^{-1} of A.

3.3   A Least Squares Filter

This Maple session is about matrices, the way to introduce them into a Maple session will be discussed and how Maple can be made to employ matrices for attacking practical problems. There is a large number of matrix functions known to Maple, some of which will be presented in this session. The worksheets MatrW3a.mws and MatrW3b.mws will go into the manipulation of matrices and vectors in a more systematic way than we need to adopt in the present demonstration.

The Maple sessions of this chapter and other chapters are meant to demonstrate that Maple can be very helpful to the user in his attempt to penetrate the core of a difficult mathematical problem. Even if we do not enter much deeper into the heart of the matter than we would without the use of a CA system, it certainly could speed up the learning process significantly. That is why at times we must make an effort and leave the surface of a problem to explore deeper layers. Therefore, it is just possible that you do not fully comprehend at first the intentions and meaning of the Maple procedures that are presented to you in the Maple sessions. However, the accompanying worksheets will put things right soon enough. After finishing working through these, a second reading of the Maple session could then be more profitable.

3.3.1   Matrices and Vectors

We load all available matrix functions in a single stroke with the Maple command:

```
>  with(linalg):
```

```
Warning, new definition for norm
Warning, new definition for trace
```

Matrices can be introduced using the `matrix` function, which is part of the `linalg` package.

```
>  A := matrix(3,4,(i,j) -> 1 + 2*i - 3*j);
```

$$A := \begin{bmatrix} 0 & -3 & -6 & -9 \\ 2 & -1 & -4 & -7 \\ 4 & 1 & -2 & -5 \end{bmatrix}$$

```
>  A, evalm(A);
```

$$A, \begin{bmatrix} 0 & -3 & -6 & -9 \\ 2 & -1 & -4 & -7 \\ 4 & 1 & -2 & -5 \end{bmatrix}$$

In order to evaluate a matrix, the `evalm` procedure should be used, otherwise the matrix is merely evaluated to its name.

Apart from the `matrix` procedure, the `linalg` package also contains a `vector` command. The first argument of the `vector` procedure determines the number of vector components. Apparently, Maple does not distinguish row vectors from column vectors, because, as you will see below, Maple displays a vector as a list of its components, arranged in a row and separated by commas. The output of Maple's `vector` procedure should always be seen as a one-dimensional list. On the other hand, a column vector really is a 3×1 matrix; here two dimensions are involved. The next lines verify all this.

```
>   b := vector(3,[1,2,3]); c := matrix(1,3,[1,2,3]);
```

$$b := [1,\, 2,\, 3]$$

$$c := \begin{bmatrix} 1 & 2 & 3 \end{bmatrix}$$

```
>   evalm(b&*A);
```

$$[16,\, -2,\, -20,\, -38]$$

```
>   evalm(transpose(A)&*b);
```

$$[16,\, -2,\, -20,\, -38]$$

```
>   evalm(c&*A);
```

$$\begin{bmatrix} 16 & -2 & -20 & -38 \end{bmatrix}$$

```
>   evalm(transpose(A)&*c);
```

```
Error, (in linalg[multiply]) non matching dimensions for
vector/matrix product
```

Note the difference between the list output and the row vector output; the former uses commas to separate elements, the latter does not. First, in `b&*A`, Maple treats the vector `b` as a 1×3 matrix, while in `transpose(A)&*b`, the vector `b` is suddenly seen as a 3×1 matrix! Of course, this is all for the benefit of matching dimensions in vector-matrix multiplication.

The worksheet MatrW1a.mws contains a further discussion on row and column vectors. Also, Gaussian elimination is included and some other simple applications of matrix analysis.

3.3.2   Removing Noise from a Data Set

In the remainder of this Maple session, we shall be occupied with the least squares method applied to the process of removing, or filtering out so-called noise from a given data set.

Consider the following problem. We start from a large given set of N points $P_i = (t_i, b_i)$ $(i = 1, \ldots, N)$ in the plane, which can be viewed as the set of (inexact) observations of an event (or function) f, so that b_i is approximately equal to $f(t_i)$ for $i = 1, \ldots, N$. Our objective is to find a polynomial of fixed degree n that best fits the observed values, in the sense that it does better than all other polynomials of the same degree. Such a polynomial will also give us good approximations (we hope) of other, unobserved values of the function f. Moreover—and this is crucial—we hope to be able to smooth down the irregularities caused by non accurate observations. Our choice of n depends on the overall pattern in which the points P_i are arranged, and we shall use the least squares approximation to obtain a best fit. Therefore, the problem we set out to solve is to compute the least squares solution to the linear system

$$Ax = b,$$

where $A = (a_{ij})$ is the $N \times (n + 1)$ matrix with elements $a_{ij} = t_i^{j-1}$ and b is a vector with components b_i.

Let as first consider a simple example. Suppose we have the use of 100 observations of the sine function on the interval $[0, 2\pi]$. These observations contain small errors, usually referred to as noise (think of the graph of a noisy electronic signal). The noisy character of the sine data can be simulated by adding to each sine value a random value between -0.2 and 0.2. We use Maple's random generator **rand** to generate the additional noise.

```
>  t := vector(100,i -> 2*Pi*i/100):
```
```
>  b := vector(100,i -> sin(t[i]) + 0.2*(rand(101)()-50)/100):
```

Now we shall try to retrieve the true sine curve from the noisy data by computing the best cubic polynomial fit in the least squares sense.
The noisy sine curve is shown below in figure 3.1.

```
>  plot([seq([t[i],b[i]],i=1..100)]);
```

The Maple command **leastsqrs** solves the least squares problem. Of course, we could instead use **linsolve** to solve the system of normal equations.

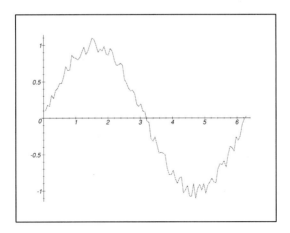

Figure 3.1: Sine function on $[0, 2\pi]$ with added noise

Like so:

```
>  A := matrix(100,4,(i,j) -> t[i]^(j-1)):
>  a := leastsqrs(A,b);
```

$$a := [-.2083613791, 1.900805884, -.8760808616, .09292997638]$$

Maple's `leastsqrs` gives a vector output of polynomial coefficients.

```
>  i := 'i':  p := t -> sum(a[i+1]*t^i,i=0..3);
```

$$p := t \to \sum_{i=0}^{3} a_{i+1} t^i$$

```
>  plot({sin(x),p(x)},x=0..2*Pi);
```

In figure 3.2 the sine function is plotted, superimposed by the graph of the least squares solution. Despite the rather sizeable noise in the sine values, the retrieved curve is not bad at all, at least it is a great improvement on its noisy counterpart. We realize of course that the example may seem rather unfair, knowing that the sine function behaves very much like a cubic polynomial on any interval of length 2π anyway.

Now assume more realistically that our data do not permit good polynomial approximations of low degree. We then could try to filter out the noise by replacing each point $P_i = (t_i, b_i)$ of the data set by another point $(t_i, p_i(t_i))$ obtained by applying the cubic polynomial least squares technique to the original point and its closest neighbours, say five to the left, and five to the right. Here p_i is the least squares cubic polynomial associated with the point P_i; observe that p_i changes from point to point. The first five and the last five data points of our set naturally need special treatment, as there are fewer neighbouring points available.

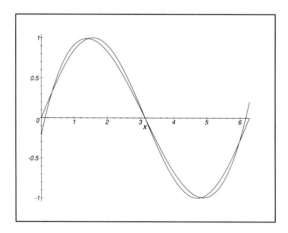

Figure 3.2: The sine function and its cubic least squares approximation

Let us first generate a 200-point data set on the interval $[0, 1]$. We use a strongly fluctuating data function to assist us.

```
> datafunction := x -> exp(-(10*x-2)^2) + exp(-2*(10*x-4)^2) +
> exp(-4*(10*x-6)^2) + exp(-8*(10*x-8)^2);
```

$$datafunction := x \rightarrow e^{(-(10x-2)^2)} + e^{(-2(10x-4)^2)} + e^{(-4(10x-6)^2)} + e^{(-8(10x-8)^2)}$$

```
> p1 := plot(datafunction(x),x=0..1):   p1;
```

The right-hand plot of figure 3.3 shows the graph of the function `datafunction`.

Next we generate the data set of function values with noise.

```
> N := 200:   argset := [seq(i/N,i=1..N)]:   _seed := 123456:
> funcset := [seq(evalf(datafunction(i/N) +
> 0.2*(rand(N+1)() - N/2)/N),i=1..N)]:
> dataset := zip((a,b) -> [a,b],argset,funcset):
> plot(dataset);
```

Next to the graph of the data function in figure 3.3, the noisy data is unmistakable.

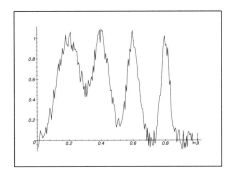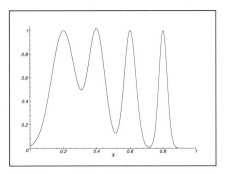

Figure 3.3: Dataset with and without noise

We shall use the least squares technique described in detail above to smooth down the rough edges from `dataset`. The Maple code is given below.

```
>  nfuncset := [ ]:  k := 'k':
>  for k to 5 do nfuncset := [op(nfuncset),funcset[k]] od:
>  for k from 6 to N-6 do
>  A := matrix(11,4,(i,j) -> argset[k+i-6]^(j-1)):
>  b := vector(11, i -> funcset[k+i-6]):
>  a := leastsqrs(A,b):
>  m := 'm':  p := t -> sum(a[m+1]*t^m,m=0..3):
>  nfuncset := [op(nfuncset),evalf(p(argset[k]))] od:
>  for k from N-5 to N do
>  nfuncset := [op(nfuncset),funcset[k]] od:
>  ndataset := [zip((a,b) -> [a,b],argset,nfuncset)]:
```

To save time we have performed the computations and saved the results into the file `filter.m` by means of the Maple instruction:

```
>  save ndataset, 'c:/Maple/Book/R5/Chapter3/filter.m':
```

This file can be read with the command `read`. The point is that reading this file takes much less time than performing the computations.

```
>  read 'c:/Maple/Book/R5/Chapter3/filter.m':
```

The next figure (figure 3.4) shows the graph of the original data function superimposed by that of the new data set. Except for a few points at the beginning and at the end of the interval, and those at the function's extremes, the result is quite satisfactory.

```
>  p2 := plot(ndataset,color=black):
>  plots[display]({p1,p2});
```

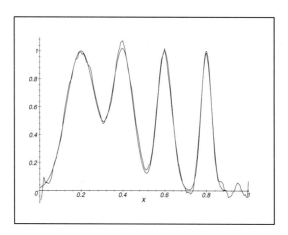

Figure 3.4: Least squares approximation of the noisy data set compared to its pristine original

The subpackage `fit` of Maple's `stats` package also contains a least squares procedure, called `leastsquare`. This procedure is very suitable for curve-fitting in the least squares sense. We might just as well have used this procedure for the application given above. However, wishing to avoid the black-box character of the latter, we chose for a more transparent approach.

3.4   Worksheets and Assignments

The worksheets MatrW3a.mws and Matr3b.mws are closely related to the previous Maple session in so far as only topics from the fields of Matrix Theory and Linear Algebra are considered. The worksheets mentioned are integrally incorporated in slightly adjusted from. This is also true for the assignment worksheets MatrA3a.mws and MatrA3b.mws.

3.4.1   Worksheet 3a. Matrices

Main topics of this worksheet include the basics of matrix introduction and manipulation under the Maple system. Further, we shall meet many of Maple's standard matrix functions, we shall look at Gaussian elimination and backsubstitution, and some other elementary problems of Linear Algebra will be discussed as well.

• Introducing a Matrix

As you should know by now, the `linalg` package will put at our immediate disposal all matrix functions Maple has to offer. We begin with a restart to clear Maple's internal memory.

```
>   restart:  with(linalg):
```

A matrix is not a number, but a collection of numbers or expressions grouped or structured in a special way. On the other hand, a set is a collection without any structure. Further, a list has the one-dimensional structure of a sequence, and a matrix consists of rows and columns (both lists), which give the matrix its two-dimensional structure. This explains why Maple uses the two-dimensional array data structure for the definition of a matrix. The elements of an array are arranged by a double index system.

There are many different ways to introduce a matrix into a Maple session. One direct way is:

```
>   A := matrix([[1,2,3,4],[8,7,6,5],[1,0,-2,3]]);
```

The 3×4 matrix A is explicitly given by its successive rows. Another way is to provide all its elements in a long list from top left to bottom right. But then the size of A should be given explicitly as well.

```
>   A := matrix(3,4,[1,2,3,4,8,7,6,5,1,0,-2,3]);
```

Each specific matrix element can be extracted by using a double index system, row number first. The instruction

```
>   A[2,3];
```

shows the matrix element on the intersection of the second row and the third column. An individual matrix element can be changed by assigning a new value to it.

```
>   A[2,3] := 9;
```

Now verify that this change really has taken effect.

```
>   A = evalm(A);
```

Apparently, calling just A (note that no back quotes are used around A in the left-hand side) returns A unevaluated without showing its elements. The letter `m` in `evalm` comes from 'matrix' of course. The `evalm` command reveals the values of all elements of many types of matrix expressions, such as sums and products of matrices.

```
>  evalm(A + A);
```

This deviating property of matrix evaluation has a peculiar effect on assignments
like

```
>  B := A;
```

Each element of B gets the same value as the corresponding element of A, which
is to be expected really. What is more surprising is that new changes on the
elements of A automatically effect B in the same way!

```
>  evalm(A), evalm(B); A[2,3] := 6; evalm(A), evalm(B);
```

To avoid this happening we have Maple's copy command.

```
>  C := copy(A);
>  evalm(A), evalm(C); A[3,4] := 11; evalm(A), evalm(C);
```

Observe that the change in A has no effect on the matrix C.

The elements of a matrix often show a certain regularity. In many cases such a
regular pattern can be considered the result of a function prescription applied to
each pair of indices (i, j). Maple enables the user to insert a prescription as part
of the matrix definition. For example:

```
>  f := (i,j) -> 1/(i+j-1);
>  H := n -> matrix(n,n,f);
```

This defines the so-called Hilbert matrices $H(n)$.

```
>  H(4);
```

It is not absolutely necessary to introduce a matrix in the completely explicit way
of giving all its elements as we did before. A symbolic matrix is obtained when
elements are not explicitly given. Of course, the size of the matrix must then be
specified.

```
>  A := matrix(2,3); evalm(A);
```

It is also possible to instruct Maple to provide a symmetric (symbolic) matrix.
However, this can not be done by means of the matrix command, the array
procedure should be used instead. After introducing a symmetric matrix A in
this way, it is easy to check that A is indeed symmetric.

```
>  A := array(1..3,1..3,'symmetric');
>  i := 'i'; j := 'j'; A[i,j] - A[j,i];
```

First we have made sure that both i and j are indeterminate.

Other special matrices are zero matrices and identity matrices. A zero matrix
is a matrix of only zero elements. It can be defined by inserting a single 0 at
the position where we normally type the matrix elements, or where the element
prescription goes.

```
>  ZeroMatrix := (m,n) -> matrix(m,n,0);
>  ZeroMatrix(2,3);
```

Identity matrices are not automatically provided by Maple, the user himself has
to create them.

```
>  Id1 := n -> array(1..n,1..n,'identity');
>  Id2 := n -> matrix(n,n,(i,j) -> if i=j then 1 else 0 fi);
>  Id1(3), Id2(4);
```

A disadvantage of both methods is that the size has to be specified. It would be
nice to have a single symbol for all identity matrices. The symbol I (capital i) is
generally reserved for this purpose. But Maple has another use for it, namely the
complex number $i = \sqrt{-1}$. Fortunately, the designers of Maple invented another
symbol, or rather procedure, that produces a universal identity matrix, namely
&*(). Assisted by Maple's `alias` function, we can now create a more natural
symbol, such as Id, which is short for identity.

```
>  alias(Id = &*());
```

Recall that Maple uses the &* symbol for matrix multiplication, in contrast to the
single * which stands for scalar multiplication. One reason for this difference is
that the usual multiplication symbol * is only used for commutative operations,
and, as you know, matrix multiplication is not commutative. The distinction
between commutative and non-commutative is important in connection with the
automatic simplification of complicated expressions.

```
>  A := matrix(7,5); evalm(A&*Id - Id&*A);
```

Note that in the second expression above the symbol Id is used for two different
identity matrices, one of size 5×5, the other of size 7×7.

• Computations with Matrices

In order to test hypotheses like: "matrix multiplication is non-commutative",
it is often convenient to use random matrices. The procedure `randmatrix`
produces such matrices. A number of options, such as `sparse`, `symmetric`,
and `anti-symmetric` are available. Recall that an anti-symmetric matrix A
satisfies the condition $A^t = -A$, and that most elements (let us say at least
80%) of a sparse matrix are zero.

```
> A := randmatrix(5,5); B := randmatrix(5,5);
> equal(A&*B - B&*A,matrix(5,5,0));
```

We may conclude that, generally speaking, the matrix products AB and BA do not coincide.

With `equal(A,B)` Maple checks that both matrix arguments A and B are equal.

At this point you could put your knowledge to the test by completing **assignment 1** and **assignment 2** of worksheet MatrA3a.mws. In **assignment 1** (see page 77) random matrices are used to test a certain hypothesis, and **assignment 2** (see page 78) considers lower triangular matrices.

You should now be familiar with the process of creating matrices. The definitions of matrix addition and matrix multiplication are known to you as well. Power matrices and a matrix's inverse follow suit.
Introduce the following matrices and take a look at the way the matrix C is composed; pay special attention to the placing of parentheses.

```
> A := matrix(2,3,[1,2,3,4,5,6]);
> B := matrix(2,2,[1,-1,3,-1]);
> C := (2*(B^3 + inverse(B))&*A)/5:  evalm(C);
```

On clicking the right mouse button on one of the matrices, a menu of common matrix functions pops up. Note that for the square matrix B there are more procedures available than for the other two matrices.

• Solving a System of Linear Equations

Next we shall solve a system of linear equations by matrix computation. Let us choose a matrix of coefficients A and a constant vector b.

```
> A := matrix(3,3,[1,2,3,2,5,3,1,0,8]);
> b := vector([5,3,17]);
```

It can hardly be called a remarkable achievement to have Maple solve the system $Ax = b$. The command `linsolve` will do it.

```
> x := linsolve(A,b);
```

As we wish to gain more insight into the reduction process Gaussian elimination is based on, we shall take another approach. Therefore we first create the augmented matrix:

```
> A_b := augment(A,b);
```

Now apply row reduction to this augmented matrix. First exchange the first and third rows, then subtract the first row twice from the second row, and after that subtract the first row from the third row. This is put into effect by the three instructions:

```
> swaprow(%,1,3);
> addrow(%,1,2,-2);
> addrow(%,1,3,-1);
```

The Maple commands `swaprow` and `addrow` speak for themselves. You see zeros appear in the first column. Next subtract $\frac{2}{5}$ times the second row from the third row, and after that multiply the last row by 5. Now we have obtained the row reduced form of the augmented matrix used in the Gaussian elimination process to extract a solution.

```
> addrow(%,2,3,-2/5);
> R := mulrow(%,3,5);
```

Applying `backsub` (back substitution) to the reduced form `R` immediately gives the solution.

Verify this by typing:

```
> backsub(R); equal(backsub(R),x);
```

Finally, the reduced row-echelon form can be obtained directly from the augmented matrix by means of the Maple procedure `rref`, which is short for 'reduced row-echelon form'.

```
> evalm(rref(A_b));
```

In assignment 3 of worksheet MatrA3a.mws (see page 78) the reduced row-echelon form of a matrix is used to compute the inverse of a matrix.

3.4.2 Assignments 3a. Matrices

The assignments in this subsection relate to the topics discussed in worksheet MatrW3a.mws.

1. (a) Use the procedure `randmatrix` to introduce two random 4×4 matrices M and N.

   (b) Compare the matrices $(M^t)^{-1}$ and $(M^{-1})^t$.

   (c) Use the matrices M and N to test the hypothesis:

   "$\det(A + B)$ is generally not equal to $\det(A) + \det(B)$."

(d) Compare $\det(kM)$ and $\det(kN)$ with $\det(M)$ and $\det(N)$, respectively, for any constant k. What is the relation between $\det(kA)$ and $\det(A)$ for an arbitrary 4×4 matrix A and $k \in \mathbb{R}$?

2. A square matrix $A = (a_{ij})$ is called lower triangular if $a_{ij} = 0$ for all pairs (i, j) with $i < j$.

(a) Write the Maple code for a function

```
>  g := proc(i,j)  ...  end;
```

that assigns to (i, j) a random integer in the interval $[0, 100]$ if $i \geq j$, and 0 otherwise.
You can use the command `rand(100)()` to obtain a random integer in the interval $[0, 100]$.

(b) Apply function g of part (a) to generate two 6×6 lower triangular random matrices P and Q. Verify that their product PQ is again lower triangular.

3. Determine the inverse of the 4×4 Hilbert matrix $H(4)$ by computing the reduced row-echelon form of the matrix formed by $H(4)$ augmented with the identity matrix. Check your answer by calculating the product of $H(4)$ and the computed inverse.

The command `submatrix` can be useful to extract a specified submatrix from a matrix. Use Maple's help system to see some examples of the use of this `submatrix` procedure.
The Hilbert matrices $H(n)$ can be introduced as follows:

```
>  H := n -> matrix(n,n,(i,j) -> 1/(i+j-1));
```

3.4.3   Worksheet 3b. Vectors

In this worksheet (MatrW3b.mws) we continue the discussion started in MatrW3a.mws in so far as matrices are concerned, although here the calculus of vectors shall get our main attention. We shall learn several ways of introducing vectors into a Maple session, and how to work with vectors under Maple. For matrix computation Maple knows many specialized commands, and likewise for vector computation. In summary, we shall be concerned with Maple's standard vector functions, the standard inner product and its corresponding vector norm, linear (in)dependence and bases, the Gram-Schmidt orthogonalization process, and several other elementary topics in the field of vector and matrix analysis.

• **Vectors versus Matrices**

We need to load the `linalg` package again, so that all standard matrix and vector functions can be used right away. We begin with a restart of the Maple system to clear Maple's internal memory.

```
> restart:  with(linalg):
```

To the Maple system, all matrices are two-dimensional arrays, even those of size $m \times 1$ and $1 \times n$, which really are vector formats. Hence, in order to call any matrix element, two indices are needed, a row index number and a column index number. In contrast, vectors are one-dimensional arrays. A vector can be defined explicitly by providing its size (or vector dimension) together with a list of elements. For example:

```
> v := vector(4,[1,2,3,4]);
```

The vector dimension can be dropped here. At first it seems as if we are looking at a row vector, but then, the commas show that this vector actually is a list and not a 1×4 matrix. So let us compare our vector v with a proper row vector and an ordinary list of four numbers.

```
> fourlist := [1,2,3,4]; rowvector := matrix([[1,2,3,4]]);
```

Maple's `equal` command will tell us whether these three objects are equivalent by Maple standards.

```
> equal(v,fourlist), evalm(v - fourlist);
> equal(v,rowvector);
```

The error message speaks for itself. Further, the vectors v and `fourlist` are indistinguishable, both being one-dimensional arrays of the same size and with the same entries. On the other hand, `rowvector` is a matrix which to Maple is never a vector. Let us emphasize that the use of the predicate 'row' or 'column' in combination with 'vector' is only meaningful in the framework of matrices. A vector is simply a list, that is all there is to it. This is confirmed by the output of the following Maple lines:

```
> Id4 := diag(1,1,1,1):  # this is the 4x4 identity matrix
> evalm(v&*Id4); evalm(Id4&*v); # v is a vector
> evalm(Id4&*rowvector); # 'rowvector' is a matrix
```

Note the error message as a result of the third input line.

● **Introducing a Vector**

A column or a row of a given matrix, viewed as an ordered collection of objects, can be given the structure either of a vector or of a (sub)matrix.
Let us first define a symbolic matrix. Notice the definition: it gives the matrix and its elements in more or less the same way as we normally would give them: capital A for the matrix and lower case a for its elements.

```
>  A := matrix(3,5,(i,j) -> a[i,j]);
```

The code

```
>  row_3 := row(A,3); column_4 := col(A,4);
```

defines the third row and the fourth column of A as individual vectors or lists. Moreover, the Maple code

```
>  subvector(A,1..2,3); subvector(A,2,2..5);
```

extracts as separate vectors the first two elements of the third column of A, and the last four elements of A's second row respectively. It thus becomes important to determine the size or dimension of a given vector. This is provided for by the function vectdim.

```
>  vectdim(%);
```

On clicking the right mouse button on Maple's output of the vector above and selecting Dimension in the menu that pops up, a new input line appears with the same result.

For matrices similar Maple functions are available. It takes no time to find out the precise function of each of the following Maple commands:

```
>  rowdim(A); coldim(A);
>  SubM := submatrix(A,1..3,2..4);
```

Conversely, vectors of equal dimension can be joined to build up a matrix. The Maple input

```
>  S := seq(col(A,i),i=2..4);
```

singles out columns 2, 3 and 4 of matrix A and puts them into a sequence of vectors. After this, we stack these vectors into a matrix. The stacking process, that is putting the vectors as rows on top of one another, is accomplished by applying Maple's stackmatrix[1] command.

```
>  evalm(stackmatrix(S));
```

_____

[1] The stack command of Release 4 has been renamed stackmatrix in Release 5.

The **augment** function has the effect of arranging a sequence of vectors side by side as columns into a matrix.

> `equal(augment(S),SubM);`

It applies to vectors just as it does to matrices: a function prescription may be used in the definition of such objects. In order to build a 10-vector of square roots, just type:

> `u := vector(10,i -> sqrt(i));`

Now turn to **assignment 1** of worksheet MatrA3b.mws (see page 84), and perform the manipulations on the vector u as specified.

The components of a vector need not be given explicitly at the definition stage, this can be postponed to later or altogether omitted. So you could start with a symbolic vector, and fill in the components later if you wish.
Give the next couple of instructions to see how this works.

> `v := vector(5):`
> `evalm(v);`
> `v[5] := 3;`
> `evalm(v);`

Vectors are evaluated in the same way as matrices: if a vector is assigned to a name, like v, then the **evalm** command should be used to view the elements of the vector v.

• Computations with Vectors

So far we have only considered the definition of vectors. Let us now continue with a few applications.

If A is a matrix and x a vector, the product Ax may be interpreted as a linear combination of A's columns, provided A and x have matching dimensions of course. Given a set S of vectors of equal dimension, how can we find out whether this set is linearly independent or not? We could proceed in the following way. Join the vectors of S together into a matrix A, so that the columns of A are the vectors of S. Next solve the system $Ax = 0$. Now suppose this system is only trivially solvable, which means there is only one solution, the zero solution. Then the vectors of S must be independent. The problem of finding a linear expression for a given vector b in terms of the vectors of S, can be solved similarly.
Let us illustrate this by means of an example.

First we generate five random vectors with single digit components. These vectors are put into a sequence SR.

```
>  for j to 5 do v[j] := vector(5,i -> rand(10)()) od:
>  SR := seq(evalm(v[i]),i=1..5);
```

Next the vectors of SR are joined together to form a matrix A. Moreover, let b be a vector of 1's. Now our first objective is to solve the system $Ax = b$.

```
>  A := augment(SR); b := vector(5,1);
>  c := linsolve(A,b);
```

The resulting vector c expresses b as a linear combination of the columns of A.

```
>  j := 'j':  b = sum(v[j]*c[j],j=1..5);
```

Verification is quickly achieved:

```
>  evalm(%);
```

Let us repeat that the product Ax can be viewed as the linear combination of the column vectors of A in which the components of x act as coefficients. Formulated in another way, the components of the product vector Ax are standard inner products of the row vectors of A and x.

Recall that the standard inner product or dot product of two vectors is the sum of the products of their corresponding components. The Maple command for this inner product is innerprod.

```
>  x := vector(5):  y := vector(5):
>  innerprod(x,y);
```

The linalg[norm] procedure gives a vector norm; the type of vector norm may be specified with an extra parameter. Thus

```
>  norm(x,2);
```

gives the Euclidean norm (the usual length function) of the vector x and the supnorm (or maxnorm) is invoked by adding the parameter infinity.

```
>  norm(x,'infinity');
```

Here you can stop for a moment and work with innerprod and norm in the course of completing assignment 2 of worksheet MatrA3b.mws (see page 84).

We showed above how it can be checked that a given vector is expressible as a linear combination of vectors taken from a given set. Linear dependence of a set of vectors may be examined analogously. A closely related problem is the determination of a basis for the span of a dependent set.

Let us begin with generating a set of vectors S. Stack them into a matrix M and calculate the reduced row-echelon form of M. Matrix theory tells us that the non-zero rows of this echelon matrix form a basis for the span of S. The next lines of Maple code cover the entire process.

```
> v := 'v':  # empty the vector v, and define new vectors vi
> for i to 8 do v.i := vector(10,j -> i^2+j^2+i*j+1) od:
> S := seq(v.i,i=1..8):  # build a sequence of vectors vi
> M := stackmatrix(S):
> RM := rref(M):
> Basis := {seq(row(RM,i),i=1..rank(RM))};
```

The Maple command **rowspace** gives the same basis directly.

```
> rowspace(M);
```

Maple also possesses a built-in **basis** instruction.

```
> basis([S]);
```

If the vectors of the set S are arranged as columns, side by side, and the row reduction process is applied to the matrix thus formed, the reduced row-echelon form should clearly show that each vector of S is a linear combination of its first three vectors. Can you confirm this?

```
> rref(augment(S));
```

The following Maple instructions are instrumental in finding these linear combinations:

```
> MS := augment(seq(v.i,i=1..3)):
> for i from 4 to 8 do c.i := linsolve(MS,v.i) od;
```

Finally, by Maple's **GramSchmidt** procedure we obtain an orthogonal basis for the span of S—note the combination of upper and lower case characters. Recall that the vanishing of the inner product of any two basis vectors is characteristic for an orthogonal basis.

```
> GS := GramSchmidt([S]);
```

Just a final check:

```
> for i to 2 do
> for j from i+1 to 3 do
> print(innerprod(GS[i],GS[j]))
> od od;
```

Assignment 3 of worksheet MatrA3b.mws (see page 84), in which the column space of a matrix has a prominent place, provides the opportunity of trying out some of the vector processes mentioned.

3.4.4   Assignments 3b. Vectors

The worksheet MatrA3b.mws contains the complete text of the assignments associated with the worksheet MatrW3b.mws.

1. Use Maple's help facility to get some information about the use of the `map`
   command. Now generate the 10-vector z with $z_i = \ln(\sqrt{i})$. You should do
   this by applying the `map` command to the vector

   ```
   >  u := vector(10,i -> sqrt(i));
   ```

   Also use the `map` command together with the `evalf` procedure in order to
   convert each element of z to its numerical value.

2. (a) For indeterminate α and β, compute the inner product of the vectors
   x and y, where

   $$x = [\alpha, \beta, -\alpha, -4\beta] \quad \text{and} \quad y = [-2\beta, 5\alpha, 3\beta, \alpha].$$

   Under what condition are the vectors x en y orthogonal? To verify
   your answer you can compute the angle between x and y using the
   `angle` procedure.

   (b) Use the vectors x and y to verify the Theorem of Pythagoras, that is
   to say, check that

   $$\|x + y\|^2 = \|x\|^2 + \|y\|^2,$$

   where the notation $\| \cdot \|$ stands for the Euclidean norm.

3. Given the matrix B below. Further, let $\mathbb{V}$ be the subspace of $\mathbb{R}^4$ spanned
   by the column vectors of B; this makes $\mathbb{V}$ the column space of B. Answer
   the following questions and give the Maple code that inspired your answers.

   $$B = \begin{pmatrix} -14 & -2 & 8 & -16 & -5 \\ 5 & 8 & -1 & 0 & 9 \\ 9 & -6 & -12 & 18 & 19 \\ 14 & 8 & -17 & 18 & -16 \end{pmatrix}$$

   (a) Can the last column vector of B be expressed as a linear combination
   of the first four column vectors?

   (b) Is $\mathbb{V}$ spanned by the first four column vectors of B?

   (c) Do the first, third, and fifth column vectors of B constitute a linear
   independent set?

   (d) Do the final three column vectors of B make up a basis for $\mathbb{V}$?

   (e) Is it true that $\mathbb{V} = \mathbb{R}^4$?

3.5   Exercises

1. Use symbolic 3×3 matrices A, B and C to verify the associativity of matrix multiplication, that is: $(AB)C = A(BC)$.

2. Verify with 5×5 random matrices A, B and C that

   (a) $(A + B)C = AC + BC$,   (b) $\det(AB) = \det(A) \cdot \det(B)$.

3. Explain Maple's reaction to the instruction:

   ```
   >   matrix(10,10,10);
   ```

4. When applying the Maple command `evalf` to a matrix A, you might expect to get a view of all matrix elements in the active floating point representation. Unfortunately, this is not so. It is possible however to obtain such a viewing of numerical matrix elements by proper use of the `map` function. What is the precise procedure?

5. Let $A = (a_{ij})$ be the $m \times n$ matrix with $a_{ij} = 1/(i + j - 1)$. Thus A is the Hilbert matrix $H(n)$ in case $m = n$. Determine bases for the null space and the column space of A in the following situations:

   (a) $(m, n) = (10, 10)$,   (b) $(m, n) = (15, 5)$,   (c) $(m,) = (12, 20)$

6. Let $a = (a_1, \ldots, a_n)$ be an arbitrary vector and let A be the associated $1 \times n$ matrix with row vector a. Show that the orthogonal complement of a in $\mathbb{R}^n$ coincides with the linear subspace of solutions of the linear system $Ax = 0$. Use the Maple commands `stackmatrix`, `rref` and `backsub` to give a parametric description of the space of all vectors $x \in \mathbb{R}^8$ that are perpendicular to the vector $a = (1, -2, 3, -4, 5, -6, 7, -8)$.

7. The 8×5 matrix $A = (a_{ij})$ is defined by $a_{ij} = 1/(i + j - 1)$. Further, $b = (1, 2, 3, 4, 5, 6, 7, 8)$. Calculate the orthogonal projection u of b onto A's column space and use the result to obtain the least squares solution of $Ax = b$ by solving the system $A^t Ax = A^t b$. Compare your answer with Maple's output of `leastsqrs(A,b)`.

8. Let the matrix

$$A = \begin{pmatrix} 21 & 22 & 23 \\ 24 & 25 & 26 \\ 27 & 28 & 29 \end{pmatrix}$$

   be given. In order to determine real coefficients c_0, c_1 and c_2 for which

$$A^3 + c_2 A^2 + c_1 A + c_0 \mathrm{Id} = 0,$$

first choose possible candidates for these coefficients by solving a suitable linear system. Next check out your choice by means of the substitution $x = A$ into a suitably chosen polynomial $p(x)$.

NB. The so-called Cayley-Hamilton theorem asserts that a relation as suggested above exists. The polynomial $p(x)$ is the characteristic polynomial of A.

9. As you probably know, two vectors of equal dimension are said to be orthogonal (or perpendicular) if their dot product vanishes. With dot product we mean the standard inner product.

   Write a Maple procedure that returns the orthogonal projection of a given vector u onto another given vector v. You can use either one of Maple's `dotprod` or `innerprod` commands. Moreover, include type-checking on both u and v. Use two random vectors u and v to verify that v and the difference of u and the orthogonal projection of u onto v are perpendicular.

3.6   Survey of Used Maple Expressions

Below you will find a new selection of important Maple expressions and commands reflecting our own personal tastes.

expression		brief explanation
`&*`	–	matrix multiplication
`*`	–	scalar multiplication
`&*()`	–	identity matrix of arbitrary size
`array(1..m,1..n,[])`	–	two-dimensional array or $m \times n$ matrix
`op(expression)`	–	gives the sequence of operands of the Maple expression `expression`
`symmetric, antisymmetric` `identity, sparse`	–	optional parameters for two-dimensional arrays
`inverse(A);`	–	inverse of the matrix A
`linsolve(A,b);`	–	gives the exact solution of the system $Ax = b$
`leastsqrs(A,b);`	–	gives the least squares solution of the system $Ax = b$
`randmatrix(m,n);`	–	generates an $m \times n$ matrix with random elements (integers in the interval $[-100, 100]$)

expression		brief explanation
`randvector(n);`	–	gives a n-vector with random elements (integers in the interval $[-100, 100]$)
`augment(A,B,...);`	–	joins two or more matrices or vectors together horizontally
`stackmatrix(A,B,...);`	–	joins two or more matrices or vectors together vertically
`equal(A,B);`	–	determines whether the matrices A and B are equal
`rref(A);`	–	gives the reduced row-echelon form of the matrix A

In this chapter the following Maple commands where introduced, most of which are contained in the `linalg` package for linear algebra procedures:
`addrow, backsub, basis, col, coldim, colspace, GramSchmidt, innerprod, mulrow, norm, rank, row, rowdim, rowspace, submatrix, subvector, swaprow, transpose, vector, vectdim.`

4

Counting and Summation

The previous chapters should have given you some idea of the possibilities of computer algebra for Analysis and Linear Algebra. In this chapter, we shall focus on another field of application. In contrast to the continuous (or limit) processes we have encountered so far, in the present chapter we shall work with finite processes such as ordinary counting. We shall have occasion to look into the ways Maple can assist us with counting and summation processes, both numerical and symbolic. The examples we have chosen are mainly taken from the fields of combinatorics and discrete probability theory.

4.1 Introduction

Combinatorics, the study of 'intelligent counting', is part of Discrete Mathematics. In this field binomial coefficients emerge in many ways and in many places. For example, when counting the possibilities of choosing some fixed number of elements from a given finite set, or when calculating discrete probabilities, the binomial coefficient plays an essential role. Therefore, it should not come as a surprise that we first pay ample attention to examples which are dominated by binomial coefficients. Finally, we shall consider the computation of discrete probabilities and the random generator used by Maple.

Just as we did in the previous chapters, we shall first review the most important notions we intend to use in this chapter and with it lay down the particular definitions we shall adopt.

4.2   Selected Concepts from Discrete Mathematics

The term binomial coefficient hardly needs any further explanation, the name speaks for itself. Of course, we refer to the coefficients of the terms $a^k b^{n-k}$ in Newton's binomium:

$$(a+b)^n = \sum_{k=0}^{n} \binom{n}{k} a^k \, b^{n-k}.$$

Later on we shall see that Maple works with a much wider definition than commonly used. However, the next definition is more than sufficient for our purposes:

$$\binom{x}{k} := \frac{x(x-1)\ldots(x-k+1)}{k!},$$

whenever it makes sense, so for $k \in \mathbb{N} \cup \{0\}$ and $x \in \mathbb{R}$.

In case both arguments k and n of $\binom{n}{k}$ are natural numbers ($k \leq n$), an important interpretation of $\binom{n}{k}$ is provided by the number of different ways in which k objects can be chosen from a collection of n distinct objects.

The principle of mathematical induction is well-known. We shall encounter the strong version of this principle which can be stated as follows. Generally speaking, mathematical induction provides a method for proving a statement $E(n)$, depending on a natural number n, for all $n \geq n_0$ simultaneously. Now let m be a fixed natural number. First we examine $E(n)$ for the m smallest values of n, i.e. for $m = n_0, n_0 + 1, \ldots, n_0 + m - 1$, and check its validity for these values of m. If all m statements are true we try to deduce the statement $E(n+1)$ for some arbitrary $n \geq n_0 + m - 1$ from the truth of its m predecessors $E(n-m+1), \ldots, E(n)$. This assumption, namely that $E(j)$ is true for all $j = n - m + 1, \ldots, n$ is called the induction hypothesis. If this works out we have succeeded in proving in a single stroke the correctness of $E(n)$ for all $n \geq n_0$. For $m = 1$ the strong version reduces to the 'ordinary' (or weak) version of mathematical induction.

Equally well known is the notion of power series . The adjective 'formal' is used in connection with power series to emphasize that the corresponding expression should be considered a single, undivided object. Although the expression is written in terms of some unknown x, it is not seen as a function of x. For every function f with derivatives of all orders at $x = x_0$, such a formal power series is defined in some neighbourhood of x_0 in the domain of f by the expression

$$\sum_{k=0}^{\infty} c_k \, (x - x_0)^k, \quad \text{with } c_k = \frac{f^{(k)}(x_0)}{k!} \text{ for } k = 0, 1, \ldots.$$

This formal power series is uniquely defined by its list of coefficients $(c_k)_{k=0}^\infty$. Convergence properties do not play any part in the context of formal power series. It may be helpful to compare the difference between a formal power series and its functional counterpart with the difference between 'polynomial' and 'polynomial function'. Here 'formal power series' corresponds with 'polynomial' and 'power series as a function of x' with 'polynomial function'; of course, for the latter, convergence is essential.

Formal power series are very useful for discovering and proving binomial identities: if two seemingly different functions happen to have the same formal power series, then their corresponding series of coefficients are equal too!

For example, the formal power series

$$\sum_{k=0}^\infty \binom{\alpha}{k} x^k$$

is uniquely defined by the binomial coefficients $\binom{\alpha}{k}$. We also know that this power series comes from the Taylor-Maclaurin expansion of the function

$$(1+x)^\alpha.$$

Since

$$(1+x)^\alpha (1+x)^\beta = (1+x)^{\alpha+\beta},$$

the series of binomial coefficients $(\binom{\alpha+\beta}{k})_{k=0}^\infty$ coincides with the series of coefficients of the product series

$$\sum_{k=0}^\infty \binom{\alpha}{k} x^k \cdot \sum_{k=0}^\infty \binom{\beta}{k} x^k = \sum_{k=0}^\infty p_k x^k,$$

where

$$p_k = \sum_{i=0}^k \binom{\alpha}{i} \binom{\beta}{k-i}.$$

This leads to the well-known VanderMonde identity

$$\binom{\alpha+\beta}{k} = \sum_{i=0}^k \binom{\alpha}{i} \binom{\beta}{k-i}.$$

Another topic we shall bring up for discussion in this chapter is the generation and application of random numbers. To give a precise definition of the notion of 'random' is not so easy. The intuitive meaning however is not hard to describe. When we speak of a random sequence of (independent) random numbers distributed in some specific way, we are saying that each number is brought forth by chance, independently of all other numbers of the sequence, and that each number belongs to some given interval with the same fixed probability. In other words, the numbers of a random sequence are independent realizations of a random variable with given probability function. In the forthcoming discussions we shall only consider discrete probability functions.

A random generator is an algorithm for rendering random sequences. Computer generated random sequences can not be random in the full meaning of the word because they are obtained by a purely deterministic process. We call such sequences pseudo-random but more often than not we shall leave out the predicate 'pseudo'. Maple uses a random generator based on the so-called linear-congruential method.

Most pseudo-random sequences are constructed as follows. We first choose a large natural number m, the modulus (often a prime number), an integer a, the multiplier $(0 \leq a < m)$, an integer c, the increment $(0 \leq c < m)$, and some initial value X_0 called seed. Then the random numbers of the sequence $(X_n)_{n \geq 1}$ are successively obtained by the linear congruence

$$X_{n+1} \equiv aX_n + c \pmod{m}, \quad n \geq 0,$$

starting with X_0. This means that X_{n+1} is the non-negative remainder after division by m of the integer $aX_n + c$. Suitable choices of m, a and c will provide a sequence that is 'as random as possible' within the limitations of the linear-congruential method; the degree of randomness can be determined by applying several statistical tests.

Random sequences are used to simulate processes in which probability plays an essential role. To understand the evolution of natural processes, simulation can often be very useful, especially if it is all but impossible to get meaningful observations. Such processes can be found everywhere; for example in nuclear physics but also in operations research. An extensive discussion of the 'random' concept can be found in the classical book of Knuth [13].

4.3   Binomial Coefficients

We start this Maple session with the binomial coefficient. We shall show by example how Maple works with it and how we can use Maple to derive identities in which binomial coefficients appear. We shall also consider Maple's random generator and use Maple for improving our perception of the De Moivre-Laplace limit theorem. Roughly, this theorem asserts that for large values of the parameter n the binomial distribution $B(n, p)$ behaves like a normal distribution with mean $\mu = n\,p$ and variance $\sigma^2 = n\,p\,(1 - p)$.

4.3.1 Maple's `binomial` Function

Because the binomial coefficient is the main subject of this session, it is quite natural to first find out the extent of Maple's knowledge of it.

```
>  restart: help(binomial);
```

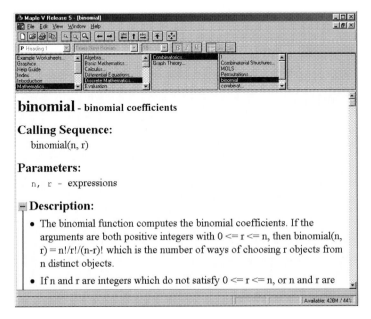

Figure 4.1: Maple's help window for `binomial`

As you can see from the help window, the first argument of the Maple function `binomial(n,k)` does not need to be a natural number. Moreover, the Γ-function is also involved in the definition of binomial coefficients. This is not really surprising once you realize that $\Gamma(n+1) = n!$ for non-negative integers n. Maple knows this too; indeed

```
>  convert(n!,GAMMA);
```
$$\Gamma(n+1)$$

But also for some unusual combinations of integers n and k does `binomial(n,k)` give unexpected answers. This is apparent from the output of the following instructions:

```
>  binomial(5,2),binomial(5,-2),binomial(-5,2),binomial(-5,-2);
>  binomial(2,5),binomial(2,-5),binomial(-2,5),binomial(-2,-5);
```
$$10,\ 0,\ 15,\ 0$$
$$0,\ 0,\ -6,\ -4$$

Even if we stick to the wider definition given in section 4.2 of this chapter (see page 90) so that $\binom{x}{k}$ also makes sense for $x \in \mathbb{R}$, then still four out of eight answers provided by Maple are surprising to a degree.

In order to understand what Maple is doing, it is necessary to look at the Maple code for the function `binomial(n,k)`. We indicated before how this can be done.

```
>  interface(verboseproc=2); print(binomial):
```

proc(*n::algebraic, k::algebraic*)
    local *b, i*;
    global *_BinomialK, _BinomialB, _BinomialN*;
    option '*Copyright (c) 1992 by the University of Waterloo. All rights reserved.*';
        if type(*n, integer*) **and** type(*k, integer*) **then**
            if $k < 0$ **then if** $0 \le n$ **then** 0 **elif** $n - k < 0$ **then** 0
        else binomial(*n, n − k*) **fi**
            else

                $\cdots$ *Here we left out a large number of lines* $\cdots$

            elif $k = 0$ **or** $k = n$ **then** 1
            elif $k = 1$ **or** $k = n − 1$ **then** n
            elif type(*n − k, integer*) **and** $n − k < 0$
        and signum(*n*) $= 1$ **and** signum(*k*) $= 1$ **then** 0
            elif type(*n − k, integer*) **and** $n − k < 0$
        and signum(*n*) $= −1$ **and** signum(*k*) $= −1$ **then** 0
            elif type(*n + k, integer*) **and** signum(*n*) $= 1$
        and signum(*k*) $= −1$ **and** is(*n, integer*) **and**
            is(*k, integer*) **then** 0
            else 'binomial(*n, k*)'
            fi
        end

The complete code will now appear on the screen. Here we only show the first and final lines of this code. From these lines you can read off that Maple interprets the coefficient $\binom{-2}{-5}$ as $\binom{-2}{-2-(-5)} = \binom{-2}{3} = -4$. Moreover, the Γ-function is used when n is integral and k is a rational number with denominator 2.

4.3.2   Two Binomial Identities

How does Maple handle $\binom{n}{k}$? What we mean is, how much does Maple know about the typical properties of $\binom{n}{k}$?

Would Maple know the following basic binomial identity?

```
> binomial(n+1,k) = binomial(n,k)+binomial(n,k-1);
> evalb(%);
```

$$\mathrm{binomial}(n+1,k) = \mathrm{binomial}(n,k) + \mathrm{binomial}(n,k-1)$$
$$\textit{false}$$

Again we see that `evalb` gives no definite answer; of course this is not surprising considering that both expressions are not literally the same. However, some slight manipulation with `expand` and `simplify` enables Maple to identify the resulting expressions as equal.

```
> evalb(simplify(expand(%%)));
```

$$\textit{true}$$

Let us now look at a different, less familiar expression.

```
> s := (m,n) -> sum(binomial(m,k)/binomial(n,k),k=0..m):
> Sum(binomial(m,k)/binomial(n,k),k=0..m) = s(m,n);
```

$$\sum_{k=0}^{m} \frac{\mathrm{binomial}(m,\,k)}{\mathrm{binomial}(n,\,k)} = \frac{n+1}{n+1-m}$$

We have discovered an unusual identity. Or rather, Maple has done that. Is it correct? We tacitly assumed m to be a non-negative integer, because only then does summing over $k = 0, \ldots, m$ make sense. Furthermore, n cannot be smaller than m (at least not when n is integral) for in that case the above summation is not defined. One has to take care!

If n and m are integral and $n \geq m \geq 0$, this identity can be proved formally by mathematical induction on n. This is so, because

```
> 's(m,n+1)' = m/(n+1)*'s(m-1,n)'+1;
```

$$s(m,\,n+1) = \frac{m\,s(m-1,\,n)}{n+1} + 1$$

which does not take too much effort to prove. Indeed, increasing the summation variable in the second finite sum by 1, gives the first one without its $k = 0$ term. Thus

```
> Sum(binomial(m,k)/binomial(n+1,k),k=0..m) -
> Sum(m*binomial(m-1,k)/((n+1)*binomial(n,k)),k=0..m-1) =
> simplify(s(m,n+1)-m/(n+1)*s(m-1,n));
```

$$\left(\sum_{k=0}^{m} \frac{\text{binomial}(m, k)}{\text{binomial}(n + 1, k)}\right) - \left(\sum_{k=0}^{m-1} \frac{m \, \text{binomial}(m - 1, k)}{(n + 1) \, \text{binomial}(n, k)}\right) = 1$$

The strong version of mathematical induction can now be directly applied with the desired result. By the way, the identity in question is correct for all real values of n for which all parts are properly defined.

It is important to realize that in this example Maple's output has been instrumental in convincing us of the identity's correctness and in proving it as well.

Once again, the main point of this example is this: Maple, and other CA systems just the same, possess large amounts of mathematical knowledge, much of it hidden. In order to fully profit from this knowledge, one must use the system with care and understanding, and most of all, one should not gratuitously accept all that is shown on the screen, a warning that really applies to all computer output. Nevertheless, the information supplied by the CA system can often lead to an improved perception of the problem or at least to sensible directives for further exploration.

4.3.3   The Binomial Series

We now take a short excursion into the field of Analysis.
The binomial series expansion is a direct generalization of the Binomial Theorem. In the Taylor-Maclaurin expansion of the function

```
> f := x -> sqrt(1+x);
```

$$f := x \rightarrow \sqrt{1 + x}$$

the binomial coefficients $\binom{\frac{1}{2}}{k}$ play an important role. The formal power series of this function at $x = 0$ is equal to

```
> Sum(binomial(1/2,k)*x^k,k=0..infinity);
```

$$\sum_{k=0}^{\infty} \text{binomial}(\tfrac{1}{2}, k) \, x^k$$

Let us verify this answer.

The power series expansion of $f(x)$ at $x = 0$ is known to Maple and with the command `taylor` we can bring to the screen as many terms as we wish.

```
> taylorseries := taylor(f(x),x=0,12);
```

$$taylorseries := 1 + \frac{1}{2} x - \frac{1}{8} x^2 + \frac{1}{16} x^3 - \frac{5}{128} x^4 + \frac{7}{256} x^5 - \frac{21}{1024} x^6 +$$
$$\frac{33}{2048} x^7 - \frac{429}{32768} x^8 + \frac{715}{65536} x^9 - \frac{2431}{262144} x^{10} + \frac{4199}{524288} x^{11} -$$
$$\frac{29393}{4194304} x^{12} + \frac{52003}{8388608} x^{13} + O(x^{14})$$

The third parameter of the `taylor` procedure—here 12— should produce as many terms[1]. Note that the remainder term is nicely written with Landau's O-symbol. Finally we have to check that the taylor coefficients and the binomial coefficients agree. For that purpose we need the procedure `coeftayl` which has to be loaded separately.

```
> readlib(coeftayl):
> for j from 0 to 49 do
> if not coeftayl(f(x),x=0,j) = binomial(1/2,j) then
> ERROR('A difference is found at index ',j) fi od;
> 'value of j' = j;
```
$$value\ of\ j = 50$$

We don't get any error messages and j ran through all values from 0 up to 50 since the final value of j is 50. This shows that the first 50 terms of the taylor series have indeed the expected binomial coefficients.

4.3.4 The De Moivre-Laplace Limit Theorem

In the next example we again have to subtly steer Maple towards our ultimate goal, which is an improved perception of the De Moivre-Laplace limit theorem. This theorem is about a sequence (X_n) of stochastic variables, binomially distributed with parameter n and probability p, $(0 < p < 1)$. Thus

```
> P(X[n]=k) = binomial(n,k)*p^k*(1-p)^(n-k);
```

$$P(X_n = k) = \text{binomial}(n,\ k)\, p^k\, (1 - p)^{n-k}$$

---

[1]But by a strange bug in Maple V, initially 14 terms are produced instead of 12; when the procedure is repeated the expected number of terms is given!

Further, let (Y_n) be the associated sequence of stochastic variables

```
>  Y[n] := (X[n] - n*p)/sqrt(n*p*(1-p));
```

$$Y_n := \frac{X_n - np}{\sqrt{np(1-p)}}$$

Then the limit theorem claims the following limit identity to be true:

```
>  limit(P('Y[n]' <= x),n=infinity) =
>  1/sqrt(2*Pi)*Int(exp(-t^2),t=0..x);
```

use capital (L)

$$\lim_{n \to \infty} P(Y_n \le x) = \frac{1}{2} \frac{\sqrt{2}\int_{-\infty}^{x} e^{(-t^2)}\, dt}{\sqrt{\pi}}$$

This clearly means that for large values of n, the binomial distribution $\mathrm{B}(n, p)$ behaves like a normal distribution $\mathrm{N}(np, np(1-p))$. Can Maple help us to verify the correctness of this statement?

Let us first take a closer look at this asymptotic relation from a practical point of view. Hence the following experiment. Tossing a coin 50 times, we count the number of times 'cross' comes up. This number is counted by the stochastic variable X. Obviously, the variable X is binomially distributed with mean $np = 50 \times 0.5 = 25$ and variance $np(1 - p) = 50 \times 0.5^2 = 12.5$. We repeat this experiment 200 times and arrange the results in a histogram. We then try to match up the density function of the corresponding normal distribution with the data in our histogram. Of course, our experiment will be simulated with the use of Maple's random generator. In worksheet CountW4b.mws Maple's random generator is discussed in some detail.

The following procedure counts the number of crosses:

```
>  crosstoss := proc() local i;
>  add(rand(2)(),i=1..50) end;
```

$$crosstoss := \mathbf{proc}()\ \mathbf{local}\ i;\ \mathrm{add(rand(2)(),}\ i = 1..50)\ \mathbf{end}$$

Next we repeat this process 200 times and collect the information in the data set crossdata.

```
>  crossdata := []:
>  for j from 1 to 200 do
>  crossdata := [op(crossdata),crosstoss()] od:
```

For the creation of a histogram, we shall use the packages stats (statistics) and plots and the subpackage statplots of stats.

```
>  with(stats): with(plots): with(statplots):
>  data := transform[tallyinto](crossdata,
```

```
>    [seq(i..i+1,i=0..49)]):

>    histogram(data);
```

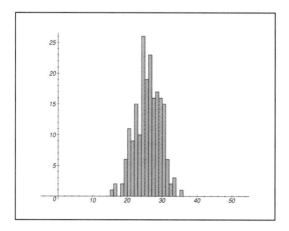

Figure 4.2: Histogram of `crossdata` points

The resulting graph indeed resembles to some extent that of a normal distribution with mean 25 and variance 12.5; see figure 4.2.

It is not easy to judge how many data points are needed for a really convincing normal distribution likeness. Increasing the number to 1000 would certainly improve this appreciably. But then the time factor would also increase considerably of course.

The histogram is now to be compared with the graph of the density function of a normal distribution with the same mean and variance.

Both graphs can be jointly displayed in a figure using the command `display` from the `plots` package. To expose the differences more clearly, the normal curve gets a different color and the `style` value is changed from the default `style = patch` to `style = line`. See figure 4.3.

```
>    normalplot := plot(200/sqrt(Pi*25)*exp(-(x-25)^2/2/(12.5)),
>    x=0..50,color=black):

>    display({histogram(data),normalplot},style=line);
```

Finally, we may also attempt to increase our insight into the theoretical background to the theorem. Let us state once more the limit identity on which the theorem is based. But first we give the mean μ and standard deviation σ of (X_n).

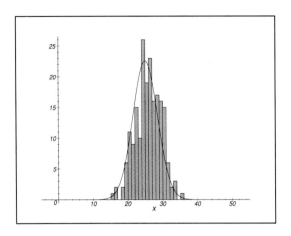

Figure 4.3: Histogram and density function

```
>  n := 'n':   mu := n/2; sigma := sqrt(n/4);
```

$$\mu := \frac{1}{2}\,n$$

$$\sigma := \frac{1}{2}\,\sqrt{n}$$

```
>  limit(P('Y[n]'<=y),n=infinity) =
>  1/sqrt(2*Pi)*Int(exp(-t^2/2),t=0..y);
```

$$\lim_{n\to\infty} P(Y_n \leq y) = \frac{1}{2}\,\frac{\sqrt{2}\displaystyle\int_{-\infty}^{y} e^{(-1/2\,t^2)}\,dt}{\sqrt{\pi}}$$

If Y_n tends to $y = (x - \mu)/\sigma$ then X_n/x tends to 1. Hence, in the limit, a change in Y_n, induced by a change in X_n, is measured by

```
>  Limit('sigma'*P(Y[n]='y'),n=infinity) = simplify(
>  limit(binomial(n,mu+sigma*y)/2^n*sigma,n=infinity));
```

$$\lim_{n\to\infty} \sigma P(\frac{X_n - n\,p}{\sqrt{n\,p\,(1-p)}} = y) = \frac{1}{2}\,\frac{\sqrt{2}\,e^{(-1/2\,y^2)}}{\sqrt{\pi}}$$

and this is just the density function of the standard normal distribution. Apparently, Maple has no problems with this limit!

Maybe it will be more evident if we take another approach. We give the probability function $P(X_n = x)$ with parameter n the name f. Thus

```
>  f := (x,n) -> binomial(n,x)/2^n;
```

$$f := (x,\, n) \to \frac{\text{binomial}(n,\, x)}{2^n}$$

Next we consider the relative change in $f(\mu + \sigma y, n)$ as a function of y. In the resulting expression we let n tend to infinity.

```
>  Limit(Diff('f(mu+sigma*y,n)',y)/'f(mu+sigma*y,n)',
>  n=infinity) = limit(diff(f(mu+sigma*y,n),y)/f(mu+sigma*y,n),
>  n=infinity);
```

$$\lim_{n\to\infty} \frac{\frac{\partial}{\partial y} f(\mu + \sigma y, n)}{f(\mu + \sigma y, n)} = -y$$

Hence, in the limit, the probability function $f(\mu + \sigma y, n)$ (as a function of y) can be found as the solution to the differential equation

$$g'(y) = -y\,g(y)$$

with $g(0) = g_0$, for an appropriate value of g_0. The Maple command `dsolve`[2] will help us find this solution.

```
>  dsolve(diff(g(y),y)/g(y) = -y,g(y));
```

$$g(y) = e^{(-1/2\,y^2)}\,\_C1$$

Finally, the constant _C1 is obtained from

```
>  Int(exp(-1/2*y^2)*_C1,y=-infinity..infinity) = 1;
```

$$\int_{-\infty}^{\infty} e^{(-1/2\,y^2)}\,\_C1\,dy = 1$$

and hence

```
>  _C1 := solve(value(%),_C1);
```

$$\_C1 := \frac{1}{2}\frac{\sqrt{2}}{\sqrt{\pi}}$$

so that

$$g(y) = \frac{e^{(-1/2\,y^2)}}{\sqrt{2\pi}}$$

is the sought after density function of the standard normal distribution.

---

[2]The `dsolve` procedure has been extensively rewritten in Release 5, many new result forms have been added, and its options are slightly different too.

4.4 Worksheets and Assignments

In the worksheets CountW4a.mws and CountW4b.mws we consider in more detail
how Maple handles counting problems.

4.4.1 Worksheet 4a. Symbolic Summation

Everyone knows that counting plays an important role in mathematics, at least
in certain branches of mathematics. Examples are discrete mathematics, combinatorics and discrete probability theory. Set in a more general context, counting
becomes summation: adding finitely many or even a countably infinite number
of objects. Also in other parts of mathematics not mentioned above summation
processes are often encountered. Mostly one would prefer to work with simple
expressions for finite and infinite sums so that manipulating them becomes easier.

In this worksheet we shall be concerned with the way Maple handles definite
(finite or infinite) and indefinite or symbolic summation; the meaning of this will
become clear in due course.

- **Some Familiar Summation Formulas**

The calculation of arithmetic and geometric sums is no great feat for Maple:

```
>  restart:
>  Sum(a+v*k,k=0..n-1) = factor(sum(a+v*k,k=0..n-1));
>  Sum(a*r^k,k=0..n-1) = factor(sum(a*r^k,k=0..n-1));
```

The purpose of using the Maple command `factor` here is to try and write as
products the expressions produced by Maple for both summations, in the way we
would do that ourselves, unaided by a machine.

Also the next well-known infinite sums are calculated fast and efficiently by
Maple.

```
>  Sum(a*r^k,k=0..infinity) = sum(a*r^k,k=0..infinity);
>  Sum(1/k!,k=0..infinity) = sum(1/k!,k=0..infinity);
>  Sum(1/k^2,k=1..infinity) = sum(1/k^2,k=1..infinity);
```

So far Maple succeeded each time. But sometimes, no simple expression for a
finite summation is known, or, even if it is public knowledge, such an expression
may not be known to Maple. Therefore Maple is unable to produce a simplification.

• Indefinite Summation

Because binomial coefficients are closely connected with counting—especially with combinatorial counting—and because so many beautiful, finite expressions involving binomial coefficients exist, we shall take a rather arbitrary selection from the almost inexhaustible supply of combinatorial identities.

We first consider the following indefinite sum:

```
> Sum(binomial(n+k,k),k) = sum(binomial(n+k,k),k);
```

Maple offers an answer. But what does it mean, or more to the point, what question does it answer?

Indefinite summation could be described as the discrete version of indefinite integration. Turning it around, indefinite integration—or finding a primitive for a function on a given interval—is something like 'continuous summation'; the integration symbol is a styled S, the first letter of Summation.

So, indefinite (discrete) summation means that one tries to write the 'summand' (the object of the summation process, in our case, the function `binomial(n+k,k)` with summation variable k) as the difference between two consecutive terms of a suitable sequence, as in

$$r(k+1) - r(k),$$

where k is again the summation variable. Summation of such differences is very easy because of the following telescoping effect: in the corresponding definite sum with k running from a to $b - 1$, cancellation occurs of all but the first and last terms. Consequently, what remains is the difference

$$r(b) - r(a).$$

The function r (or better, the sequence induced by r) is the discrete counterpart of the primitive in the continuous case. For instance, recalling the Fundamental Theorem of Calculus, observe that

```
> f := 'f':  Int(f(x),x=a..b) = F(b) - F(a);
```

and compare this expression with

```
> Sum(f(k),k=a..b-1) = F(b) - F(a);
```

Indefinite summation is as difficult as indefinite integration. The point is to get hold of a suitable sequence $(r(k))$ (the 'discrete' primitive), provided such a sequence exists. Maple uses ingenious tools in which hypergeometric series play an essential role. It is beyond the scope of this book to give any details.

What does the related sequence $(r(k))$ of the previous example look like anyhow? To find out, we recall the well-known binomial identity:

```
>   binomial(n+1,k) = binomial(n,k) + binomial(n,k-1);
```

with $1 \le k \le n$. Replacing n by $n + k$ we also have

```
>   binomial(n+k,k) = binomial(n+k+1,k) - binomial(n+k,k-1);
```

From this it is immediately clear that the $r(k)$ of our example must be equal to

```
>   r(k) = binomial(n+k,k-1);
```

Maple gives precisely this answer; try it out, if you like, with

```
>   expand(rhs(%));
```

In assignment 1 of worksheet CountA4a.mws (see page 106) you will find an indefinite sum that has no secrets for Maple.

• Finding a Simple Expression for a Binomial Sum

We now turn to a combinatorial expression which Maple does not recognize at first.
We define the following sequence (remember that, by definition, $\binom{n}{k} = 0$ for non-negative integers k and n with $k > n$):

```
>   s := n -> sum((-1)^k*binomial(n-k,k),k=0..n):
>   n := 'n':   's(n)' = s(n);
```

Maple can not simplify this expression, and therefore returns $s(n)$ unaltered. Apparently Maple does not know what to do with this specific indefinite sum. It is up to us to try and find a simple expression for $s(n)$ for general n. With the next for-loop we generate the first 25 elements of the sequence $(s(n))_{n \ge 1}$.

```
>   v := 1:   for n from 1 to 24 do v := v,s(n) od;   v;
```

Only three different values occur, namely -1, 0, 1. Also a definite regularity emerges: the pattern $1, 1, 0, -1, -1, 0$ is periodically repeated. It seems that for all $n \ge 1$ the following relation holds:

$$s(n + 1) - s(n) + s(n - 1) = 0.$$

Let us first try to verify this by direct computation, but first we have to 'empty' n of its numerical value ($=25$) by assigning its own name to it.

```
>   n := 'n'; s(n+1) - s(n) + s(n-1);
```

You probably agree that the expression you are looking at now does not obviously vanish. So we are left to our own devices, as Maple does not really offer any assistance with finding a proof for the identity: $s(n+1) - s(n) + s(n-1) = 0$ for general n. Fortunately, this happens to be surprisingly simple. We only need to consider a slight adaptation of the standard binomial identity we used before. Summation of the identity (verify that it really is an identity!)

```
>   (-1)^k*binomial(n+1-k,k) = (-1)^k*binomial(n-k,k) -
>   (-1)^(k-1)*binomial('n-1-(k-1)',k-1);
```

gives just what we want. Since $s(0) = 1$ and $s(1) = 1$, the sequence $(s(n))$ is uniquely determined by the recurrence relation

$$s(n+1) = s(n) - s(n-1).$$

Allowing complex numbers, a much simpler expression for $s(n)$ is possible. This expression is obtained by solving the recurrence relation above with the Maple procedure rsolve.

```
>   n := 'n':
>   rsolve({t(n)=t(n-1)-t(n-2),t(0)=1,t(1)=1},t(n));
```

It is tempting to use the notation $s(n)$ in the procedure rsolve instead of a different one like $t(n)$. Using the former incites Maple to work with the previously defined $s(n)$ and something must surely go wrong. Try it and see!

With complex evaluation (evalc) we can give $s(n)$, or rather $t(n)$, a nicer appearance.

```
>   s(n) = evalc(%);
```

Still a surprising formula, don't you agree?

Now try and complete **assignment 2** of worksheet CountA4a.mws (see page 106), in which a simple expression is required for yet another binomial sum.

• Procedures Involving Symbolic Summation

A final remark about symbolic summation. We have mentioned before that Maple's function sum is based on symbolic summation and therefore rather slow when merely numerical summation results are required. Also in recursive procedures involving symbolic summation, one can expect to run into all sorts of memory and run-time trouble.

Suppose we wish to compute some of the elements of the sequence (c_n) where

$$c_n = \sum_{k=0}^{n-1} \frac{\binom{n-k}{k}}{c_k^2}, \quad c_0 = 1.$$

In view of its symbolic character, it is better to avoid the `sum` command. Instead, we calculate the elements by means of the following procedure, in which the `add` command is used for numerical summation:

```
>  c := proc(n) option remember; local k;
>  add(binomial(n-k,k)/c(k)^2,k=0..n-1);
>  end;
```

After setting $c(0) := 1$, this procedure enables us to calculate other elements of the recurrence quickly and reliably.

```
>  c(0) := 1; c(20); evalf(c(20));
```

On the other hand, when the command `sum` is used recursively inside a procedure, a 'too many levels of recursion' error message is issued, whether the option remember is included or not. It takes only a moment to try this and be convinced!

```
>  c := proc(n) option remember; local k;
>  sum(binomial(n-k,k)/c(k)^2,k=0..n-1);
>  end;
```

A similar recursive sequence involving symbolic summation is the subject matter of **assignment 3** of worksheet CountA4a.mws (see page 107).

4.4.2   Assignments 4a. Symbolic Summation

The assignments in this worksheet are meant as exercises associated with the worksheet CountW4a.mws of the previous section.

1. Use Maple to evaluate the following indefinite sum:

   ```
   >  Sum(k^3*3^k,k) = sum(k^3*3^k,k);
   ```

   What does Maple's answer mean? Use this answer to compute

   $$\sum_{k=0}^{49} k^3 3^k.$$

2. Define the sequence (s_n) as follows:

   ```
   >  s := n -> sum((-4)^k*binomial(n+k,2*k),k=0..n);
   ```

   Compute s_n for $n = 0, 1, \ldots, 10$ (use Maple's `seq` command). The sequence satisfies a second order linear recurrence relation:

   $$s_n = c_1 s_{n-1} + c_2 s_{n-2}.$$

In order to determine c_1 and c_2 you should solve the system $Ax = b$ with A and b defined in the following way:

```
>  with( linalg ):
>  A := matrix(5,2,(i,j) -> s(i+j-2));
>  b := vector(5,i -> s(i+1));
```

Use Maple's `rsolve` procedure to solve the recurrence. Finally, the `factor` command can be useful to give Maple's answer a nicer appearance.

3. In the process of computing some elements of the sequence

$$t(n) := \sum_{k=0}^{n-1} \frac{1}{t(k)^2} \quad \text{with } t(0) := 1 \text{ and } n \in \mathbb{N},$$

you may run into serious problems. These are caused most likely by the difficulties the Maple system has when the `sum` command is placed inside a recursive procedure. But also when the `add` command is used, Maple calculates exact values for this sequence's elements as all of them are rational numbers; the problem now is that the size of these rational numbers grows very rapidly.

(a) Create a procedure

```
>  t := proc(n) option remember;  ...  end;
```

which computes the exact value of $t(n)$. Use this procedure to compute $t(9)$. Don't forget to define $t(0) := 1$.

(b) Now write a similar procedure

```
>  tN := proc(n) option remember;  ...  end;
```

with this difference that this time the elements of the sequence $(t(n))$ are calculated numerically, instead of exactly (symbolically). This procedure should use the `evalf` function.

To prove that your method is correct you only need to calculate $tN(100)$, but before you do that it makes sense to save this worksheet, because if your procedure does not work correctly, you will probably want to stop the calculation, and this may only be possible by pressing the <Ctrl>, <Alt>, and <Del> keys simultaneously. The point is that in that case the computation might take a few hours!

4.4.3   Worksheet 4b. Counting and Random Numbers

In this worksheet we shall look into Maple's way of producing random numbers and we will try to get an impression of the degree of true randomness of Maple's random generator.

As you know, random numbers are used in investigations of processes containing a stochastic component; especially if simulation can not be avoided, a random generator is an absolutely essential tool. We repeat the remark we made earlier that random generators used in real life are not random in the true sense of the word but only pseudo-random. This is because purely deterministic tools, like computer algorithms, are used to generate random numbers. However, we shall not make a point of holding on to the correct term of pseudo-random when no confusion seems likely. From now on we shall use the term random even if pseudo-random would be more appropriate.

• Maple's Random Procedure

Almost all commonly used random generators are based on the same linear-congruential method. This is also true for Maple's random generator. The method is explained briefly in section 4.2. Let us have a quick look at Maple's random algorithm.
With this in mind, give the following instructions:

```
>  restart:
>  print(rand);
```

You see that rand is a procedure, but nothing more is revealed. To look at this procedure in more detail, we need the following instruction:

```
>  interface(verboseproc=2):
```

Now repeat your earlier instruction:

```
>  print(rand);
```

As its structure is rather simple, the algorithm is easy to read. Some constants are involved: a prime number (the modulus)

```
>  p := 10^(12)-11;
>  isprime(%); # Is p really prime?
```

the multiplier

```
>  a := rand();
```

the increment

```
>  c := 10^(12);
```

and the

```
>  'seed' := _seed;
```

Furthermore, the algorithm shows that the command **rand()** without parameters generates a random integer of at most 12 digits conform the principle:

$$X_{n+1} \equiv a\,X_n + c \pmod{p},$$

with initial value X_0 =_seed. Although you are probably familiar with the notation $\pmod{p}$, let us remind you of its meaning: the remainder after division of the expression $a\,X_n + c$ (usually much larger than p) by p is assigned to X_{n+1}. This non-negative remainder is smaller than p and hence a 12-digit number or less. Further, by default, _seed has the value 1, but may be redefined. The underscore _ attached to the variable's name tells us that this is a global variable, internally used by Maple.

Let us verify all this carefully. We start with assigning the value 1 to the seed and then apply the random generator **rand()** ten times.

```
>  _seed := 1:  random_sequence := [seq(rand(),i=1..10)];
```

Exactly the same sequence is obtained with the following lines of Maple instructions:

```
>  X[0] := a:  for k to 9 do X[k] := a*X[k-1] mod p od:
>  random_sequence_2 := [seq(X[k],k=0..9)];
```

Clearly there is nothing unpredictable about the random generator!

Maple's **rand** procedure makes use of the **irem** ('integer remainder') procedure. The effect of **irem** is the same as that of **mod** mentioned above. You can try this out by means of

```
>  evalb(irem(a*X[5]+c,p) = a*X[5]+c mod p);
```

It may also strike you that as soon as the variable _seed is set to 1 again, the same random numbers are generated as before. Therefore, whenever Maple is (re)started, the same random sequence is produced until the variable _seed is reset to an integer value different from 1.

Furthermore, we observe that **rand(n)**—now supplied with the integer argument n—is itself a random *procedure*, and not a random *number*. See for yourself:

```
>  rand(100000);
```

On the screen a procedure is shown, not a random number. But with the instruction: `rand(100000)()`—note the trailing empty procedure brackets—a random integer of at most 5 digits is generated.

>   `rand(100000)();`

You can stop here for a moment in order to complete **assignment 1** of worksheet CountA4b.mws (see page 113). This assignment is about a random bit generator, that is a random procedure which produces only zeros and ones.

In summary we can say that in general the numbers generated by Maple's random generator are arbitrary integers of a predetermined number of digits. In theory, the numbers generated by `rand(N)()` are uniformly distributed in $[0, N-1]$. Thus, one gets uniformly distributed numbers in $[0, 1]$ with

>   `N := 10^(12):   evalf(rand(N)()/(N-1));`

From the above you will have gathered that suitable choices for the modulus p and the multiplier a are vital for an acceptable random behaviour of the numbers produced by the random generator.

If one does not choose a prime number for p, then the period of the random sequence will in general be considerably smaller than p, so that the numbers will reappear in exactly the same order long before this is strictly necessary. Sooner or later a repetition must occur because there are only finitely many different numbers available as there are exactly p distinct remainders modulo p.

The generated sequence can be tested for randomness by means of the appropriate statistics. In Knuth [13, section 3.6] you can read which conditions a good random sequence should satisfy.

• Generating Normally Distributed Random Numbers

Maple also offers the means of generating realizations of stochastic variables with other distribution functions than the uniform one. The most popular distribution functions are included in the package `stats` and its sub-packages. The instructions `with(stats)`, `with(describe)` and `with(random)` produce lists of procedures included in these packages or sub-packages.

>   `with(stats); with(describe); with(random);`

Now turn to **assignment 2** of worksheet CountA4b.mws (see page 113), and investigate a list of uniformly distributed random numbers.

In our next exercise we shall build a histogram based on a list of 400 standard normally distributed random numbers so that we may roughly check by eye the standard normal form. It makes sense to suppress the output of this list of data. Why?

```
>  random_list := [normald[0,1](400)]:
```

We first check whether the values of mean and standard deviation of the finite data set are conform the theoretical values of 0 and 1 respectively.

```
>  mean(random_list); standarddeviation(random_list);
```

Next we shall distribute the data over $20 = \sqrt{400}$ classes. We first calculate the range of the sequence and then divide this range into 20 sub-intervals of equal length, the classes. To take care of the placement of all numbers in their proper destination intervals (otherwise an error will occur later on), right endpoints will be rounded upwards and left endpoints downwards to 4 significant digits.

```
>  left := floor(lhs(range(random_list))*10^3)*0.001;
>  right := ceil(rhs(range(random_list))*10^3)*0.001;
```

The spread then equals

```
>  h := right - left;
```

This gives the following list of classes:

```
>  classlist := [seq(left+k*h/20..left+(k+1)*h/20,k=0..19)]:
```

Finally, the random numbers are distributed over the 20 classes by means of the command `tallyinto`.

```
>  data := transform[tallyinto](random_list,classlist):
```

The histogram planned is now produced by [3]

```
>  statplots[histogram](data);
```

• **Testing a Sequence for Random Behaviour**

As a final task for this worksheet we shall consider sequences of bits (sequences of zeros and ones) and check them for acceptable random behaviour. The precise meaning of this can not be easily expressed in a few words. Therefore our inspection will be of a rather limited scope.
We start with generating a random sequence of 50 bits.

```
>  N := 50:
>  randombits := [seq(rand(2)(),i=1..N)];
```

---

[3] the `statplots` sub-package has been completely rewritten in Release 5; check the help pages for details.

At first glance, this sequence does look perfectly random. But what should we look for in a random sequence? Well, first of all, on average, in each block of successive bits, the frequency of both zeros and ones should be approximately 0.5. Further, no fixed patterns should be identifiable. This last observation is rather vague and can be interpreted in many ways.
Let us begin to check the frequency of zeros and ones.

```
> add(randombits[i],i=1..50)*0.02;
```

Here the `add` command is used to calculate the sum of the elements of the bit sequence `randombits`.

Although a sequence of alternating zeros and ones could hardly be called random, it has the correct $(0, 1)$-frequency. Based on this observation, we could count the number of switches from 0 to 1 and vise versa. Theoretically, the mean of this number of switches for a random sequence of length N equals $\frac{1}{2}(N - 1)$, which is 24.5 for $N = 50$. Hence, a number of switches deviating considerably from 24.5 should cast serious doubts on the randomness of our sequence.
The number of switches can be computed by mod 2 addition of each pair of consecutive bits; the grand total of ones thus obtained is the required number of switches.

The following example is concocted for the purpose of showing that there is more to randomness than meets the eye. The $(0, 1)$-sequence below looks rather random, even under close scrutiny. However, its number of bit-switches is far too large to pass any serious test of randomness.

```
> bitsequence :=
> [1,0,1,0,1,1,0,1,1,1,0,1,0,0,0,1,0,1,1,0,1,0,0,1,1,
> 1,0,1,0,1,0,1,1,0,1,0,0,1,0,1,1,0,1,0,0,0,0,1,1,0];
```

We now calculate the number of bit-switches for this sequence.

```
> switchsequence := [seq(bitsequence[i] + bitsequence[i+1]
> mod 2,i=1..49)]:
> add(switchsequence[i],i=1..49);
```

The theoretical probability of at least this number of switches in a sequence of length 50 is

```
> with(statevalf):  dcdf[binomiald[49,0.5]](49-switchcount);
```

which is far too small to suggest that this bit-sequence is a random sequence.

By the way, the command `dcdf` stands for 'discrete cumulative distribution function', and its argument $(49 - \mathtt{switchcount})$ means that the probability of at least `switchcount` bit-switches is calculated.

In **assignment 3** of worksheet CountA4b.mws (see page 113) you can now apply the $(0, 1)$-switch test to a randomly generated sequence of bits.

Admittedly, we looked into the phenomenon of random bit sequences only briefly and rather superficially, but it must have given you at least some idea of the possibilities of Maple's random generator for the creation and use of random sequences.

4.4.4 Assignments 4b. Counting and Random Numbers

The next assignments are related to the notions of random generator and random sequence such as they were discussed in worksheet CountW4b.mws.

1. (a) Write a procedure

    ```
    >  rand3 := proc() ...  end;
    ```

    that first generates three random numbers X, Y and Z and then returns the product XYZ mod 2.
    So the procedure **rand3** should return 1 if XYZ is odd and 0 if XYZ is even.

   (b) Use your **rand3** procedure to generate a list of 1000 bits (zeros and ones). Use Maple's **seq** procedure.

   (c) Compute the number of ones by calculating the sum of the elements of the list. Is **rand3** a good random bit generator in your opinion? Or rather, is the frequency of both zeros and ones approximately 0.5?

2. Generate a list of 400 uniformly distributed numbers in $[0, 1]$. Suppress the output of this list. Use the **uniform** procedure from the **random** subpackage of the **stats** package.

   Next compute the mean and the variance of this data set using procedures from the **describe** subpackage of the **stats** package.
   Are these values conform the theoretical values of $\frac{1}{2}$ and $\frac{1}{12}$ respectively ?

3. In the following input line we use the **rand(2)()** command to generate a random bit sequence of length 100:

    ```
    >  randombitsequence := [seq(rand(2)(),i=1..100)];
    ```

   Apply the $(0, 1)$-switch test (discussed in Worksheet 4b) on this **randombitsequence**. Does **randombitsequence** exhibit acceptable random behaviour?

4.5   Exercises

1. Use Maple to find simple expressions—that is expressions consisting of a single term—for

   (a) $\displaystyle\sum_{k=0}^{n} \binom{k+r}{k}$, and

   (b) $\displaystyle\sum_{k=0}^{n} \binom{r}{k} \left(\frac{r}{2} - k\right)$.

   Here r is some positive integer.

2. Use the technique of generating functions—this is the method we have used to derive the VanderMonde identity in section 4.2—to show that

$$\sum_{k=0}^{n} \binom{r}{k} \binom{r}{n-k} (-1)^k = (-1)^{\frac{1}{2}n} \binom{r}{\frac{1}{2}n}$$

   for any even positive integer n and $r \in \mathbb{R}$. Verify this identity with Maple.

3. In order to find a simple expression for the finite sum

$$f_n := \sum_{k=1}^{n} (-1)^{k+1} \binom{n}{k} \frac{1}{k},$$

   we consider the functional expressions

$$f_n(x) := \sum_{k=1}^{n} (-1)^{k+1} \binom{n}{k} \frac{x^k}{k},$$

   depending on the variable x with parameter $n \in \mathbb{N}$. Calculate the derivative of $f_n(x)$ by term-by-term differentiation. This derivative can be put into a rather simple form. From the identity

$$f_n = f_n(1) = \int_0^1 f_n'(x)\, dx,$$

   a simple expression for the difference $f_n - f_{n-1}$ $(n > 1)$ may be deduced. Use this expression to determine f_n for general n.

4. Check that

$$\binom{2n}{n} \equiv (-1)^n \qquad (\text{mod } 2n + 1)$$

   is true in case $2n + 1$ is a prime number. The reverse is not true: the congruence can also be valid for composite numbers $2n + 1$. However, such an occurrence is extremely rare. Give an example with $n < 3000$.

5. Let (X, Y, Z) be a triad of uniformly distributed random numbers in $[0, 1]$. What is the probability that these numbers represent the lengths of the sides of a triangle? Generate 1000 random triads to estimate this probability. Note that three positive numbers represent the lengths of the sides of a triangle if and only if the sum of each pair is larger than the third number.

6. The movements of a point P in the plane are described as follows: starting at the origin $(0, 0)$, it moves in one step from $(x, y) \in \mathbb{Z}^2$ with equal probability $\frac{1}{4}$ to one of the four neighbouring points $(x + 1, y)$, $(x - 1, y)$, $(x, y + 1)$, or $(x, y - 1)$. Calculate the mean of the squared distance from P to the origin after n steps.

7. The numbers $f(n)$, defined by

$$f(n) = \sum_{k=0}^{n} \binom{n + k}{n - k}, \quad \text{for } n \in \mathbb{N}$$

satisfy a recurrence relation. Can you find it?
Such a relation may be found by solving the linear system $Ax = 0$ with matrix of coefficients

$$A = (a_{ij})_{3 \times 3}, \quad \text{with } a_{ij} := f(i + j + n).$$

If, for different values of n, always the same solution is obtained for this linear system, a recursive relation is likely to exist. Why is this so? A formal proof is not required. Also solve the recurrence relation.

8. On the assumption that the sequence $(R(n))$ is a random sequence of integers, the three consecutive elements $R(n), R(n + 1), R(n + 2)$ satisfy the inequalities

$$R(n + 2) < R(n + 1) < R(n),$$

with probability $\frac{1}{6}$, because each of the six possibilities are equally probable.

Using Maple's random generator `rand()`, generate 20 integral random sequences of length 200 and verify that your results are conform the above mentioned expected (mean) value.

9. Consider the most significant digit of the product XYZ, where X, Y and Z are uniformly distributed positive integers. As leading zeros are always discarded, the most significant digit is never 0. The question is whether all nine non-zero digits have equal probability of occurring as the leading digit of the product XYZ. From the literature it can be learned that the digit 1 occurs far more often than the digit 9.

Make use of Maple's random generator to count the frequencies of 1 and 9 in 1000 random samples of triads of random numbers (X, Y, Z).

10. The decimal expansion of the number π seems to carry on in a completely arbitrary way. Up to the present time nobody ever discovered any pattern in this expansion. It may therefore be possible, at least in principle, to base a good random bit-sequence generator on this decimal expansion.

We proceed as follows: first we fix the seed at an arbitrary position in the decimal expansion of π. Next, as our bit-sequence generator runs through the successive digits of π, it produces a 1 if the present digit is odd and a 0 otherwise.

Give the Maple code of your random bit-sequence generator that works conform the specifications given above and check its usefulness by applying the $(0, 1)$-switch test (discussed in Worksheet 4b) on a few random sequences produced by your generator.

4.6   Survey of Used Maple Expressions

The following list contains the most important Maple expressions and commands used in this chapter. Just as in the foregoing chapters, completeness is not pursued. Some expressions appear only in worksheets CountW4a.mws and CountW4b.mws of this chapter.

expression		short explanation
`binomial(n,k)`	–	gives the number $\binom{n}{k}$
`convert(expr,form)`	–	converts the expression `expr` to type `form` (many possibilities)
`plots[display](plots,options)`	–	puts all `plots` (list or set) together in a single picture
`expr mod p`	–	calculates remainder of `expr` after division by $p \in \mathbb{N}$, $p > 1$
`dsolve(dv,f(x))`	–	solves the differential equation dv for $f(x)$
`rand`	–	procedure to generate random numbers
`rand()`	–	generates a 12 digit random integer (default)
`rand(N)`	–	procedure to generate random numbers in the interval $[0, N-1]$ $(N \in \mathbb{N})$

expression	short explanation
rand(N)()	– generates a random integer in the interval $[0, N-1]$
dcdf[distr](x)	– gives the probability $P(X \leq x)$ when the random variable X has the distribution distr

The Maple expressions, used for the first time in this chapter are:
add, binomiald, ceil, coeftayl, describe, dsolve, evalc, histogram, irem, mean, random, range, standarddeviation, statevalf, statplots, tallyinto, taylortransform.

5

Derivative and Integral

A fter having completed a first tour of applications embracing several
branches of mathematics, we turn to Mathematical Analysis again. We
are now in a position to put to good use the knowledge of functions and
series, and of limits and continuity, picked up in a previous chapter. In this
chapter, the emphasis is on differentiation and integration of functions and the
possibilities a computer algebra system provides for gaining more insight into
these fundamental concepts of Analysis.

5.1 Introduction

We shall see that Maple has no problems calculating the derivatives of complicated functions. A large collection of integration techniques is at Maple's disposal;
hence Maple is able to compute many standard and non-standard integrals ef-
fortlessly. In spite of this, things go wrong regularly, mostly for understandable
reasons. We shall give an example of such an occurrence. Moreover, we shall
study a very peculiar function which happens to be continuous on the entire real
line but almost nowhere differentiable. Getting a reliable picture of its graph will
obviously pose quite a few problems, as no tangents can be drawn. Nevertheless,
we will succeed in providing some pictures of this unusual function, and thus
remove some of the mystery that surrounds it.

5.2   Further Concepts from Analysis

A function $f : \mathbb{R} \to \mathbb{R}$ defined in some neighbourhood of a point a is differentiable at a if a number A exists such that

$$f(a + h) = f(a) + ha + \mathcal{O}(h^2) \quad (h \to 0),$$

where $\mathcal{O}$ is Landau's O-symbol . This at first glance unusual definition is equivalent with the standard definition of differentiability, because division by h gives

$$\frac{f(a + h) - f(a)}{h} = A + \mathcal{O}(h) \quad (h \to 0),$$

and the precise meaning of this identity is that the differential quotient of the left-hand side tends to A as h tends to 0. Therefore, the number A is the value of the derivative of f at the point a, usually written as $A = f'(a)$.

This definition immediately shows that continuity is a consequence of differentiability. Another advantage of the definition of differentiability given above is that here we clearly see the first step towards the very important power series expansion known as the taylor expansion:

$$f(a + h) = \sum_{k=0}^{n} \frac{f^{(k)}(a)}{k!} h^k + R(f, h, n),$$

where we assume f to have a k-th order derivative $f^{(k)}$ at a for each $k = 1, \ldots, n$. Further, the remainder term satisfies

$$R(f, h, n) = \mathcal{O}(h^{n+1}) \quad (h \to 0).$$

As you probably know, the remainder term can be given a very precise form that explicitly shows its dependence on f, h and n. We refer to the standard integral form of the remainder. We shall return to this shortly.

It is impractical to repeat at this point the definition of integration in extenso. Very briefly we say that a (bounded) function $f : [a, b] \to \mathbb{R}$ is integrable over the interval $[a, b]$ if the so-called Riemann sum,

$$\sum_{i=1}^{n} f(\xi_i) \Delta x_i, \quad \text{with } \Delta x_i = x_i - x_{i-1} \text{ and } \xi_i \in (x_{i-1}, x_i) \text{ for } i = 1, \ldots, n,$$

tends to a limit L, where the limit process runs over all partitions $V = \{a = x_0 < x_1 < \cdots < x_n = b\}$ of $[a, b]$ with $\max_{1 \leq i \leq n} \Delta x_i \to 0$. The value of the integral of f over $[a, b]$ is by definition equal to the limit L; in the usual notation:

$$L = \int_a^b f(x) \, dx.$$

Note the similarity in notation between the Riemann sum with summation symbol Σ and the integral with 'continuous summation' symbol $\int$.

Unfortunately this definition of integral is not very useful for the practical process of integration. For this the Fundamental Theorem of Calculus suggests a much better approach. It provides a direct link between differentiation and integration in the following way.

Let f be integrable over $[a, b]$ and put

$$F(x) = \int_a^x f(t)\, dt, \quad x \in [a, b].$$

The function F is properly defined by this integral expression. It is continuous on the whole of $[a, b]$ and even differentiable at those points $x \in [a, b]$ where the integrand f is continuous, and $F'(x) = f(x)$ at such points x.

Furthermore, a function G is called a primitive for f on the interval I if the following two conditions are met:

1. I belongs to the domain of definition of both f and G,

2. G is differentiable at every point of I, and $G'(x) = f(x)$ for $x \in I$.

The function F therefore is a primitive for f on $[a, b]$, provided the latter is continuous on the whole of $[a, b]$. Moreover, all primitive functions for f on this interval $[a, b]$ are equal up to an additive constant. Well-known techniques such as partial integration and integration by substitution can be very useful in the process of explicitly generating primitives, but only in a limited number of cases these methods are successful. Maple has at its disposal a large number of integration techniques, all of which are part of the Risch-algorithm. This powerful and resourceful algorithm is no match for the average integration specialist.

We return for a moment to the taylor series and the integral form of its remainder term we hinted at before. Repeated application of partial integration to the right-hand side of

$$f(a + h) - f(a) = \int_a^{a+h} f'(x)\, dx,$$

yields the following expression for the remainder term:

$$R(f, h, n) = \frac{(-1)^n \int_a^{a+h} (t - a - h)^n\, f^{(n+1)}(t)\, dt}{n!}.$$

This formula usually serves as the starting point from which many well-known representations of the remainder term (such as the one named after Lagrange) can be derived immediately.

For any function having derivatives of all orders on an interval I, a taylor series is defined in some neighbourhood of each internal point a of I. If the remainder term converges on this neighbourhood to 0 for $n \to \infty$, then the series converges to $f(a)$.

Conversely, the sum function of a power series is analytic on any open interval contained in its domain of convergence, which means that it has derivatives of all orders.

What about the differentiation properties of a series the terms of which are differentiable functions of x, but quite different from ordinary powers of x? We shall see that such a series need not be differentiable. A well-known example is the function of Riemann; this function is everywhere continuous and almost nowhere differentiable. It is defined by the following power series:

$$\sum_{k=1}^{\infty} \frac{\sin(k^2\,\pi\,x)}{k^2}.$$

In the next section we shall closely examine this function. As it is hard to imagine what the graph of this function looks like, we shall need some ingenuity in the process of revealing its true character.

5.3   Riemann's Non-differentiable Function

As announced above, in this session we shall discuss the notions of derivative and integral. We shall take a look at Maple's ability to differentiate and integrate. Modern computer tools are very skillful in finding primitives; they are generally much faster and much better equipped than we will ever be. Moreover, a potential primitive found by the computer can simply be checked by direct computation of its derivative.

Again we shall occasionally experience Maple's failure to produce a correct answer to a fair question, or worse, its refusal to give an answer at all. Despite this, from misleading formulas we can often extract useful information putting us on the right track towards a correct answer.

5.3.1   Investigating the Riemann Function

We shall begin with the concept of differentiation. In the previous section we went over its definition in detail. Worksheet DerivW5a.mws also considers this, but in a rather different way.

Most elementary functions are differentiable at each point of their domains. Sometimes they are differentiable everywhere except at one point—such as the absolute value function `abs(x)` at $x = 0$—or with the exception of a few points. Functions that are discontinuous at many points are of course not differentiable at these points, because differentiability implies continuity. On the other hand there are functions that are continuous everywhere but nowhere or 'almost' nowhere differentiable. There is a good chance that you never set eyes on such functions but that will change, because we will take a look at the non-differentiable Riemann function we mentioned before. This function should not be confused with the Riemann ζ-function. The latter, known to Maple as `Zeta`, is usually defined by

$$\zeta(s) = \sum_{n=1}^{\infty} \frac{1}{n^s},$$

whereas the non-differentiable Riemann function we have in mind we defined in the previous section by

```
>   f := x -> sum(sin(n^2*Pi*x)/n^2,n=1..infinity);
```

$$f := x \rightarrow \sum_{n=1}^{\infty} \frac{\sin(n^2 \pi x)}{n^2}$$

It is immediately clear that we are looking at a properly defined function. Indeed, the sine function takes only values between -1 and 1, which guarantees the absolute convergence of the series defining f by providing the absolute upper bound $\zeta(2)$.

```
>   Sum(1/n^2,n=1..infinity) = Zeta(2);
```

$$\sum_{n=1}^{\infty} \frac{1}{n^2} = \frac{1}{6} \pi^2$$

We shall show that the Riemann function $f(x)$ is indeed continuous at every real point x. It therefore stands to reason that we might get an impression of the behaviour of this function from its graph. Now the function $f(x)$ is almost nowhere differentiable, and we are curious to see if and how this shows up in the graph of f. So our aim is to get a picture which closely resembles the true graph of f. By the way—and this is a serious warning—one should not expect the graph of a function to disclose any information of a continuous nature. A graph is no more than a finite collection of points in the plane, possibly connected by artificially created line segments, from which differentiability can never be read off. Besides, a nowhere differentiable function does not admit a tangent line at any point of its graph, and it therefore most likely behaves in a very unpredictable way! But, let us not anticipate unduly.

Maple is unable to symbolically evaluate the series that defines the Riemann function f. This is not surprising as there is for general x no simple representation for this series. In order the compute f's function values anyway—or rather to approximate these—we need to proceed numerically. Therefore we give the following 'numerically adjusted' definition:

```
>  f := x -> evalf(Sum(sin(n^2*Pi*x)/n^2,n=1..infinity));
```

$$f := x \rightarrow \text{evalf}\left(\sum_{n=1}^{\infty} \frac{\sin(n^2\,\pi\,x)}{n^2}\right)$$

The capital letter S in Sum is used to prevent useless symbolic summation. Using this new definition, Maple gives

```
>  'f(0.5)' = f(0.5);
```

$$f(0.5) = 1.233700550$$

Although Maple is capable of calculating the value of $f(0.5)$, this is an exception, at most other points Maple cannot evaluate f. Consequently, generating a plot is most certainly out of the question. Apparently, the infinite summation poses a serious problem in this respect. Replacing in the definition of f the infinite summation by a suitable partial sum of the corresponding series, we have to decide how many terms of this partial sum we need to secure acceptable approximations of f's function values.

We shall leave the decision on the number of terms to later, and meanwhile continue our investigations with a new version of f, properly adjusted to our needs. This new function has an additional argument N, which gives the number of terms of the partial sum that replaces the series used in the original definition.

```
>  Pf := (N,x) -> evalf(Sum(sin(n^2*Pi*x)/n^2,n=1..N));
```

$$Pf := (N, x) \rightarrow \text{evalf}\left(\sum_{n=1}^{N} \frac{\sin(n^2\,\pi\,x)}{n^2}\right)$$

First we take a look at the graph of $Pf(500, x)$ for $x \in [-0.3, 2.3]$. As the sine function is periodic, there is no point in making this interval any larger. We shall also give the run time.

```
>  starttime := time():
>  plot(Pf(500,x),x=-0.3..2.3,numpoints=1000);
>  runtime := time() - starttime;
```

$$runtime := 6.765$$

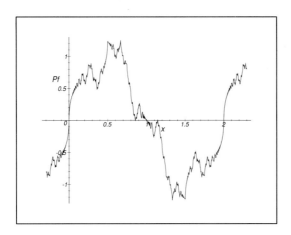

Figure 5.1: Approximation of the Riemann function on $[-0.3, 2.3]$

Indeed, this shows rather chaotic behaviour! We observe many sharp edges and we clearly see vertical tangents, e.g. at $x = 0$ and $x = 2$. It also appears that the line through $(1, 0)$ with slope $-\frac{1}{2}$ is tangent to the graph at this point. We should be aware however of the fact that we are looking at the graph of an approximating function, not of the Riemann function itself. The question remains whether or not the function $Pf(500, x)$ gives a reliable picture of the Riemann function $f(x)$. To answer this question, we have to examine the difference function $f(x) - Pf(N, x)$. This also will enable us to show that $f(x)$ is continuous at every $x \in \mathbb{R}$.

For arbitrary N and x we define the remainder function by

```
>  R(N,x) := combine(f(x) - Pf(N,x));
```

$$R(N, x) := \sum_{n=N+1}^{\infty} \frac{\sin(n^2 \pi x)}{n^2}$$

[handwritten note: Maple 7: doesn't work unless you previously do "assume(N::posint)"]

Maple's `combine` function is used to enforce combining corresponding terms of both summations. Hence

```
>  abs('R(N,x)') <= Sum(1/(n^2),n=N+1..infinity);
```

$$|R(N, x)| \leq \sum_{n=N+1}^{\infty} \frac{1}{n^2}$$

From this inequality it can be deduced that the absolute remainder is bounded from above by $\frac{1}{N}$. Indeed, for $M \geq N + 1$, we have

```
>  Sum(1/n^2,n=N+1..M) < sum(1/(n*(n-1)),n=N+1..M);
```

$$\sum_{n=N+1}^{M} \frac{1}{n^2} < -\frac{1}{M} + \frac{1}{N}$$

from which the assertion is an immediate consequence.

In general, this estimate of the remainder function $R(N, x)$ cannot be improved. So, in the computation of $f(x)$-values by means of the values $Pf(500, x)$ of the adapted function, only two decimal digits can be trusted. On an interval of length 2.6 with function values between -1.3 and 1.3, this should be sufficient to give a reliable picture of the Riemann function.

Analogously we find that for each x, y and N,

```
>  N := 'N':
>  abs('f'(x) - 'f'(y)) <= abs('Pf'(N,x) - 'Pf'(N,y)) + 2/N;
```

$$|f(x) - f(y)| \le |Pf(N, x) - Pf(N, y)| + \frac{2}{N}$$

Moreover, for fixed N, the function $Pf(N, x)$ is as a finite sum of differentiable functions itself differentiable as a function of x.
As we pointed out before, the graphs of the functions $Pf(N, x)$ and $f(x)$ look very much alike. However, $f(x)$ is almost nowhere differentiable while $Pf(N, x)$ is differentiable everywhere. There seems to be a contradiction here, but as we have stressed before, the matter of differentiability of functions can not be decided on by merely considering their graphs.

Having established the fact that $Pf(N, x)$ is differentiable at every point, we may apply the mean value theorem for this function on any interval $[x, y]$.

```
>  'Pf'(N,x) - 'Pf'(N,y) = subs(t=xi,diff(Pf(N,t),t))*(x-y);
```

$$Pf(N, x) - Pf(N, y) = \left(\sum_{n=1}^{N} \pi \cos(n^2 \pi \xi) \right) (x - y)$$

where ξ lies between x and y.

In combination with the preceding inequality, this expressing yields

```
>  abs('f'(x) - 'f'(y)) <= N*Pi*abs(x-y) + 2/N;
```

$$|f(x) - f(y)| \le N\pi \, |x - y| + \frac{2}{N}$$

for any x, y, and $N > 0$. In particular, N may be chosen in any way we like. Provided $x \neq y$, a sensible choice is

$$N = \frac{1}{\sqrt{|x - y|}}.$$

Now we obtain an inequality from which the (uniform) continuity of f immediately follows.

```
>   abs('f'(x) - 'f'(y)) <=
>   factor(subs( N = 1/sqrt(abs(x-y)),rhs(%)));
```

$$|f(x) - f(y)| \leq \sqrt{|x - y|}(\pi + 2)$$

which holds for any x, $y \in \mathbb{R}$.

The Riemann function has many interesting properties. Here we are mainly interested in properties related to differentiation. It is known that the Riemann function $f(x)$ is differentiable at rational points $x = p/q$ with p and q odd and relatively prime. The derivative at these points is always equal to $-\frac{1}{2}$. At all other points x, be it rational or irrational, $f(x)$ is not differentiable. These statements are not easy to prove. This is born out by the fact that it took until 1971 before the differentiability problem of the Riemann function could be settled once and for all. At that time the Riemann function had been around for a hundred years!

We return to the graph of $f(x)$, or rather of $Pf(500, x)$.

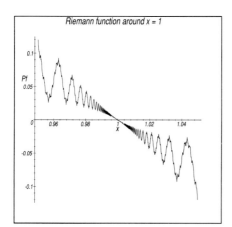
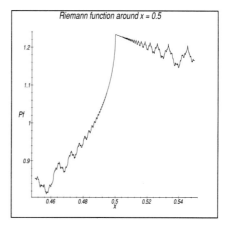

Figure 5.2: The Riemann function locally

Figure 5.2 above pictures the graphs of $f(x)$ in a neighbourhood of the point $x = 1$ and in a neighbourhood of $x = \frac{1}{2}$. What these figures show is clearly in accordance with the facts mentioned above.

```
>  plot(Pf(500,x),x=0.95..1.05,numpoints=1000,
>  title='Riemann function around x = 1');

>  plot(Pf(500,x),x=0.45..0.55,numpoints=1000,
>  title='Riemann function around x = 0.5');
```

Taking a closer look at the graph of $f(x)$ by zooming in locally, we would see the same graphical pattern, whatever the magnification. This so-called fractal characteristic is another indication of the non-differentiable character of $f(x)$. In figure 5.3 below a closeup is given of the graph of $f(x)$ at $x = \frac{1}{2}$.

```
>  plot(Pf(500,x),x=0.49..0.51,numpoints=1000,
>  title='Riemann function at x = 0.5');
```

The fractal character mentioned above is very much visible in the parameter curve defined by $\{(Pg(N, t), Pf(N, t)) \mid 0 \leq t \leq 2\}$, where the function Pg is just like Pf, except that the sine function in the defining expression is replaced by the cosine. Hence

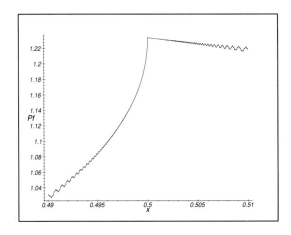

Figure 5.3: Close-up of the Riemann function at $x = \frac{1}{2}$

```
>  Pg := (N,x) -> evalf(Sum(cos(n^2*Pi*x)/n^2,n=1..N));
```

$$Pg := (N,\, x) \to \text{evalf}\left(\sum_{n=1}^{N} \frac{\cos(n^2\, \pi\, x)}{n^2}\right)$$

The Maple code for this parameter curve is

```
>   Riemannplot := plot([Pg(1000,t),Pf(1000,t),t=0..2],
>   numpoints=2000):
```

Depending on the hardware you are using, the generation of so many points could take a long time. As in the present case, it is sometimes quite useful to save the data points in a Maple file so that they can be read and used at any time and in any future session without the bother of having to generate them again. The point is that reading a very large data set is very much quicker than generating an equally large number of data points. In the input lines below it is shown how Maple's **save** command can be used to write **Riemannplot** to a Maple file **Riemann.m** in the directory **c:/Maple/Book/R5/Chapter5**. Note the unix-like forward separators (/) in the directory name; instead you could use double backward separators (\\).

```
>   save Riemannplot, 'c:/Maple/Book/R5/Chapter5/Riemann.m':
```

This file can be read with the command **read**. **Riemannplot** can then be reproduced by just calling it by name.

```
>   read 'c:/Maple/Book/R5/Chapter5/Riemann.m':
>   Riemannplot;
```

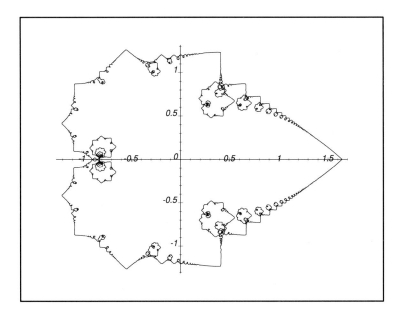

Figure 5.4: Parameter curve $\{(Pg(N, t), Pf(N, t)) \mid 0 \leq t \leq 2\}$ with $N = 1000$

5.3.2   Finding a Primitive Function

After the generous attention we have given to matters of differentiability, we shall now turn to integrability for a change.

Maple is in command of a very powerful integration engine based on the cele-brated Risch algorithm. In a practical sense, Maple should therefore be perfectly capable of finding virtually all primitives a well-trained integration expert could come up with, and in addition cope with a multiple of large and complex cases which are forever beyond the reach of any human. In the worksheet DerivW5b.mws examples can be found showing Maple's capabilities in this field.

But there are also limitations to what Maple can do, and things go wrong occa-sionally. Let us remind you of the fact that there is nothing strange about an integrable function having seemingly different primitives on different intervals. For example, the function x^{-1} has a primitive $\ln x$ on each interval contained in the positive reals, and $\ln(-x)$ on each interval contained in the negative reals.

In the next example, Maple needs a hand, as it cannot find an acceptable primitive all by itself.
We shall try and find a primitive for the function

```
>  w := x -> sqrt(1+sin(x)):   w(x);
```

$$\sqrt{1 + \sin(x)}$$

Clearly this function is defined on the whole of $\mathbb{R}$, it is even continuous on the reals. Hence w has a primitive on each finite interval, and up to an additive constant, this primitive is unique.

```
>  p_w := unapply(int(w(x),x),x);
```

$$p\_w := x \to 2\,\frac{(\sin(x) - 1)\,\sqrt{1 + \sin(x)}}{\cos(x)}$$

Maple does come up with a primitive[1]. Observe that the expression returned by Maple is not defined at the zeros of the cosine function. So we should have a closer look at the answer Maple provides. Let us first check its derivative.

```
>  diff(p_w(x),x);
```

$$2\,\sqrt{1 + \sin(x)} + \frac{\sin(x) - 1}{\sqrt{1 + \sin(x)}} + 2\,\frac{(\sin(x) - 1)\,\sqrt{1 + \sin(x)}\,\sin(x)}{\cos(x)^2}$$

---

[1]We like to point out that by previous releases of Maple V entirely different expressions are returned.

```
> simplify(normal(%));
```

$$\sqrt{1 + \sin(x)}$$

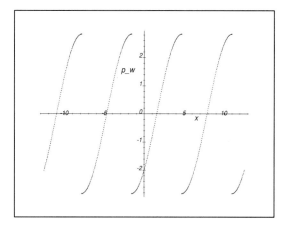

Figure 5.5: Maple's 'primitive' function for $\sqrt{1 + \sin x}$ has discontinuities

This at least checks out. Next let us take a look at the graph of Maple's primitive.

```
> plot(p_w(x),x=-4*Pi..4*Pi,numpoints=500,style=point);
```

From figure 5.5 it is obvious that the function p_w(x) has a discontinuity at all points $x = -\frac{1}{2}\pi + 2k\pi$. This ties in with our earlier observation regarding the vanishing of the denominator of p_w(x). Therefore, the primitive Maple finds is unacceptable in view of the fact that a primitive of a continuous function should be differentiable, and hence continuous at all points of the function's domain.

There is no alternative but to try and find a primitive under our own steam. There are several options[2]; a possible approach runs by means of the well-known substitution rule, where $y = \sin x$ seems the obvious choice. We use the procedure changevar from the Maple student package. Since we only want to use this specific procedure, there is no need for loading the entire package.

```
> I1 := student[changevar](sin(x)=y,Int(w(x),x),y);
```

$$I1 := \int \frac{\sqrt{1+y}}{\sqrt{1-y^2}}\,dy$$

---

[2]We have noticed that in this particular situation different sessions may give different outputs and/or expressions requiring individual 'manual' help in order to reach the desired result.

From the start, we should have serious doubts about the expression Maple returns, because it tacitly assumes that $\cos x = \sqrt{1 - \sin^2 x}$ and therefore ignores the sign of $\cos x$. Further examination of this expression shows its drawbacks even more clearly.

The indefinite integral $I1$ will be evaluated when we use the Maple command `value`.

> `I2 := value(I1);`

$$I2 := -2\,\frac{\sqrt{1 - y^2}}{\sqrt{1 + y}}$$

Here y still stands for $\sin x$ and is therefore not larger than 1. Close inspection of this expression in y now shows that it is real and non-positive, and that it could easily be simplified. Maple often has trouble simplifying complicated expressions involving square roots. So instead of calling Maple's `simplify` function, we first square our expression, then simplify, take the square root again, and finally change its sign.

> `I3 := -sqrt(simplify((I2)^2));`

$$I3 := -2\,\sqrt{-y + 1}$$

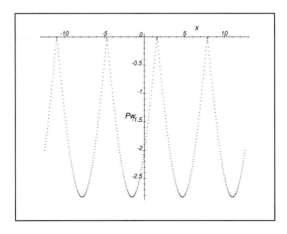

Figure 5.6: Another periodic 'primitive' function for $\sqrt{1 + \sin x}$

This may be an indication—note our careful formulation—that the function

> `Pw := unapply(subs(y=sin(x),I3),x);`

$$Pw := x \rightarrow -2\,\sqrt{-\sin(x) + 1}$$

is a primitive for the function w. On the other hand, Pw cannot possibly be a primitive, because any primitive should be an increasing function in view of the fact that w is non-negative, but unfortunately Pw is periodic. The graph of Pw should clearly shows this.

```
>    plot(Pw(x), x=-4*Pi..4*Pi,numpoints=500,style=point);
```

Indeed, figure 5.6 confirms our suspicions.

We have after all made no progress since Maple's first attempt, the function p_w(x). So what should our conclusion be? The first primitive Maple obtained is certainly correct on any interval that is free of any discontinuity point $-\frac{1}{2}\pi+2k\pi$. The explanation lies in the constant: a primitive of a continuous function on a given interval is unique up to a suitable additive constant. Hence, for every interval between two successive discontinuity points we need a different constant, suitably chosen so that the continuous primitive expression found by Maple, and properly adjusted by these constants, can be joined together into a single continuous, monotonically increasing function on $\mathbb{R}$. At long last, this will give the primitive F we have been looking for. If we also require F to satisfy the condition $F(0) = 0$, then F will take the shape

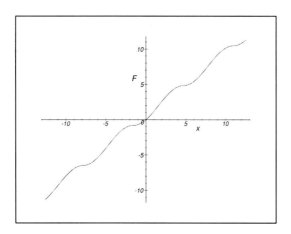

Figure 5.7: Primitive function for $\sqrt{1+\sin x}$ on $(-4\pi, 4\pi)$ passing through the origin

```
>    F := x -> 2 + p_w(x) + 4*sqrt(2)*floor((x+Pi/2)/2/Pi):   F(x);
```

$$2 + 2\,\frac{(-1+\sin(x))\,\sqrt{1+\sin(x)}}{\cos(x)} + 4\,\sqrt{2}\,\mathrm{floor}\left(\frac{1}{2}\,\frac{x+\frac{1}{2}\,\pi}{\pi}\right)$$

We end this Maple session with the graph of F on the interval $(-4\pi, 4\pi)$ (see figure 5.7).

```
>  plot(F(x),x=-4*Pi..4*Pi,numpoints=500);
```

We point out that the function F has the function value $2 + (4\,k - 2)\,\sqrt{2}$ at $x = -\frac{1}{2}\pi + 2k\pi$ $(k \in \mathbb{Z})$. This is a direct consequence of the following limit:

```
>  Limit('F'(x),x=-Pi/2) = limit(F(x),x=-Pi/2);
```

$$\lim_{x \to (-1/2\,\pi)} F(x) = 2 - 2\,\sqrt{2}$$

5.4 Worksheets and Assignments

The subject matter of worksheet DerivW5a.mws is differentiation, whereas the main topic of worksheet DerivW5b.mws is practical integration with Maple. As usual, the Maple output is suppressed with one or two exceptions.

5.4.1 Worksheet 5a. Differentiation

In this worksheet we shall have a closer look at the process of differentiating functions of one variable. Maple offers efficient techniques for symbolic differentiation of rather complicated functions. Moreover, applications like the mean value theorem, the taylor expansion of a function around a point and the differentiation rules of de l'Hôpital will be reviewed.

- **Computing a Derivative**

As you know from section 5.2, the derivative of a function f at the point x is usually defined as the value of the limit

```
>  restart:
>  Limit((f(x+h)-f(x))/h,h=0) = limit((f(x+h)-f(x))/h,h=0);
```

Even before the existence of the limit is established, Maple assigns the symbolic value D(f)(x) to it, which we would normally write as $f'(x)$. The expression returned by Maple shows that Maple is aware of the notion of derivative, and that its notation for the derivative of the function f is the symbol $D(f)$. Let us check that this conclusion is justified.

With this in mind we choose functions with derivatives that are non-trivial and easy to remember at the same time, such as the natural logarithm and the sine function.

```
> f := ln; g := sin;
> D(f); D(g);
```

The output clearly shows that the `D` operator gives the prescription for the derived function. There is another Maple command associated with differentiation: `diff`. This procedure differentiates a given expression with respect to a single variable. The result is an expression, not a function (prescription)! There is of course no difference between the expressions `diff(f(x),x)` and `D(f)(x)`.

```
> Diff(f(x),x) = D(f)(x); Diff(g(x),x) = D(g)(x);
> evalb(diff(f(x),x) = D(f)(x));
```

Here we used the inert `Diff` instead of `diff` to get on screen the unevaluated form of the derivative. Note that this derivative is written with round delta's ∂ which is the usual notation for partial differentiation. This is in agreement with the use of the procedure `diff` as a way to differentiate any expression with respect to any one of its variables.

As you will see below, the operator `D` can differentiate composite functions by means of the chain rule.

```
> Diff(f(g(x)),x) = D(f@g)(x);
```

We next turn to functions that are non-differentiable at some points. An obvious choice is the absolute value function which has no derivative at the origin.

```
> f := abs:  D(f)(x); D(f)(0);
```

Although Maple returns a general formula, it knows that `abs` is not differentiable at 0. The notation $F(n, x)$ stands for the n-th order derivative of the function F with argument x. In particular, $abs(1, x)$ is the first order derivative of `abs(x)`. The limit definition of the derivative should give a similar result.

```
> Limit((f(x+h) - f(x))/h,h=0) = limit((f(x+h) - f(x))/h,h=0);
```

If we assume x to be negative (or positive) then Maple can determine this limit.

```
> assume(x<0):
> Limit((f(x+h)-f(x))/h,h=0) = limit((f(x+h)-f(x))/h,h=0);
> Diff('f(x)','x') = D(f)(x);
```

When piecing together different prescriptions into a single function prescription with the procedure `piecewise`, we have to take great care and check the values of the derivative given by Maple at the knots.

```
> x := 'x':
> f := x -> piecewise(x>1,x^2-1,x>-1 and x<=1,x,-1);
> plot(f(x),x=-2..2,style=point);
```

The graph of f reveals that this function is discontinuous at $x = 1$ and continuous but non-differentiable at $x = -1$. Yet Maple gives the derivative at all real points. So this can not be correct at $x = 1$ and $x = -1$.

```
> D(f); D(f)(1), D(f)(-1);
```

In **assignment 1** of worksheet DerivA5a.mws (see page 140) the derivative of the function $x^2 \sin(1/x)$ is investigated at $x = 0$.

• The Mean Value Theorem

Recall that the derivative can be graphically represented as a direction. To be more precise, the derivative $f'(x)$ is the slope of the tangent to the graph of the function f at the point $(x, f(x))$. This tangent—or rather, the corresponding linear function—is the best linear approximation of the function at the point of contact.

With Maple's `plot` command we make a picture of the graph of the function $f(x) = x^2$ on the interval $[-1, 2]$ together with its tangent at the point $x = 1$.

```
> f := x -> x^2:
> plot(f(x),D(f)(1)*(x-1) + f(1),x=-1..2);
```

We take this function and its tangent to illustrate the mean value theorem. This theorem says that the chord connecting two points of the graph of a differentiable function, has a slope which is equal to the value of the derivative of the function at some intermediate point. Thus

```
> meanv := ('f'(b)-'f'(a))/(b-a) = 'D(f)'(c);
```

for a certain c between a and b. The plot we made earlier shows that in this particular situation there is only one solution for c on the interval $[-1, 2]$.

```
> a := -1:  b := 2:  xi := solve(meanv,c);
```

The following Maple code brings together in one picture the chord, the tangent and the graph of f:

```
> plot({f(x),D(f)(xi)*(x+1)+f(-1),
> D(f)(xi)*(x-xi)+f(xi)},x=-2..3);
```

• The Taylor Expansion

A direct generalization of the mean value theorem is Taylor's theorem which expresses $f(x + h)$ as a sum of ascending powers of the increment h. Recall the

definition of the derivative we gave in section 5.2. First we make the function
symbol f neutral again.

```
>  f := 'f':   x := 'x':
>  f(x+h) = f(x) + D(f)(x)*h + r(x,h);
```

The remainder $r(x, h)$ satisfies

$$\lim_{h \to 0} \frac{r(x, h)}{h} = 0,$$

or rather $r(x, h) = \mathcal{O}(h^2)$ $(h \to 0)$, where $\mathcal{O}$ stands for the O-symbol of Landau .

Maple knows all about the taylor expansion, even of unspecified functions, in
which case this expansion can only be given symbolically of course.

```
>  taylor(f(x+h),h);
```

Note that only the first six terms are given. If you want to see more terms (or
fewer, whatever the case may be), then you should add the required number of
terms n as an additional parameter as in `taylor(f(x+h),h,n)`.

The subject of **assignment 2** of worksheet DerivA5a.mws (see page 140) is the
taylor expansion. Several taylor polynomials of the same function around the
same point but of different degrees are compared.

The taylor expansion can help us to compute limits of type

$$\lim_{x \to a} \frac{f(x)}{g(x)},$$

where $f(a) = g(a) = 0$. Probably, seeing this type of limit made you instantly
think of the well-known rules named after the Marquis de l'Hôpital. With these
rules the limits of such quotients of functions can be determined by considering
the corresponding limits of the quotients of their derivatives. Let us now examine
this more closely.
The functions

```
>  f := x -> sin(Pi*x); g := x -> x^2 - x;
```

both have value 0 at $x = 1$. The quotient $f(x)/g(x)$ therefore is not defined at
this point. But both derivatives of f and g do not vanish at $x = 1$. This is
illustrated in the following figure:

```
>  plot({f,g},0.5..1.5);
```

Observe that the best linear approximation of f at $x = 1$ differs from that of g
at the same point. These best linear approximations are:

```
>  rf := h -> f(1) + D(f)(1)*h; rg := h -> g(1) + D(g)(1)*h;
```

Hence for $h \neq 0$ we have approximately

$$\frac{f(1+h)}{g(1+h)} \approx \frac{rf(h)}{rg(h)},$$

or, properly evaluated,

```
>  'f'(1+h)/'g'(1+h) = rf(h)/rg(h);
```

by approximation. All this means that

```
>  Limit('f'(x)/'g'(x),x=1) = limit(rhs(%),h=0);
```

We let Maple verify this by means of the limit computations:

```
>  Limit('f'(x)/'g'(x),x=1) = limit(f(x)/g(x),x=1);
>  Limit('D(f)'(x)/'D(g)'(x),x=1) = limit(D(f)(x)/D(g)(x),x=1);
```

You should realize that this whole process collapses in case the limit of the quotient of derivatives does not exist or is undetermined. This would surely have been so if D(g)(1) had vanished. For example, as in

```
>  Limit('f'(x)/'g'(x)^2,x=1) = limit(f(x)/g(x)^2,x=1);
```

because

```
>  'D(f)'(1) = D(f)(1);  'D(g^2)(1)' = D(g^2)(1);
```

so that the conditions of l'Hôpital's theorem are not fulfilled.

As you know, sometimes l'Hôpital's rule must be applied several times to get the desired result. In these cases, it is almost always better and faster to use taylor expansions of the denominator and numerator.

Now complete **assignment 3** of worksheet DerivA5a.mws (see page 141): taylor expansions should be used in order to determine the limit of a quotient of functions.

• Investigating an Implicit Function Using the Taylor Expansion

The taylor expansion can be very useful for getting to know the behaviour of an implicit function in a neighbourhood of some point. For instance, in many situations no explicit formula can be given for the inverse of a function, even though this function itself is completely explicit. In such cases the taylor expansion frequently offers a way out.

The following elementary function L is strictly monotonically increasing, so that it has an inverse. However, this inverse function can only be given implicitly, namely as the solution $x(y)$ to the equation $L(x(y)) - y = 0$, where $x(y)$ means that x should be considered a function of y.

```
>  L := x -> ln(x^2+1)+x+1;
>  'dL/dx'(x) = factor(normal(D(L)(x)));
```

Clearly the derivative of L is positive everywhere except at $x = -1$. This means that L is strictly increasing and hence injective. However, its inverse function cannot be explicitly extracted from the identity $L(x(y)) = y$.

On the other hand, it is quite easy to obtain an explicit expression for the derivative of the inverse function and hence for all higher order derivatives as well. Keeping this in mind we differentiate the identity $L(x(y)) - y = 0$ with respect to the variable y.

```
>  alias(x=x(y)); diff(L(x)-y = 0,y);
```

The function `alias` is used here to instruct Maple that x should be considered a function of y.

Next we solve the equation so obtained for the unknown $\dfrac{\partial}{\partial y} x$.

```
>  diff(x,y) = factor(normal(solve(%,diff(x,y))));
```

Higher order derivatives can now be calculated, and thus taylor expansions of the inverse of L around any point except $x = -1$ can be constructed.

Let us consider the point $y = L(0) = 1$. First we remove x's dependency on y, so that it is an independent variable again.

```
>  alias(x=x); RootOf(L(x)=y,x); taylor(%,y=1);
```

The place holder `RootOf` is used here to somehow store the solution $x = x(y)$ of $L(x) = y$.

Now we convert the taylor expansion to a polynomial expression by removing the order term. Finally, aided by Maple's `unapply` function, this polynomial is transformed into a polynomial function.

```
>  Lpol := expand(convert(%,polynom));
>  'L^(inv)' := unapply(Lpol,y);
```

Since the function L^{inv} approximates the inverse L^{-1} of L in a neighbourhood of $y = 1$, the collection of points

$$\{(L^{\mathrm{inv}}(y), y) \mid y \text{ in some neighbourhood of } 1\}$$

gives an approximation of the function L in some neighbourhood of $x = 0$. For, in a neighbourhood of $x = 0$, the expressions $y = L(x)$ and $x = L^{-1}(y)$ carry exactly the same information about the relationship between x and y.

To verify this, let us display side by side the graph of L and a sample of 100 points of the collection of points $(L^{\text{inv}}(y), y)$.

```
>  ss := [seq('L^(inv)'(0.6+i/100),i=0..99)]:
>  ii := [seq(0.6+i/100,i=0..99)]:
>  tt := zip((a,b)->[(a,b)],ss,ii):
>  iplot := plot(tt,color=green):
>  Lplot := plot(L,-1.5..1.5,color=red):
>  plots[display]({iplot,Lplot});
```

The figure clearly shows that close to $x = 0$ both graphs agree rather well.

Finally, if L^{inv} is a good approximation to L^{-1}, then the composite function $L^{\text{inv}} \circ L$ should be more or less equal to the identity function $x \mapsto x$. This seems to be correct considering the output of

```
>  taylor((Linv @ L)(x),x = 0);
```

5.4.2   Assignment 5a. Differentiation

The assignments of DerivA5a.mws relate to the topics discussed in worksheet DerivW5a.mws.

1. We define the function s as follows:

   ```
   >  s := x -> if x=0 then 0 else x^2*sin(1/x) fi;
   ```

   (a) Look at the graph of s over $[-0.01, 0.01]$ and compute the value of the derivative of s at $x = 0$.

   (b) Now try to determine $\lim_{x \to 0} s'(x)$.
   Is the derivative s' continuous at $x = 0$? Illustrate your answer by plotting s' over $[-1, 1]$.

2. The function t is given by

   ```
   >  t := x -> exp(x^2);
   ```

   (a) Determine the taylor expansions of t around $x = 0$ with 2, 4 and 6 terms.

   (b) Convert these taylor expansions into polynomials without a remainder term using the command

   ```
   >  convert(..., polynom);
   ```

   (c) Compare the graphs of these three polynomials with the graph of t over the interval $[-1.5, 1.5]$. Which polynomial gives the best approximation?

3. Consider the functions f, g given by

$$f := x \mapsto e^{x^2} + e^{-x^2} - 2,$$
$$g := x \mapsto \cos(\cos(\pi x) - 1) - 1.$$

Calculate the taylor expansions around $x = 0$ of the two functions. Does the limit

$$\lim_{x \to 0} \frac{f(x)}{g(x)}$$

exist and if so, what is its value? How many times do you have to apply l'Hôpital's rule in order to answer these questions, in other words, what is the smallest order derivative unequal to 0 at $x = 0$ for these functions? To verify your answer you should also compute the limit directly using Maple's `limit` command.

5.4.3   Worksheet 5b. Integration

This worksheet is devoted to integration—Riemann integration, to be precise—of functions of a single variable. The variety of techniques offered by Maple for indefinite integration and numerical calculation of definite integrals is impressive; we shall pick a few lovely flowers in the luxuriant garden called Maple integration. We shall also consider examples of partial integration and of the substitution method. Finally we shall have a look at some definite integrals with limits of integration that are themselves functions of a single variable.

• Intuitive Perception of Integration

Riemann integration of a bounded function $f : x \mapsto f(x)$ on an interval $[a, b]$ is about measuring the area bounded by the graph of f, the x-axis and two vertical lines $x = a$ and $x = b$. The area below the x-axis, is counted negative. Areas bordered by the graphs of functions can only be properly defined and computed if these functions can be approximated very accurately by step functions. Therefore, integration is often visualized as a process in which an ever increasing number N of rectangles is used to collectively cover the area in question more and more accurately as N increases.

The `student` package includes some procedures which demonstrate this intuitive perception of integration. Let us begin with defining a function and then load this package.

```
> restart:
> f := x -> x^4 - 2*x^2 + 3*x + 2;
> with(student);
```

To get a first impression of this function, we quickly plot its graph over some suitable interval, say $[-2, 2]$.

```
> plot(f(x),x=-2..2);
```

A description of the process of integrating a function over an interval $[a, b]$, usually starts with the partitioning of this interval into a (finite) number of subintervals, followed by calculating the function's supremum and infimum over each subinterval, so that lower sums and upper sums can be built. If this partition is constantly refined by adding intermediate points in such a way that the maximum of the individual lengths of the subintervals tends to 0, then, provided the function is integrable over $[a, b]$, the corresponding upper sum and lower sum converge to a common limit: the (Riemann) integral of f over $[a, b]$.

Instead of lower and upper sums, we could also take middle sums to approximate the integral. A middle sum—this is a particular choice of Riemann sum—determines the total area of the rectangles with height $f(m_i)$, where m_i is the midpoint of the i-th interval. Clearly a middle sum will approximate the integral better as the number of subintervals grows. With ten subintervals of equal length on the interval $[-2, 2]$, we get the following picture:

```
> middlebox(f(x),x=-2..2,10,color=black);
```

The area covered by all ten rectangles is

```
> middlesum(f(x),x=-2..2,10);
> value(%);
```

Letting the number of subintervals (of equal length) increase from 10 to 200 with steps of 10, we see that with each step the value of the middle sum gets closer and closer to a limit value. We realize of course that this must be the value of the integral of f over $[-2, 2]$, or, in other words, the area of the region enclosed by the graph of f, the x-axis and the lines $x = -2$ and $x = 2$.

```
> MSum := [seq(evalf(middlesum(f(x),x=-2..2,10*n)),n=1..20)];
```

Also take a look at the following figure showing the graph of f and the middle sum on 400 subintervals. The rectangles are no longer individually visible; the area below the graph of f appears to coincide with the combined area of all 400 rectangles.

```
> middlebox(f(x),x=-2..2,400,color=black);
```

This rather inefficient way of calculating areas is only meant to illustrate the integration principle; fortunately there are much better ways available. The Fundamental Theorem of Calculus provides such a method.

```
>  Int('f'(x),x=-2..2) = F(2) - F(-2);
```

The function F is a primitive for f on the interval $[-2, 2]$. For polynomials like f, primitives are quickly found.

```
>  F := unapply(int(f(x),x),x);
```

Although there is hardly any need for in a trivial case like this, it is no trouble at all to quickly check the derivative of F and see that it coincides with f. This is of course the property that is most characteristic of a primitive function.

```
>  evalb(diff(F(x),x) = f(x));
```

Finally the Fundamental Theorem will give us the exact value of the integral.

```
>  Int('f'(x),x=-2..2) = F(2) - F(-2);
>  'numerical value' = evalf(rhs(%));
```

Assignment 1 of worksheet DerivA5b.mws (see page 146) takes another look at middle sums.

• Integration of Rational Functions

We have suggested before, and we repeat it here: Maple can integrate very complicated functions. It is well-known that every rational function has a primitive. In the process of indefinite integration of a rational function, partial fraction decomposition plays an essential role. Let us consider how Maple accomplishes this.

It might test your integration skills to their limits if you tried to integrate the following function by hand:

```
>  integrand := x -> (x^6 - 2*x^5 + 3*x^4 - 4*x^3 + 5*x^2 -
>  6*x + 7)/(x^5 + x^3 + x^2 + 1):
>  Int(integrand(x),x) = int(integrand(x),x);
```

It seems almost equally difficult to verify the answer. Maple can help by differentiating the result.

```
>  diff(rhs(%),x);
```

This still does not get us very far. It seems that Maple has applied partial fraction decomposition. Let us try to give the derivative a more or less normal appearance.

```
>  normal(%,'expanded');
```

Here we see the original integrand again. We could force Maple to first apply partial fraction decomposition with

```
>  convert(integrand(x),parfrac,x);
```

• Partial Integration and Integration by Substitution

A commonly used integration technique is partial integration. The procedure `intparts` of the package `student` may help us to improve our working knowledge of this standard method.

In the next lines both partial integration and substitution are used to integrate an elementary function; occasional explanations and comments are added.

```
>  with(student):
>  integral := Int(x*sin(x),x);
>  intparts(integral,x); # The factor to be differentiated is x
>  Primitive1 := value(%);
```

Verification shows that Maple's answer is correct, for instance by

```
>  diff(Primitive1,x);
```

Now try and complete **assignment 2** of worksheet DerivA5b.mws (see page 146) where the method of partial integration is applied to a similar indefinite integral.

Another integration technique is the substitution method. For this purpose the `student` package has a procedure called `changevar`.

```
>  Int(x*log(x^2 + 1),x);
>  changevar(x^2 + 1 = t,%); # Change of variable x to t
>  intparts(%,log(t));
>  value(%);
>  Primitive2 := subs(t = x^2 + 1,%); # Give t back its x-value
```

Verify Maple's answer by clicking the right mouse button on the primitive in the output region and selecting the option `Differentiate` from the pop-up menu.

Of course, Maple could have produced both primitives without any help from us.

Assignment 3 of worksheet DerivA5b.mws (see page 146) is about symbolic integration and the necessity of keeping a watchful eye on the results Maple produces.

• Numerical Integration

In many situations we are only interested in the numerical value of a definite integral. It then makes sense to call numerical integration procedures directly, instead of in a roundabout way via symbolic integration. This is done by `evalf(Int(...))` with capital I (or with `'evalf/int'`). Now symbolic integration is avoided altogether, and as this is often in vain for 'difficult' functions anyway, it saves time as well. We give an example.

```
>   Int(exp(-x^2)*cos(x),x=0..Pi) =
>   evalf(Int(exp(-x^2)*cos(x),x=0..Pi));
```

• Inside Information on Maple's Integration Methods

To get inside information on the integration methods Maple uses, the value of the Maple variable `infolevel` should be increased.

```
>   integrand2 := x -> exp(sqrt(x))/(x^2 + 1):
>   infolevel[int] := 5;
>   Int(integrand2(x),x) = int(integrand2(x),x);
```

Maple did find a primitive, but the expression returned is rather complicated. Let us try to unravel Maple's output a bit. The procedures used are stated with a brief explanation. We won't go into the precise meaning of the information provided here. The primitive produced by Maple is written as a finite sum of expressions in which the elliptic integral `Ei(n,x)` can be distinguished, and with a summation variable running through the roots of the fourth degree polynomial $z^4 + 1$.

Let us reset `infolevel` to 0. To make sure this rather involved expression is the correct primitive, we quickly check its derivative.

```
>   infolevel[int] := 0:
>   normal(diff(rhs(%%),x),'expanded');
```

• A Repeated Integral

Take a look at the following repeated integral (note the combinations of capital I and lower case i of `Int` and `int`).

```
>   Int(Int(x*y/(x^2 + y^2)^2,x=y..y^2),y=1..2) =
>   Int(int(x*y/(x^2 + y^2)^2,x=y..y^2),y=1..2);
>   Int(int(x*y/(x^2 + y^2)^2,x=y..y^2),y=1..2) =
>   int(int(x*y/(x^2 + y^2)^2,x=y..y^2),y=1..2);
```

This integral is equal to the double integral over the (x, y)-region bounded by the line $x = y$, the parabola $x = y^2$ and the line $y = 2$. The next Maple code colours this region red[3].

```
> g1 := plot(min(x,2),x=0.5..4.5,color=red,filled=true):
> g2 := plot(sqrt(x),x=0.5..4.5,color=background,filled=true):
> plots[display]([g2,g1,plot({x,2,sqrt(x)},
> x=0.5..4.5,color=black)],view=[0.5..4.5,0.5..2.5]);
```

5.4.4   Assignments 5b. Integration

The assignments below are related to Riemann integration. They are meant as exercises for the integration techniques discussed in worksheet DerivW5b.mws.

1. First define the function w by the Maple instruction

   ```
   > w := x -> 2*sqrt(1-x^2);
   ```

   Then define the sequence $(r(k))$ as follows:

   ```
   > r := k -> middlesum(w(x), x= -1..1, k);
   ```

   Compute the values of $r(10)$, $r(100)$ and $r(1000)$. The `evalf` procedure can be useful. Also determine the limit

   $$\lim_{k \to \infty} r(k)$$

   using Maple's `limit` command. Explain Maple's answer.

2. Consider the indefinite integral

   ```
   > integ := Int(x^2*cos(x),x);
   ```

   Use partial integration to obtain a symbolic value for this integral. You should use the `intparts` procedure twice. The factor to be differentiated should first be x^2 and then x.
   Verify your answer by differentiation.

3. Consider the function

   ```
   > f := x -> cos(x)*sqrt(1+cos(x)^2);
   ```

   (a) Plot the graph of f over $[-\frac{1}{2}\pi, \frac{1}{2}\pi]$.

---

[3]For some reason which eludes us, we only get the correct picture if the plot order in the first argument of `plots[display]` is exactly as shown.

(b) Use Maple to calculate the definite integral

$$\int_{-\frac{1}{2}\pi}^{\frac{1}{2}\pi} f(x)\,dx.$$

To verify Maple's answer, also calculate

$$\int_{-\frac{1}{2}\pi}^{0} f(x)\,dx \quad \text{and} \quad \int_{0}^{\frac{1}{2}\pi} f(x)\,dx.$$

Considering the plot of part (a), what is your view on the correctness of the values Maple computed?

(c) The function

```
> F := y -> Int(f(x),x=-Pi/2..y);
```

is a primitive function for f on $[-\frac{1}{2}\pi, \frac{1}{2}\pi]$. Observe the use of the inert integration procedure `Int`. Use Maple's `value` command to try and get an explicit symbolic expression for $F(y)$. You will agree that the answer is less than satisfactory. Also plot the graph of F over $[-\frac{1}{2}\pi, \frac{1}{2}\pi]$.

(d) Replace $\cos^2 x$ by $1 - \sin^2 x$ in the definition of $f(x)$ and let Maple once more try and find a primitive F for f satisfying $F(-\frac{1}{2}\pi) = 0$. Calculate $F(0)$ and $F(\frac{1}{2}\pi)$. Did Maple find the correct primitive this time?

5.5   Exercises

1. You are asked to determine the n-th order derivative, $n \in \mathbb{N}$, of the function $f(x) := \ln(x^2 + x + 1)$ at the point $x = -\frac{1}{2}$. First let Maple calculate the expression

$$\frac{f^{(n)}\left(-\frac{1}{2}\right)}{(n-1)!}$$

for different values of n.

2. The function $f(x) := x^{x^x - 1}$ is properly defined for $x > 0$.
Determine $\lim_{x \downarrow 0} f(x)$. Is it possible to define $f(0)$ so as to make f continuous on the interval $[0, \infty]$?
The function f is surely differentiable on $(0, \infty)$. Find the global maximum and the global minimum that f attains on the interval $[0, 1]$.
Observe that the Maple command `maximize` returns an incorrect global maximum for f on $[0, 1]$.

3. A primitive for the rational function

$$R(x) := \frac{x^2 + 6\,x + 6}{x^{12} + 1}$$

can be explicitly given, provided its denominator can be decomposed into linear and quadratic factors.

We expect Maple to give the complete partial fraction decomposition of $R(x)$. Unfortunately, this is not so, because on the instruction

```
>   convert(R(x),parfrac,x);
```

only a partial answer is returned. It seems that Maple needs some help with the complete factorization of the denominator of $R(x)$.

Use the command `factor` with parameters `sqrt(2)` and `sqrt(6)` to obtain the complete partial fraction decomposition. Finally find a primitive for $R(x)$.

4. The function $f : \mathbb{R} \to \mathbb{R}$ defined by $f(x) = x^2 + \sin x$, is strictly increasing on the interval $(-\delta, \infty)$ for a fixed $\delta > 0$. Find the maximal value of δ subject to this condition.

Find the first 6 terms of the taylor expansion around $x = 0$ of the inverse function of f.

5. Find a finite expression for the definite integral

$$J(m) := \int_0^{\frac{\pi}{4}} \tan^m x\,dx, \quad m = 0, 1, 2, \dots,$$

by letting Maple first determine an expression for the sum

$$J(m + 1) + J(m - 1).$$

6. The object of this exercise is to compute the double integral of the function $\sqrt{|x^2 - y|}$ over the region D in the (x, y)-plane enclosed by the parabolas $x = y^2$ and $y = x^2$. Hence

$$\iint_D \sqrt{|x^2 - y|}\,dx\,dy,$$

with $D = \{(x, y) \in [0, 1] \times [0, 1] \mid x^2 \leq y \text{ and } y^2 \leq x\}$. Computing a numerical value for this integral poses no problems. We are, however, interested in a symbolic answer. Maple is not able to produce one without assistance.

Carefully inspect Maple's output and act on what you see. Maybe a suitable substitution via `student[changevar]` will help.

7. The function f is defined as follows:

$$f(x) = x\,(x-p)\,(1+p-x),$$

with parameter $p > 1$. The word parameter refers to a quantity that, though unknown, should not be seen as a variable, but as a constant. Show that f is strictly concave on the interval $[p, \infty)$ and that f attains a unique maximum at a point of the subinterval $[p, p+1]$. Can you find out which point this is?

8. Use the differential operator D to check the chain rule. Hence verify that Maple correctly differentiates an arbitrary composite function $f \circ g$. Calculate in particular the derivative of the composite functions $f \circ g$ and $g \circ f$, where

$$f(x) := e^{1/x^2} \quad \text{and} \quad g(x) := \int_0^{\sqrt{x}} \cos t^2 \, dt.$$

Check your answers.

9. Find all k-th order derivatives for $k = 0, 1, \ldots, 10$ of the function

$$f : (-1, \infty) \to \mathbb{R}, \quad f(x) = e^{\sin(\ln(x+1))}$$

and evaluate these at the point $x = 0$. Compare your results with the coefficients of the taylor expansion of the same function around $x = 0$.

10. In order to find a primitive for a function $f : I \to \mathbb{R}$, we might consider the Maple instruction

```
>  int(f(x),x) + c;
```

where c is some constant. The result however is an expression and not a mechanism for giving the function prescription. The latter can be obtained via Maple's **unapply** command. So far, this is rather old news.
We could also try and find the prescription of a primitive function for f in quite another way, namely by means of

```
>  F := x -> int(f(x),x) + c;
```

Initially this does not seem a bad idea. Try F, $F(y)$, $D(F)$, and $D(F)(t)$. However, for numerical arguments, as in $F(1)$, things go wrong. Maple's output might suggest a possible modification of the definition given above to avoid such unwanted behaviour. As a matter of fact, you are not supposed to use the Maple procedure **unapply**.
Note the similarity between indefinite integration and definite integration with a variable upper integration limit.

11. In this chapter's Maple session, we observed that Maple was in trouble trying to find the correct primitive for the function $\sqrt{1 + \sin x}$ on $\mathbb{R}$. The following description gives an alternative for finding a primitive: first substitute $x = 2y + \frac{1}{2}\pi$ in

$$\int \sqrt{1 + \sin x}\, dx.$$

Suitable manipulations with `simplify`, `normal`, and/or `expand` will transform the integral expression so obtained into a rather simple expression in y. Which one? Use this expression to find, assisted by Maple, a primitive for the function $\sqrt{1 + \sin x}$ on $\mathbb{R}$.

5.6   Survey of Used Maple Expressions

The following list contains important Maple expressions and commands used in this chapter. Only expressions that may need additional explanation are included. Some expressions occur only in worksheets DerivW5a.mws and DerivW5b.mws included in this chapter.

expression	brief explanation
`Zeta`	– Riemann's ζ-function: $\zeta(s) = \sum_{n=1}^{\infty} \dfrac{1}{n^s}$
`evalf(Sum())`, `evalf(Int())`	– inert form: capitals are used to avoid unwanted symbolic evaluation
`D`	– differential operator: $D(f) = f'$
`diff(f(x),x)`	– determines the derivative of $f(x)$
`diff(f(x),x$k)`	– determines the k-th order derivative of $f(x)$
$F(n, x)$ in output	– n-th order derivative of the function F at argument x
`infolevel[func] := n`	– sets information level for command `func` to `n` $(= 1, 2, 3, 4,$ or $5)$

The following Maple expressions appear in this chapter for the first time (some belong to the package **student**):
`changevar`, `infolevel`, `intparts`, `middlebox`, `middlesum`, `maximize`, `parfrac`.

6

Vector Spaces and Linear Mappings

I n this closing chapter we will be engaged again with notions and techniques typical for the field of Linear Algebra, but here our attention will also be focused on the abstract structure of vector spaces and linear mappings (or linear transformations) between them. Vectors—the elements of a vector space—do not need to be ordered lists of numbers, polynomials can also be viewed as vectors. Of course, matrices continue to play a prominent role, namely as representations of linear mappings between vector spaces with predetermined bases.

6.1 Introduction

The most important concepts we shall come across in this chapter are those of eigenvalue and eigenspace, and the singular value decomposition of an arbitrary matrix.

The topic of eigenvalues of matrices and their eigenvectors comes usually at the very end of a first acquaintance with the field of Linear Algebra. The diagonalization of symmetric matrices and its applications frequently serve as a natural climax. More often than not, the so-called 'singular value decomposition' (SVD for short) is missing from a first course in Linear Algebra. This important factorization technique can be viewed as a direct generalization of the diagonalization method of symmetric matrices, because it applies to any matrix, be it non-symmetric or even non-square. The method plays an important role in numerical Linear Algebra because many essential properties a general matrix may have can be read off from its numerical SVD, such as rank, an orthonormal basis for its nullspace and an orthonormal basis for its range. In the following section we shall give more details of the SVD construction and the theory behind this factorization method. Finally, in the Maple session of section 6.3 we shall give an example of the practical application of the singular value decomposition to image processing.

6.2   Further Concepts from Linear Algebra

The present section continues the brief summary of basic concepts of Linear Algebra started in Chapter 3 with the concept of vector space. A vector space over the real numbers $\mathbb{R}$ is a collection of vectors endowed with two structures, an addition and a scalar multiplication—the elements of $\mathbb{R}$ are called scalars. Vector addition behaves very similar to ordinary addition of numbers: it is commutative and associative, a unique zero vector exists and each vector has a unique inverse, also called additive inverse or negative. The scalar multiplication has nice properties too which generalize the notion of 'multiple' in quite a natural way. For precise and complete definitions we refer to any Linear Algebra textbook.

A subspace of a vector space $\mathbb{V}$ is a subset of $\mathbb{V}$ which, endowed with the same addition and scalar multiplication as $\mathbb{V}$, is a vector space in its own right. A finite-dimensional vector space $\mathbb{V}$ is characterized by the existence of a finite basis $\mathcal{B}$; this is the name given to a finite subset of $\mathbb{V}$ of linearly independent vectors with the property that each vector in $\mathbb{V}$ can be uniquely expressed as a linear combination of the vectors of $\mathcal{B}$. In a finite dimensional vector space all bases have the same number of elements, the dimension of $\mathbb{V}$. Characteristic examples of finite dimensional vector spaces over $\mathbb{R}$ are the n-spaces $\mathbb{R}^n$. The vector space $\mathbb{P}_n$ of all polynomials with real coefficients and of degree at most n is an $(n+1)$-dimensional vector space over $\mathbb{R}$. From now on we shall only consider finite dimensional vector spaces, so that we might as well drop the predicate 'finite dimensional'.

A linear mapping (or linear map or linear transformation) is a function T from one vector space $\mathbb{V}$ to another vector space $\mathbb{W}$, with the additional property that the typical structure of $\mathbb{V}$ given by its own vector addition and scalar multiplication is mapped onto that of $\mathbb{W}$. Hence, a linear map preserves all linear relations. Necessary and sufficient conditions are that for each pair of vectors $u, v \in \mathbb{V}$ and for each scalar $r \in \mathbb{R}$ the following identities are satisfied:

$$T(u + v) = T(u) + T(v) \quad \text{and} \quad T(ru) = rT(u).$$

Note that the first $+$ in the first identity means vector addition in $\mathbb{V}$, whereas the second $+$ represents addition in $\mathbb{W}$. Likewise, the second identity involves two scalar multiplications: one in $\mathbb{V}$ and one in $\mathbb{W}$. The vector spaces $\mathbb{V}$ and $\mathbb{W}$ are called isomorphic if there is a bijective linear map $T : \mathbb{V} \to \mathbb{W}$; such a linear map T is called an isomorphism. The vector space $\mathbb{P}_n$ is isomorphic to $\mathbb{R}^{n+1}$.

Vector spaces are generally infinite collections of vectors, and therefore it is nice that every linear mapping between two (finite-dimensional) vector spaces has a finite representation, and what is more, this finite representation is unique if in both vector spaces an (ordered) basis is preselected. Such matrix representations can be manipulated more easily and a suitably chosen matrix representation can considerably simplify the derivation of characteristic properties of a linear transformation. Especially in situations where the vector spaces under consideration do not merely comprise lists of numbers, as in vector spaces such as $\mathbb{P}_n$, this is a major advantage. The relation between a linear mapping T and a matrix representation of T can be formulated very precisely. Let $T : \mathbb{V} \to \mathbb{W}$ be a linear map from vector space $\mathbb{V}$ into vector space $\mathbb{W}$, mapping each $v \in \mathbb{V}$ to $w = T(v) \in \mathbb{W}$. Further, given a basis $\mathcal{B} = \{b_1, b_2, \ldots, b_n\}$ of $\mathbb{V}$, each $v \in \mathbb{V}$ can be expressed uniquely as a linear combination of the basis vectors $b_1, b_2, \ldots, b_n$. The (column) vector, or $n \times 1$ matrix of coefficients of this linear combination, also called the coordinate vector of v relative to the basis $\mathcal{B}$, will be denoted by $[v]_{\mathcal{B}}$. So, if $v = v_1 b_1 + v_2 b_2 + \cdots + v_n b_n$ then

$$[v]_{\mathcal{B}} = (v_1, v_2, \cdots, v_n)^t.$$

Finally, the matrix A representing the linear mapping T relative to the basis $\mathcal{B}_1$ of $\mathbb{V}$ and the basis $\mathcal{B}_2$ of $\mathbb{W}$, is defined by the matrix relation

$$[T(v)]_{\mathcal{B}_2} = A[v]_{\mathcal{B}_1}.$$

If $\mathbb{V} = \mathbb{W} = \mathbb{R}^n$ and $\mathcal{B}_1 = \mathcal{B}_2$ is the standard basis of $\mathbb{R}^n$, then the relationship between T and A is simply given by $T(v) = Av$, the matrix product of matrix A and (column) vector v. In case $\mathbb{V} = \mathbb{W}$ and only one basis is mentioned, it is tacitly assumed that for both the domain and the codomain of T the same basis is chosen.

An eigenvalue of a linear mapping $T : \mathbb{V} \to \mathbb{V}$ is a scalar λ for which the equation $T(v) = \lambda v$ has a vector solution $v \neq 0$. Such a non-zero solution v is called an eigenvector corresponding to the eigenvalue λ of T. An immediate consequence of the discussion in the paragraph preceding the present one is that for any matrix representation A of T, relative to some basis $\mathcal{B}$ of $\mathbb{V}$, the equation $Ax = \lambda x$ has a non-zero vector solution $x = [v]_B \in \mathbb{R}^n$: the eigenvalues of a linear mapping are just the eigenvalues of any matrix representation.

All eigenvectors corresponding to the same eigenvalue span a subspace of $\mathbb{V}$, the so-called eigenspace corresponding to this eigenvalue. In case $\mathbb{V}$ happens to have a basis of eigenvectors of T then its matrix representation relative to this basis is a diagonal matrix with the eigenvalues of T on its main diagonal. The linear mapping T is called diagonalizable. For matrices this has the following meaning. If A is an $n \times n$ matrix, and the linear mapping $T : \mathbb{R}^n \to \mathbb{R}^n$ is defined by $T(x) = Ax$ for $x \in \mathbb{R}^n$—A is called the standard matrix (representation) of T—then A is diagonalizable if T is diagonalizable. All symmetric matrices are diagonalizable, even orthogonally diagonalizable, which means that the corresponding basis of eigenvectors is an orthonormal set. Hence a symmetric matrix A can always be written as the product

$$A = Q \Lambda Q^t$$

for a suitable orthogonal matrix Q, and diagonal matrix Λ of eigenvalues of A. The column vectors of Q are an orthonormal set of eigenvectors of A.

All matrices, even those for which no eigenvalues exist, do have so-called singular values. In a sense these singular values take the place of eigenvalues.

The definition of the concept of singular value is surprisingly simple: the singular values of A are the square roots of the eigenvalues of the symmetric matrix $A^t A$. This matrix is symmetric and positive (semi-)definite, which implies that all its eigenvalues are non-negative. Therefore the singular values of a matrix are properly defined and always non-negative. Moreover, there are as many positive singular values as the rank of the matrix A. It is a direct consequence of the definition of eigenvalue that the matrices $A^t A$ and $A A^t$ have exactly the same eigenvalues, the corresponding eigenvectors however are different. For a given $m \times n$ matrix A, let the set of $\mathbb{R}^m$-vectors $\{u_1, u_2, \ldots, u_m\}$ be an orthonormal set of eigenvectors of $A A^t$—the so-called left singular vectors of A—and let the vectors $v_1, v_2, \ldots, v_n \in \mathbb{R}^n$ constitute an orthonormal set of eigenvectors of $A^t A$, called the right singular vectors of A. Moreover, let the vectors be ordered in such a way that for each i the vectors u_i and v_i correspond to the same eigenvalue σ_i. Then A can be written as the product

$$A = U \Sigma V^t,$$

where, by definition, U and V are orthogonal matrices with left and right singular vectors respectively for column vectors, and Σ is the $m \times n$ diagonal matrix of singular values of A. These singular values are usually put in order of magnitude, from large to small. It is quite natural to compare this decomposition with the one of symmetric matrices as described above.

Expanding A's singular value decomposition, it is straightforward to see that A can also be written as a sum of rank 1 matrices:

$$A = \sum_{i=1}^{\text{rank}(A)} \sigma_i \, u_i \, v_i^{\,t},$$

the so-called SVD expansion.

In fact a matrix's SVD reveals a lot about its structure and properties. Assuming that the singular values are arranged in order of magnitude, and that the vectors u_i and v_i are the left and right singular vectors respectively corresponding to the singular value σ_i, the SVD of a matrix A gives

- the rank r of A. This is the number of non-zero singular values.
- an orthonormal basis $\{u_1, u_2, \ldots, u_r\}$ for the range of A.
- the dimension of the null space of A. This is the number of zero singular values.
- an orthonormal basis $\{v_{r+1}, v_{r+2}, \ldots, v_n\}$ for the null space of A.

6.3 Diagonalization and the SVD

Without doubt you remember, but let us repeat anyway, that most Maple functions and procedures about matrices and vectors are not automatically available at the start of a Maple session. They can be loaded all together in a single stroke with the command

```
> with(linalg):
```

6.3.1 A Simple Orthogonal Projection

We begin this session with a thorough examination of an elementary linear mapping.

Let $T : \mathbb{V} \to \mathbb{W}$ be the orthogonal projection of $\mathbb{V} = \mathbb{R}^5$ onto the hyperplane

$$\mathbb{W} = \{x \in \mathbb{V} \mid x_1 + x_2 + x_3 + x_4 + x_5 = 0\}.$$

The vector $e = (1, 1, 1, 1, 1)^t$ is normal to this hyperplane, i.e. e is perpendicular to all lines in the hyperplane $\mathbb{W}$. In other words, the vector e is orthogonal to all vectors of the subspace $\mathbb{W}$ of $\mathbb{R}^5$. We define

```
> e := vector(5,1):  T := x -> x + t*e;
```

$$T := x \to x + t\,e$$

where t should be chosen such that $T(x)$ and e are orthogonal. Hence (we first introduce the symbolic 5-vector x)

```
> x := vector(5):  t := x -> solve(innerprod(x+s*e,e),s);
```

$$t := x \to \text{solve}(\text{innerprod}(x + s\,e, e), s)$$

The orthogonal projection T can now be represented as

```
> T := x -> evalm(x+t(x)*e);
```

$$T := x \to \text{evalm}(x + t(x)\,e)$$

Is T really a linear transformation? To check this, we take a look at the expressions

$$T(u+v) - T(u) - T(v) \quad \text{and} \quad T(ru) - rT(u),$$

where u and v are symbolic vectors and r is a symbolic scalar. Both expressions should evaluate to the null vector, which is indeed the case.

```
>  u := vector(5):   v := vector(5):
>  evalm(T(u+v) - T(u) - T(v));
```

$$[0, 0, 0, 0, 0]$$

```
>  evalm(T(r*u) - r*T(u)):  map(simplify,%);
```

$$[0, 0, 0, 0, 0]$$

Next we wish to determine the matrix representation of T relative to the standard basis $\mathcal{B}_1$ of $\mathbb{V}$ and the basis $\mathcal{B}_2$ of $\mathbb{W}$, which we shall choose as follows:

```
>  B2 := [seq(vector(5,j -> if j=i then 1
>  elif j=i+1 then -1 else 0 fi),i=1..4)];
```

$$B2 := [[1, -1, 0, 0, 0], [0, 1, -1, 0, 0], [0, 0, 1, -1, 0], [0, 0, 0, 1, -1]]$$

Note that we use square brackets instead of braces. The reason is, that by doing this the order in which the elements of the basis $\mathcal{B}_2$ have been defined remains fixed.

The next step is to bring together into a matrix B the vectors of $\mathcal{B}_2$, treated as columns. The Maple command **augment** does just that.

```
>  B := augment(op(B2));
```

$$B := \begin{bmatrix} 1 & 0 & 0 & 0 \\ -1 & 1 & 0 & 0 \\ 0 & -1 & 1 & 0 \\ 0 & 0 & -1 & 1 \\ 0 & 0 & 0 & -1 \end{bmatrix}$$

The next stage of the process will find the matrix representation A of T. For each basis element b of the standard basis $\mathcal{B}_1$, we need to express $T(b)$ as a linear combination of elements of the basis $\mathcal{B}_2$. The vectors so obtained of coordinates of $T(b)$ relative to the basis $\mathcal{B}_2$ make up the columns of the matrix A.

For the sake of convenience we first introduce the identity matrix. Then we solve the system $Bx = T(b)$ for each element b of the standard basis of $\mathbb{R}^5$.

```
>  Id := array(1..5,1..5,'identity'):
>  A := augment(seq(linsolve(B,T(col(Id,i))),i=1..5));
```

$$A := \begin{bmatrix} \dfrac{4}{5} & \dfrac{-1}{5} & \dfrac{-1}{5} & \dfrac{-1}{5} & \dfrac{-1}{5} \\[2mm] \dfrac{3}{5} & \dfrac{3}{5} & \dfrac{-2}{5} & \dfrac{-2}{5} & \dfrac{-2}{5} \\[2mm] \dfrac{2}{5} & \dfrac{2}{5} & \dfrac{2}{5} & \dfrac{-3}{5} & \dfrac{-3}{5} \\[2mm] \dfrac{1}{5} & \dfrac{1}{5} & \dfrac{1}{5} & \dfrac{1}{5} & \dfrac{-4}{5} \end{bmatrix}$$

On theoretical grounds we know that $T(x) = BAx$. This is easily verified. It is equally simple to check that for each $x \in \mathbb{R}^5$ the vectors BAx and e are orthogonal. We shall carry out both checks.

```
>  equal(B&*A&*x,T(x)); innerprod(B&*A&*x,e);
```

$$true$$
$$0$$

Now, instead of the basis $\mathcal{B}_1$ of $\mathbb{V}$, we choose $\mathcal{B}_2$ augmented with e, thus $\mathcal{B}_1 = \{\mathcal{B}_2, e\}$. Observe that this new $\mathcal{B}_1$ is indeed a basis for $\mathbb{V}$. The matrix of T relative to the new basis $\mathcal{B}_1$ of $\mathbb{V}$ and the basis $\mathcal{B}_2$ of $\mathbb{W}$ is much simpler than A, namely

```
>  evalm(A&*augment(B,e));
```

$$\begin{bmatrix} 1 & 0 & 0 & 0 & 0 \\ 0 & 1 & 0 & 0 & 0 \\ 0 & 0 & 1 & 0 & 0 \\ 0 & 0 & 0 & 1 & 0 \end{bmatrix}$$

which is almost an identity matrix. Taking this simplification process one step further, we could conceive of T as a linear mapping of $\mathbb{V}$ to itself, instead of a linear transformation that maps $\mathbb{V}$ to $\mathbb{W}$. Then, relative to the new ordered basis $\mathcal{B}_1 = \{\mathcal{B}_2, e\}$, the matrix representation of T would have the following form:

```
> C := stackmatrix(%,[0,0,0,0,0]);
```

$$
C := \begin{bmatrix} 1 & 0 & 0 & 0 & 0 \\ 0 & 1 & 0 & 0 & 0 \\ 0 & 0 & 1 & 0 & 0 \\ 0 & 0 & 0 & 1 & 0 \\ 0 & 0 & 0 & 0 & 0 \end{bmatrix}
$$

This matrix representation of $T : \mathbb{V} \to \mathbb{V}$ immediately reveals that T has only two eigenvalues: 1 and 0. Moreover, based on earlier observations, we know that $\mathbb{W}$ is the eigenspace associated with the eigenvalue 1 and that the eigenspace associated with 0 is spanned by the vector e.

The new basis $\mathcal{B}_1$ is not orthonormal, not even orthogonal. With the Maple procedure GramSchmidt, an implementation of the Gram-Schmidt orthogonalization process, we can convert $\mathcal{B}_1$ into an orthogonal basis. After that, each vector of the so obtained orthogonal basis for $\mathbb{R}^5$ can be normalized by means of the normalize command. This command only applies to vectors and not to sets of vectors, so that we need Maple's map procedure to complete the normalization process.

At long last, the matrix Q is the orthogonal matrix formed by putting together as columns the elements of the orthonormal basis of eigenvectors of $T : \mathbb{V} \to \mathbb{V}$, obtained in the way described above.

```
> B1 := [op(B2),evalm(e)];
```

$$
B1 := [[1, -1, 0, 0, 0], [0, 1, -1, 0, 0], [0, 0, 1, -1, 0], [0, 0, 0, 1, -1], [1, 1, 1, 1, 1]]
$$

```
> GramSchmidt(B1);
```

$$
[[1, -1, 0, 0, 0], [\tfrac{1}{2}, \tfrac{1}{2}, -1, 0, 0], [\tfrac{1}{3}, \tfrac{1}{3}, \tfrac{1}{3}, -1, 0], [\tfrac{1}{4}, \tfrac{1}{4}, \tfrac{1}{4}, \tfrac{1}{4}, -1], [1, 1, 1, 1, 1]]
$$

```
> Q := augment(op(map(normalize,%))):  orthog(Q);
```

$$
true
$$

Finally, the matrix $F := QCQ^{-1}$ is the standard matrix representation of T. Hence, $T(x) = Fx$ and the linear mapping $T : \mathbb{V} \to \mathbb{V}$ is orthogonally diagonalizable.

```
>  F := evalm(Q&*C&*(1/Q));
```

$$
F := \begin{bmatrix}
\dfrac{4}{5} & \dfrac{-1}{5} & \dfrac{-1}{5} & \dfrac{-1}{5} & \dfrac{-1}{5} \\[2mm]
\dfrac{-1}{5} & \dfrac{4}{5} & \dfrac{-1}{5} & \dfrac{-1}{5} & \dfrac{-1}{5} \\[2mm]
\dfrac{-1}{5} & \dfrac{-1}{5} & \dfrac{4}{5} & \dfrac{-1}{5} & \dfrac{-1}{5} \\[2mm]
\dfrac{-1}{5} & \dfrac{-1}{5} & \dfrac{-1}{5} & \dfrac{4}{5} & \dfrac{-1}{5} \\[2mm]
\dfrac{-1}{5} & \dfrac{-1}{5} & \dfrac{-1}{5} & \dfrac{-1}{5} & \dfrac{4}{5}
\end{bmatrix}
$$

```
>  equal(F&*x,T(x));
```

$$true$$

We certainly realize that the process just described is not the most natural way of showing that T is diagonalizable. The roundabout way we presented served another purpose, namely that of viewing the problem from different angles.

The matrix A representing $T : V \to W$ relative to the old basis $\mathcal{B}_1$ of V and the basis $\mathcal{B}_2$ of W is not square. Therefore, we can not work with eigenvalues and eigenvectors as they do not exist. Despite this, we saw that an almost diagonal matrix representation of T exists.

6.3.2   Singular Value Decomposition

Although for $T : V \to W$ eigenvalues are not defined, T has singular values. As a reminder, we refer the reader to section 6.2 (page 154), where the concept of singular value is discussed in some detail. The singular values of a matrix can be calculated with the Maple command singularvals.

```
>  singularvals(A); evalf(%);
```

$$[\frac{1}{2}\sqrt{5} + \frac{1}{2}, \frac{1}{2}\sqrt{5} - \frac{1}{2}, \frac{1}{10}\sqrt{50 + 10\sqrt{5}}, \frac{1}{10}\sqrt{50 - 10\sqrt{5}}]$$

$$[1.618033989, .6180339890, .8506508084, .5257311121]$$

The SVD of the 4×5 standard matrix representation A of the linear mapping $T : V \to W$ is given by[1]

---

[1]In Release 4 the instruction Svd(A,U,V) returns an unevaluated A.

```
> Svd(A,U,V);
```

$$
\mathrm{Svd}\left(\begin{bmatrix}
\dfrac{4}{5} & \dfrac{-1}{5} & \dfrac{-1}{5} & \dfrac{-1}{5} & \dfrac{-1}{5} \\[6pt]
\dfrac{3}{5} & \dfrac{3}{5} & \dfrac{-2}{5} & \dfrac{-2}{5} & \dfrac{-2}{5} \\[6pt]
\dfrac{2}{5} & \dfrac{2}{5} & \dfrac{2}{5} & \dfrac{-3}{5} & \dfrac{-3}{5} \\[6pt]
\dfrac{1}{5} & \dfrac{1}{5} & \dfrac{1}{5} & \dfrac{1}{5} & \dfrac{-4}{5}
\end{bmatrix}, U, V\right)
$$

Maple has only recorded the definitions, no values are returned (note the capital first letter in the procedure name[2]). Values are only assigned after the instruction evalf. By the way, U and V have the same meaning as in section 6.2: the column vectors of U are the left singular vectors of A, which are, by definition, the eigenvectors of AA^t, and the column vectors of V are the right singular vectors of A, which are the eigenvectors of A^tA.

```
> evalf(%);
```

$$[1.618033989, .8506508084, .6180339887, .5257311121]$$

```
> evalm(U);
```

$$
\begin{bmatrix}
-.3717480345 & .6015009550 & -.6015009550 & -.3717480345 \\
-.6015009550 & .3717480345 & .3717480345 & .6015009550 \\
-.6015009550 & -.3717480345 & .3717480345 & -.6015009550 \\
-.3717480345 & -.6015009550 & -.6015009550 & .3717480345
\end{bmatrix}
$$

```
> evalm(V);
```

$$
\begin{bmatrix}
-.601500955 & .511667273 & -.371748034 & -.195439507 & .447213595 \\
-.371748034 & -.195439507 & .601500955 & .511667273 & .447213595 \\
.132340\,10^{-15} & -.632455532 & -.974633\,10^{-15} & -.632455532 & .447213595 \\
.371748034 & -.195439507 & -.601500955 & .51166727 & .447213595 \\
.601500955 & .511667273 & .371748034 & -.19543950 & .447213595
\end{bmatrix}
$$

---

[2]This is however not the inert counterpart of a presumed command svd; the latter does not exist.

As a result of the SVD expansion of A, the matrix $\Sigma = U^t A V$ should be diagonal.

```
>  Sigma := evalm(transpose(U)&*A&*V);
```

$$\Sigma := \begin{bmatrix} 1.618033989 & 0 & 0 & 0 & 0 \\ 0 & .8506508083 & 0 & -.7\,10^{-10} & 0 \\ -.2\,10^{-9} & 0 & .6180339888 & .5\,10^{-10} & 0 \\ 0 & -.4\,10^{-10} & -.4\,10^{-10} & .5257311122 & -.4\,10^{-10} \end{bmatrix}$$

Because the answer is given in numerical format, deviations will occur with a magnitude depending on the precision of Maple's internal calculations.

The Maple procedure **singularvals** does not give the singular values in order of magnitude, in contrast to the evaluated result of the procedure **Svd**. This is the reason why we prefer to take the singular values from the matrix Σ.

```
>  for i from 1 to 4 do sigma[i] := Sigma[i,i] od;
```

$$\sigma_1 := 1.618033989$$
$$\sigma_2 := .8506508083$$
$$\sigma_3 := .6180339888$$
$$\sigma_4 := .5257311122$$

The following Maple code calculates the SVD expansion of A.

```
>  evalm(convert([seq(sigma[i]*col(U,i)&*transpose(col(V,i)),
>  i=1..4)],'+'));
```

$$\begin{bmatrix} .8000000001 & -.1999999999 & -.1999999999 & -.2000000001 & -.2000000003 \\ .6000000001 & .6000000002 & -.4000000000 & -.4000000002 & -.4000000001 \\ .4000000001 & .4000000002 & .4000000000 & -.6000000002 & -.6000000001 \\ .2000000003 & .2000000001 & .1999999999 & .1999999999 & -.8000000001 \end{bmatrix}$$

```
>  map(convert,%,fraction);
```

$$\begin{bmatrix} \dfrac{4}{5} & \dfrac{-1}{5} & \dfrac{-1}{5} & \dfrac{-1}{5} & \dfrac{-133333333}{666666664} \\[2mm] \dfrac{3}{5} & \dfrac{3}{5} & \dfrac{-2}{5} & \dfrac{-2}{5} & \dfrac{-2}{5} \\[2mm] \dfrac{2}{5} & \dfrac{2}{5} & \dfrac{2}{5} & \dfrac{-3}{5} & \dfrac{-3}{5} \\[2mm] \dfrac{133333333}{666666664} & \dfrac{1}{5} & \dfrac{1}{5} & \dfrac{1}{5} & \dfrac{-4}{5} \end{bmatrix}$$

We used the Maple command `convert` with parameter `fraction` for converting the numerical elements of the expansion matrix into (rational) fractions. Only at two places round-off errors cause small deviations from the original matrix A.

The SVD expansion of a matrix enables us to find for each natural number $p \leq \mathrm{rank}(A)$ the matrix of rank p which, in a natural way, comes closest to the original matrix A. We shall not elaborate here on the exact meaning of closeness, the example below speaks for itself. The matrix we have in mind, say A_p, is constructed by taking the first p terms (corresponding to the p largest singular values) in the SVD expansion of A. Hence

$$A_p = \sum_{i=1}^{p} \sigma_i\, u_i\, v_i{}^t, \quad p \leq \mathrm{rank}(A).$$

It is time to take a look at an example of such a p-close approximation. The VanderMonde matrix below has rank 6. Two of its singular values are extremely small. This means that, although of full rank, this matrix is almost singular, and what is more, almost a rank 4 matrix.

```
>  VdM := vandermonde([1,1/2,1/3,1/4,1/5,1/6]);
>  'rank'= rank(VdM), 'determinant' = evalf(det(VdM));
>  singularvals(VdM): 'singular values' = allvalues(%);
```

$$VdM := \begin{bmatrix} 1 & 1 & 1 & 1 & 1 & 1 \\ 1 & \dfrac{1}{2} & \dfrac{1}{4} & \dfrac{1}{8} & \dfrac{1}{16} & \dfrac{1}{32} \\ 1 & \dfrac{1}{3} & \dfrac{1}{9} & \dfrac{1}{27} & \dfrac{1}{81} & \dfrac{1}{243} \\ 1 & \dfrac{1}{4} & \dfrac{1}{16} & \dfrac{1}{64} & \dfrac{1}{256} & \dfrac{1}{1024} \\ 1 & \dfrac{1}{5} & \dfrac{1}{25} & \dfrac{1}{125} & \dfrac{1}{625} & \dfrac{1}{3125} \\ 1 & \dfrac{1}{6} & \dfrac{1}{36} & \dfrac{1}{216} & \dfrac{1}{1296} & \dfrac{1}{7776} \end{bmatrix}$$

$$rank = 6, \quad determinant = -.1786122542\,10^{-9}$$

$$singular\ values = ([.00001250381122], [.0007560896196], [.01809484698],$$
$$[.2191175513], [1.585434311], [3.005489634])$$

Taking the first four terms only in the SVD expansion of the matrix `VdM` gives a matrix `VdM_4` of rank 4. This rank 4 'twin' is almost equal to the original `VdM` in spite of the fact that the latter is of rank 6.

```
> Svd(VdM,U,V): evalf(%):
> Sigma := evalm(transpose(U)&*VdM&*V):
> VdM_4 := evalm(convert([seq(Sigma[i,i]*col(U,i)&*
> transpose(col(V,i)),i=1..4)],'+')):
> deviation := evalf(evalm(VdM - VdM_4),3);
```

$$
deviation := \begin{bmatrix}
0 & 0 & 0 & 0 & 0 & 0 \\
0 & 0 & 0 & 0 & 0 & 0 \\
0 & 0 & 0 & -.0003 & -.0002 & .00021 \\
0 & 0 & -.0002 & .0002 & .00017 & -.000203 \\
0 & 0 & -.0002 & .00015 & .00010 & -.000132 \\
0 & 0 & .0002 & -.00019 & -.000130 & .000170
\end{bmatrix}
$$

It is always wise to check your answers. So[3]

```
> rank(VdM_4);
```

$$4$$

```
> singularvals(VdM_4);
```

$[.5942772267\,10^{-5}\,I,\ .00002576525805,\ .01809482233,\ .2191175508,\ 1.585434310,$
$3.005489635]$

We see that the latter result does not entirely agree with the theoretically predicted values. The discrepancies must surely be the result of numerical round-off.

This nice SVD property of producing close approximations to the original matrix with considerably fewer data elements, can be used to reduce overheads when transmitting images shaped by a great many pixels. Instead of transmitting all pixel points, only a small set of suitably chosen points is selected for transmission. This choice is made carefully so as to avoid essential loss of quality. You could think of satellite pictures from outer-space (Mars) or of finger print images (data compression).

To implement such a procedure, the transferable black and white image (a photograph or a finger print) is considered to be a large $(0,1)$-matrix where a 1 corresponds to a pixel (= black point on a white background). Such a matrix will usually contain a large percentage of zeros, and is therefore called sparse. The point is now that sparse matrices have relatively few positive singular values.

---

[3]Here Release 4 erroneously gives rank 6.

We shall give an illustration of this process of data compression by generating a rather sparse $(0,1)$-matrix of size 100×100 representing a butterfly, the so-called 'Fay butterfly'. The Fay butterfly is an example of a `polarplot`, which means that the points are given in polar coordinates. The following Maple code will do the trick:

```
>  restart:
>  with(linalg):  with(plots):
>  butterflyplot := polarplot(exp(cos(t)) - 2*cos(4*t) +
>  sin(t/12)^5,t=0..24*Pi,axes=none):
>  value(butterflyplot);
```

Figure 6.1: The Fay butterfly

The reason for using the Maple command `restart` is to free as much memory as possible in order to speed up the data compression process.

The butterfly is generated by only 1535 points. The `nops` command counts the number of first-level operands (here points) in `butterflypoints`.

```
>  butterflypoints := op(1,op(1,butterflyplot)):
>  number_of_butterflypoints := nops(butterflypoints);
```

$$number\_of\_butterflypoints := 1535$$

This means that, in a square measuring 100×100 with 10000 available points, the Fay butterfly can be given a 'true to life' representation by a $(0,1)$-matrix filled for approximately 85% with zeros. With the next Maple code such a $(0,1)$-matrix is built. Because all butterfly points lie in $[-3,4] \times [-4,4]$, we first need to transform this rectangle into the square $[0,100] \times [0,100]$.

```
>   transform := p -> [round(99*(op(1,p)+3)/7+1),
>   round(99*(op(2,p)+4)/8+1)]:
>   pp := map(transform,butterflypoints):
>   butterflymatrix := array(1..100,1..100,sparse):
>   for i from 1 to nops(butterflypoints) do
>   butterflymatrix[op(pp[i])]:=1 od:
```

With the Maple command `sparsematrixplot` we can generate a graph of a sparse matrix; the non-zero elements are plotted as dots on the screen.

```
>   sparsematrixplot(butterflymatrix,
>   title = 'Butterfly (0,1)-matrix');
```

The generation of the SVD expansion takes a large amount of time. Because it requires a lot of memory, it is advisable to construct the butterfly approximation matrix column for column. To approximate the butterfly we shall only use the 25 largest singular values.

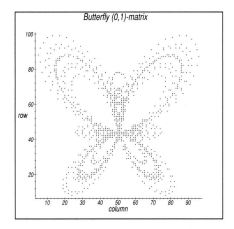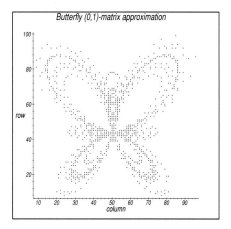

Figure 6.2: (0,1)-matrixplot of the Fay butterfly, original and approximation

The Maple code for this SVD expansion is

```
>   Svd(butterflymatrix,U,V): Sigma := evalf(%):
>   for j from 1 to 100 do vv.j :=
>   evalm(convert([seq(evalm(Sigma[i]*V[j,i]*col(U,i)),
>   i=1..25)],'+') + vector(100,0)) od:
```

```
> for j from 1 to 100 do
> vvv.j := evalm(map(a->round(a),vv.j)) od:
> butterflymatrixappr := augment(seq(evalm(vvv.j),j=1..100)):
```

Like before, it would be wise to save the results into a file, say SVD.m.

```
> save butterflymatrixappr, 'c:/Maple/Book/R5/Chapter6/SVD.m':
```

This file can be read quickly with the instruction

```
> read 'c:/Maple/Book/R5/Chapter6/SVD.m':
```

and reproduced with

```
> sparsematrixplot(butterflymatrixappr,
> title = 'Butterfly (0,1)-matrix approximation');
```

The butterfly is clearly recognizable (see figure 6.2). The difference between the butterfly $(0,1)$-matrix and its approximation, is found from

```
> difference_dots := evalm(butterflymatrix-
> butterflymatrixappr):

> number_of_diffs := convert([seq(convert([seq(abs(
> difference_dots[i,j]),j=1..100)],'+'),i= 1..100)],'+');
```

$$number\_of\_diffs := 94$$

Compared with the total number of points used in the initial $(0,1)$-matrix plot, we get a difference of only

```
> print(evalf(number_of_diffs/
> number_of_butterflypoints*100,3),' %');
```

$$6.12, \%$$

6.4 Worksheets and Assignments

The worksheet VectW6a.mws is mainly devoted to linear mappings—we sometimes speak of linear transformations instead of linear mappings, but we mean the same—and the relationship that exists between such linear mappings and matrices. In the final worksheet VectW6b.mws we concentrate on the way computations with eigenvalues and eigenspaces of matrices can be carried out under the Maple system. We shall also touch on the singular value decomposition again.

6.4.1   Worksheet 6a. Linear Mappings

Recall that a linear transformation is a function $T : \mathbb{V} \to \mathbb{W}$, which maps sums
and scalar products of vectors in $\mathbb{V}$ to corresponding sums and scalar products of
vectors in $\mathbb{W}$ (see the brief explanation in section 6.2). So, the linear mapping T
preserves the linear structure of the vector space $\mathbb{V}$, by which we refer to its vector
addition and scalar multiplication. Thinking of a vector space as the collection
of all linear combinations of a fixed number of given basis vectors helps to bring
home the point that $T(\mathbb{V})$ is a subspace of the vector space $\mathbb{W}$.

In general the vector spaces $\mathbb{V}$ and $\mathbb{W}$ are defined over the field of real numbers
$\mathbb{R}$, but other fields of scalars may also be chosen, such as the field of rational
numbers $\mathbb{Q}$ or that of complex numbers $\mathbb{C}$.

- **Linear Transformations Between Subspaces of $\mathbb{R}^n$**

How do we introduce a linear mapping T into the Maple system? Consider the
following rather simple example:

```
> restart:  with(linalg):
> T := proc(x) local ex; ex := evalm(x);
> vector([ex[1] + ex[2] - ex[3],ex[2] + ex[3] - ex[4],
> ex[3] + ex[4] - ex[1] - ex[2]])
> end;
```

Note that T immediately evaluates the input vector. That is why $T(u + v)$ is
now presented in the usual way.

```
> u := vector(4,i -> 2*i-1);
> v := vector(4,i -> (i-5)^2+2*(i-5));
> T(u); T(v); T(u+v);
```

This is also true for other, more complicated linear expressions.

```
> M := matrix(4,4,(i,j) -> i+j mod 5);
> 'T'(M&*u + innerprod(u,v)*v) = T(M&*u + innerprod(u,v)*v);
```

First we shall try and find T's standard matrix, which is the matrix representation
of T with respect to the standard bases of $\mathbb{R}^4$ and $\mathbb{R}^3$. This is rather easy because
the columns of the standard matrix are just the images of the standard basis
vectors of $\mathbb{R}^4$ under T.

Hence the following 3×4 matrix is the required standard matrix of T:

```
> A := augment(T([1,0,0,0]),T([0,1,0,0]),
> T([0,0,1,0]),T([0,0,0,1]));
```

Although we do not really doubt the correctness of this answer, it is easy and it does not take much time to check that $T(y)$ and Ay are equal for arbitrary vectors $y \in \mathbb{R}^4$.

```
> y := vector(4); equal(T(y),A&*y);
```

So this is indeed the case.

Here you can stop for a moment and have a look at **assignment 1** of worksheet VectA6a.mws (see page 170), which is about a simple linear transformation.

Next we wish to find the matrix of T relative to some other bases than the standard ones of $\mathbb{R}^4$ and $\mathbb{R}^3$. Choose in $\mathbb{R}^4$ the following basis vectors:

```
> v1 := vector(4,[2,-1,1,0]); v2 := vector(4,[1,-2,- 4,3]);
> v3 := vector(4,[1,1,1,1]); v4 := vector(4,[1,1,1,0]);
```

We put these vectors side by side as columns into the matrix B_1 and we check that they constitute a basis $\mathcal{B}_1$ for $\mathbb{R}^4$ by calculating the rank of B_1.

```
> B1 := augment(v1,v2,v3,v4); rank(B1);
```

The rank of B_1 is 4, so its columns must be linearly independent.
Now choose the following three vectors in $\mathbb{R}^3$:

```
> w1 := vector(3,[1,-3,0]); w2 := vector(3,[0,-1,0]);
> w3 := vector(3,[3,1,-1]);
```

The matrix B_2 is built from just these column vectors, and from the value of its rank it follows that the three vectors w_1, w_2 and w_3 indeed form a basis $\mathcal{B}_2$ of $\mathbb{R}^3$.

```
> B2 := augment(w1,w2,w3); rank(B2);
```

What is the relation, you may ask, between the linear transformation T and the matrix representation of T relative to the bases $\mathcal{B}_1$ and $\mathcal{B}_2$? We shall call this matrix representation $\mathrm{Mat}(T, B_1, B_2)$.
The answer is this. If $T(v_1)$, the image of the first basis vector of $\mathcal{B}_1$, is written as a linear combination of the basis elements w_1, w_2, w_3 with coefficients c_1, c_2, and c_3, then $[c_1, c_2, c_3]$ gives, by definition, the first column of the desired matrix. Now treat the other elements of the basis $\mathcal{B}_1$ analogously. All this means that the columns of the matrix $\mathrm{Mat}(T, B_1, B_2)$ are to be found as solutions to the linear systems $B_2 x = T(v_i)$ for $i = 1, \dots, 4$.

```
> for i from 1 to 4 do m.i := linsolve(B2,T(v.i)) od;
> Mat(T,B1,B2) := augment(m1,m2,m3,m4);
```

This matrix $\mathrm{Mat}(T, B_1, B_2)$ is equal to $B_2^{-1} A B_1$:

```
> evalm(inverse(B2)&*A&*B1);
```

If the vector spaces we work with happen to have large dimensions, it might be quicker to let the Maple command `genmatrix` get the standard matrix representation of a given linear mapping. This procedure requires two arguments, a list of $T(x)$-values and the list of corresponding x-values.

```
>  x := vector(4); y := T(x);
>  genmatrix([seq(y[i],i=1..3)],[seq(x[i],i=1..4)]);
```

Clearly, this is just the standard matrix representation A of the linear mapping T.

Now turn to **assignment** 2 of worksheet VectA6a.mws (see page 171), where a linear transformation and its standard matrix representation are considered.

• Linear Transformations Between Spaces of Polynomials

When considering vector spaces other than $\mathbb{R}^n$, it will become more transparent how useful the matrix representation of linear mappings can be. Let $\mathbb{P}_n$ be the linear space of polynomials of degree at most n.

Suppose we wish to find a linear mapping $L : \mathbb{P}_3 \to \mathbb{P}_2$ that maps the given polynomials p_i to the polynomials q_i, or $L(p_i) = q_i$ $(i = 1, \ldots, 4)$, where

```
>  p1 := 1 + t - t^2 + t^3; p2 := 1 + t + t^2 + t^3;
>  p3 := 1 - t + t^2; p4 := 1 + t + t^2;
>  q1 := 1 - t^2; q2 := 1 + t^2 ;
>  q3 := 1 - t; q4 := 1 + t;
```

The polynomials p_1, p_2, p_3, p_4 form a basis $\mathcal{C}_1$ for $\mathbb{P}_3$ and $\mathcal{C}_2 = \{q_1, q_2, q_3\}$ is a basis of $\mathbb{P}_2$. These statements are justified, because considering the two matrices of polynomial coefficients corresponding to these two sets of polynomials:

```
>  C1 := matrix(4,4,(i,j) -> coeff(p.j,t,i-1));
>  C2 := matrix(3,3,(i,j) -> coeff(q.j,t,i-1));
```

we find that both are non-singular as their determinants do not vanish.

```
>  det(C2); det(C1);
```

Furthermore, q_4 can be expressed as a linear combination of q_1, q_2, q_3. This is a consequence of the solvability of the linear system with matrix of coefficients C_2 and constant vector of coefficients of q_4.

```
>  linsolve(C2,[seq(coeff(q4,t,i),i=0..2)]);
```

From our previous discussion on matrix representations it now follows that the matrix representation of L relative to the bases $\mathcal{C}_1$ and $\mathcal{C}_2$, is equal to the identity matrix augmented with the solution referred to above—observe that $L(p_4) = q_4 = q_1 + q_2 - q_3$.

```
>  Mat(L,C1,C2) :=
>  augment(diag(1,1,1),[1,1,-1]);
```

Now we are ready to give the standard matrix representation $F = \mathrm{Mat}(L, \mathrm{Id}_4, \mathrm{Id}_3)$ of L.

```
>  F := evalm(C2&*Mat(L,C1,C2)&*inverse(C1));
```

A routine check shows that this matrix is the correct one. In particular, because $p_1 - p_2 + p_3 + p_4 = 2$, we have that $L(2) = q_1 - q_2 + q_3 + q_4 = 2 - 2t^2$. This can be quickly verified.

```
>  evalm(F&*[2,0,0,0]);
```

Finally we shall briefly consider a related problem.

In order to solve the equation $L(p) = 0$, we need to know the kernel or null space of the linear mapping L. Maple has a function for this.

```
>  kernel(F);
```

The next instruction provides a direct verification of Maple's output.

```
>  evalm(F&*op(%));
```

Apparently, all scalar multiples of the polynomial $t - t^2 + t^3 \in \mathbb{P}_3$ are mapped by L to the zero polynomial.

By the way, the Maple function **kernel** has exactly the same effect as the function **nullspace**.

From these examples we may safely deduce that linear mappings between finite dimensional subspaces of the space of all polynomials should be handled by way of their matrix representations.

Now try and complete **assignment 3** of worksheet **VectA6a.mws** (see page 171). The subject matter of this assignment is the differential operator working on a certain space of exponential functions.

6.4.2   Assignments 6a. Linear Mappings

1. The linear transformation $T : \mathbb{R}^2 \to \mathbb{R}^2$ is given by its standard matrix

```
>   G := matrix(2,2,[0,1,1,1]);
```

   First introduce a symbolic 2-vector s and compute the product $G\,s$.

   Next define the vector $v_0 = [0, 1]$ and compute the vectors $G\,v_0$, $G^2\,v_0$, $\ldots$, $G^6\,v_0$.

   Do you recognize the sequence of numbers that make up the elements of the vectors $G^k\,v_0$?

2. Consider the 5×5 matrix $M = (m_{ij})$, where

$$m_{ij} = j^i.$$

Verify that the columns of M form a basis $\mathcal{B}_5$ of $\mathbb{R}^5$.

Further, let $T : \mathbb{R}^5 \to \mathbb{R}^5$ map the vector $u \in \mathbb{R}^5$ to its vector of coordinates relative to the basis $\mathcal{B}_5$. Find the matrix representation of T relative to the standard basis of $\mathbb{R}^5$.

Verify your answer by using this matrix representation to compute the image vector $T([2, 4, 8, 16, 32])$.

3. Let $\mathcal{B} = \{e^x, e^{2x}, e^{3x}\}$ be a basis for the vector space $\mathbb{V}$ over the reals.

The differential operator D is a linear operator. Consider the linear mapping $D : \mathbb{V} \to \mathbb{V}$ of the vector space $\mathbb{V}$ into itself which maps each function to its derivative.

Find the matrix representation of D relative to the basis $\mathcal{B}$.

Verify your answer by applying it to the function

$$e^x + 3e^{2x} + 5e^{3x},$$

comparing the result with the derivative of this function, computed directly.

6.4.3   Worksheet 6b. Eigenvectors and Eigenspaces

The topic eigenvalues and eigenspaces is often seen as the culmination of a first introduction to Linear Algebra. Here many important concepts and principles of Linear Algebra meet, and the tools developed up till then are sufficiently powerful to prove theorems on the diagonalization of matrices and of linear mappings. This final worksheet (VectW6b.mws) is about the way Maple can assist us in finding eigenvalues and eigenspaces of matrices. Naturally, the characteristic polynomial of a matrix will be included as well as the diagonalization process of symmetric matrices. Finally we shall take a look at the computation of the singular value decomposition of a non-diagonalizable matrix.

● **Computing Eigenvalues and Eigenvectors**

As usual we begin with

```
>   restart:  with(linalg):
```

The following procedure creates a class of special matrices:

```
>   f  := (i,j) -> i+j-1;
```

For each natural number n, the command `matrix(n,n,f)` gives a nice, symmetric matrix.

We shall first work with the simplest matrix of this collection.

```
>  A := matrix(2,2,f);
```

The eigenvalues of A are the solutions to the characteristic equation of A:

```
>  charpoly(A,x); solve(%,x);
```

The command `charpoly` gives the characteristic polynomial in a variable of our own choice.

The eigenvectors v corresponding to these eigenvalues can be calculated directly using the `eigenvects` command:

```
>  eigenvects(A);
```

Maple returns a list of lists of type: [eigenvalue, multiplicity of eigenvalue, {basis of the eigenspace}].

These results can also be obtained by clicking the right mouse button on the matrix A (Maple output) and selecting `Characteristic Polynomial`, `Eigenvalues` or `Eigenvectors` from the pop-up menu.

The next example, also taken from the collection of matrices defined earlier, is less simple.

```
>  B := matrix(5,5,f);
```

The characteristic polynomial of B—or, equally, the characteristic polynomial of a linear mapping $T : \mathbb{R}^5 \to \mathbb{R}^5$ which is represented by B relative to some basis of $\mathbb{R}^5$—is usually obtained by evaluating $\det(x\,\text{Id} - B)$, where Id is the identity matrix.

```
>  alias(Id = &*()):  det(x*Id - B);
>  charpol := sort(%); evalb(charpol = charpoly(B,x));
```

Meanwhile, applying `sort`, we ordered the terms of the characteristic polynomial by decreasing degree.

The eigenvalues and corresponding eigenvectors are once more obtained by

```
>  lambda := eigenvals(B);
>  eigeninfo := eigenvects(B);
```

From Maple's output we read off that the eigenvalue 0 is a multiple zero of the characteristic polynomial of multiplicity 3. We also notice that a basis of eigenvectors corresponding to this eigenvalue comprises three vectors.

The eigenspace corresponding to the eigenvalue λ is by definition equal to the null space of the matrix $(\lambda \operatorname{Id} - B)$. Let us check this now.

```
>  EigenS := x -> nullspace(x*Id - B);
>  EigenS(lambda[1]);
>  EigenS(lambda[4]);
>  EigenS(lambda[5]);
```

• Diagonalization

All this means that for $\mathbb{R}^5$ a basis exists of eigenvectors of B, because all five eigenvectors that turned up are independent. Hence B is diagonalizable but we knew that already because B is symmetric and all symmetric matrices have this property.

The list `eigeninfo` provides us with sufficient information to verify that B is indeed similar to the diagonal matrix of its eigenvalues.

The next list of vectors gives an $\mathbb{R}^5$-basis of eigenvectors of B. We put these vectors side by side, thus forming the columns of a matrix we shall call U. Observe how we extract the eigenvectors from the list `eigeninfo`.

```
>  eigenlist := [seq(op(eigeninfo[i][3]),i=1..3)];
>  U := augment(op(eigenlist));
```

The similarity between B and the diagonal matrix of its eigenvalues is a direct consequence of the result of the following instruction:

```
>  map(normal,evalm(inverse(U)&*B&*U),`expanded`);
```

We used the Maple procedure `normal` with parameter `expanded` in combination with the `map` command to simplify the expression.
The matrix U is not orthogonal because $U^t U$ is not equal to the identity matrix.

```
>  map(normal,evalm(transpose(U)&*U),`expanded`);
```

Before continuing, take a look at assignments 1 and 2 of worksheet VectA6b.mws (see page 176). The purpose of **assignment 1** is to diagonalize a given matrix, and in **assignment 2** an example is given of the use of matrix diagonalization.

• The Gram-Schmidt Orthogonalization Process

The matrix U is not orthogonal, but we can orthogonalize the eigenspace corresponding to the eigenvalue 0 by means of the Gram-Schmidt orthogonalization procedure. Recall that eigenvectors corresponding to different eigenvalues are automatically orthogonal. However, as we do not know the exact order in which the

Maple procedure `eigenvects` will put the eigenvalues and corresponding eigenvectors, we shall apply the Gram-Schmidt procedure to the union of all three
eigenspaces. The commands `map` and `normal` are used once more to get simplified and readable expressions for all elements of the list.

```
>  GramSchmidt(eigenlist):
>  eigenlist_orthogonal := map(normal,%);
```

We have not finished yet because the basis of eigenvectors still has to be made
orthonormal, that is the length of each vector has to be normalized to 1. The `map`
command enables us to simultaneously divide each individual vector by its own
length. Recall that the length of a vector is equal to the value of its Euclidean
norm (or 2-norm). So a new list is created of mutually orthogonal eigenvectors
of B of length 1.

```
>  eigenlist_orthonormal :=
>  map(a -> a/norm(a,2),eigenlist_orthogonal);
```

This looks rather ominous because of the many radicals.
On putting the vectors of `eigenlist_orthonormal` side by side, thus forming
the columns of a matrix, we create the orthogonal matrix Q. We first verify Q's
orthogonality.

```
>  Q := augment(op(eigenlist_orthonormal)):

>  map(normal,evalm(transpose(Q)&*Q));
```

Finally we see that the matrix

```
>  Lambda := map(normal,evalm(transpose(Q)&*B&*Q),'expanded');
```

is diagonal. The next instruction verifies that the diagonal elements of Λ are the
zeros of the characteristic polynomial, and hence the eigenvalues of B.

```
>  for i from 1 to 5 do
>  simplify(subs(x=Lambda[i,i],charpol)) od;
```

The eigenvalues of square, non-symmetric, real matrices are by definition real,
in as far as they exist of course. If we consider such a real matrix over the field
of complex numbers, then all becomes more transparent. This is so, because the
eigenvalues are the zeros of the characteristic polynomial, and the characteristic
equation has exactly as many complex roots as its degree, counting multiplicities.
The Maple system is perfectly capable of performing computations with complex
numbers, and therefore eigenvalues and (complex) eigenvectors can be found for
non-symmetric matrices as well.

- **Singular Value Decomposition (SVD)**

We conclude with an example of a non-diagonalizable matrix.
The defining process for this matrix proceeds as it were in reverse order: we start
with a given polynomial and then search for a matrix having this polynomial for
its characteristic polynomial. The Maple command `companion` helps us to do
this.

The result is the so-called 'companionmatrix' of a polynomial with leading coefficient 1. The meaning of the word companion is revealed when we look at the final
column of the companion matrix: it is formed by the opposites of the coefficients
of the given polynomial, only the leading coefficient is left out.

```
>   p := (x-1)^2*(x-2)^2;
>   F := companion(p,x);
```

In order to test the companion relation between polynomial p and matrix F, we
also determine the characteristic polynomial of F in the usual way, that is by
means of $\det(x\,\mathrm{Id} - F)$.

```
>   factor(det(x*Id - F));
```

This seems to be alright. The matrix F is not diagonalizable because both
eigenspaces of the multiple eigenvalues 0 and 1 are of dimension 1. Therefore, the
number of independent eigenvectors falls short of the number needed to constitute
a basis for $\mathbb{R}^5$. We shall take a closer look at this now.

```
>   eigenvects(F);
```

Just as expected, the output is disappointing.

On the other hand, both matrices $F_l := FF^t$ and $F_r := F^tF$ are symmetric
and hence diagonalizable. Let the columns of the matrix U be the orthonormal
eigenvectors of F_l and let V be formed likewise by the orthonormal eigenvectors
of F_r. Then F can be expressed as $F = U\,\Sigma\,V^t$, where Σ is the diagonal matrix of
singular values. The singular values of F are the square roots of the eigenvalues
of F_l or F_r (both matrices have the same eigenvalues).

The command `Svd(F,U,V)` can be used to compute the singular values and the
matrices U and V.

```
>   s_values := evalf(Svd(F,U,V));
>   Sigma := diag(seq(s_values[i],i=1..5));
>   U = evalm(U);
>   V = evalm(V);
>   evalm(F) = evalm(U&*Sigma&*transpose(V));
```

Round-off errors cause small deviations from the original matrix F. The reason for these errors is that the `Svd` procedure gives only numerical approximations, not exact values.

Assignment 3 of worksheet VectA6b.mws (see below) is about the SVD of another non-diagonalizable matrix.

6.4.4   Assignments 6b. Eigenvectors and Eigenspaces

1. Diagonalize the following matrix:

   > `C := matrix(3,3,[0,1,0,0,0,1,6,-11,6]);`

   First construct a matrix P the columns of which are three independent eigenvectors of C. The `eigenvects` procedure may be useful.

   Next compute the matrix $L = P^{-1}CP$. Verify that L is a diagonal matrix of eigenvalues of C.

2. Let C, P and L be the matrices obtained in the preceding assignment 1.

   First use Maple's `evalm` procedure to compute the matrix C^{20000} directly. Then compute the matrix $PL^{20000}P^{-1}$. Make sure you suppress the output of these matrices!

   Use the `time()` procedure to determine the computing time that Maple needs in both cases. Which method is faster?

3. Define the polynomial p and its companion matrix M:

   > `p := x^3 - 1002*x^2 + 2001*x - 1000;`
   > `M := companion(p,x);`

   (a) Use Maple's `eigenvects` command to determine the eigenvalues and eigenspaces of M. Why is M non-diagonalizable?

   (b) Use the command `Svd(M,U,V)` to determine the singular value decomposition of M and note that the largest singular value σ is much larger than all other singular values.

   Determine the matrix $\sigma\,uv^t$, where u and v are the left and right singular vectors corresponding to σ. Note that u and v are the first columns of U and V respectively.

   Compare the matrix $\sigma\,uv^t$ with the original matrix M. But first round the elements of σuv^t to the nearest integer using Maple's `map` command together with the `round` procedure.

6.5   Exercises

1. The transformation $T : \mathbb{R}^n \to \mathbb{R}^{n-1}$ defined by

$$T(x_1, x_2, \ldots, x_n) = (y_2, \ldots, y_n), \quad \text{where } y_i = \sum_{j=1}^{i} x_j \text{ for } i = 2, \ldots, n$$

is a linear mapping. Verify this with Maple for $n = 5$ by showing that

$$T(u + v) = T(u) + T(v) \quad \text{and} \quad T(ru) = rT(u)$$

for each $u, v \in \mathbb{R}^5$ and $r \in \mathbb{R}$. Also determine the standard matrix representation of T.

2. The polynomials p_n ($n = 0, 1, \ldots$) are defined as follows:

$$p_n(t) = \sum_{i=0}^{n} (n - i + 1)\, t^i.$$

Further, let $\mathcal{B}_n = \{p_0, p_1, \ldots, p_n\}$. Check that $\mathcal{B}_n$ is a basis for the space of polynomials $\mathbb{P}_n$.
The function

$$T : \mathbb{P}_n \to \mathbb{R}^{n+1}$$

is defined by the rule: $T(p) = [p]_{\mathcal{B}_n}$, the vector of coordinates of p relative to the basis $\mathcal{B}_n$.
Show that T is a linear mapping. Calculate $T(t^i)$ for each $i = 0, 1, \ldots$ and find the matrix of T relative to $\mathcal{B}_n$ and the standard basis of $\mathbb{R}^{n+1}$. First experiment with some small values of n before considering the general situation.

3. For each natural number n, the $n \times n$ matrix A_n is given by

$$A_n = (a_{ij}^{(n)}) \quad \text{with } a_{ij}^{(n)} = \begin{cases} 0 & \text{if } i = j \\ 1 & \text{if } i \neq j. \end{cases}$$

For $n = 3, 4, 5, 6$, calculate the following quantities: the determinant of A_n, the characteristic polynomial of A_n, the eigenvalues of A_n and their corresponding eigenspaces.

4. Let

$$A = \begin{pmatrix} 36333 & -38841 & -26985 & -6909 \\ 2757 & -749 & -645 & 1381 \\ -19206 & 19410 & 13716 & 2364 \\ -11658 & 15602 & 11832 & 2726 \end{pmatrix}.$$

be given. First compute the characteristic polynomial of A, and then calculate the eigenvalues and eigenvectors of A. Find also a basis for the null space of A. Use the Maple commands `eigenvals` and `eigenvects`, the later with parameter `radical`. Does $\mathbb{R}^4$ have a basis of eigenvectors of A?

5. Consider the polynomial

$$p(t) = t^4 - 8\,t^3 - 78\,t^2 + 320\,t + 1925.$$

Let C be the companion matrix of p. Find the eigenvalues and eigenspaces of C. Can you give a reason for the fact that C is not diagonalizable? Determine the singular value decomposition of C and observe that the largest singular value σ is much larger than all other singular values. Determine the matrix $\sigma\,uv^t$, where u and v are the left and right singular vectors corresponding to σ. Compare the matrix $\sigma\,uv^t$ with the original matrix C.

6. The matrix

$$A = \begin{pmatrix} 12 & -8 & -4 & -4 & -8 \\ -11 & 11 & 5 & 5 & 9 \\ 2 & -2 & 0 & -2 & -2 \\ 2 & -2 & -2 & 0 & -2 \\ -1 & 1 & 1 & 1 & 3 \end{pmatrix}$$

is diagonalizable. Show this, and also find a matrix Q such that $Q^{-1}AQ$ is diagonal. Is it possible to choose Q orthogonal, subject to this condition?

7. The 5×4 matrix

$$A = \begin{pmatrix} 3 & 4x & -5 & 7 \\ 2x & -3 & 3x & -2 \\ 4 & 11x & -13 & 16 \\ 7 & -2 & x & 3 \\ x & 24 & -27 & 29 \end{pmatrix}$$

depends on the unknown x. For each value of x, find the rank, the null space and a basis for the null space of A.
Moreover, calculate the singular values of A for those values of x for which $\mathrm{rank}(A) < 4$.

8. The Dimension Theorem for linear mappings could be verified as follows: begin with constructing a completely arbitrary 10×13 matrix of arbitrary rank, let us say of rank 7. You could do this by first generating a 7×13 random matrix and subsequently adding three rows of zeros. After this, multiply the matrix so obtained from the left by another 10×10 random

matrix. Denote the resulting matrix by A and verify that its rank is 7 (with probability 1).
Next let $T : \mathbb{R}^{13} \to \mathbb{R}^{10}$ be the linear transformation with standard matrix representation A. Now calculate the dimensions of $\mathrm{Ker}(T)$ and $\mathrm{Range}(T)$.

9. The differential operator D is a linear operator. Consider the linear mapping $D : \mathbb{P}_n \to \mathbb{P}_n$ of the vector space $\mathbb{P}_n$ of all polynomials of degree at most n to itself which maps each polynomial to its derivative.
   Find the matrix representation of D relative to the standard basis of $\mathbb{P}_n$. Verify your answer by applying it to a random polynomial. Take $n = 10$.

10. Let $M = (m_{ij})$ be the 7×7 matrix with

$$m_{ij} = \begin{cases} j - i & \text{if } i \leq j \\ 1 & \text{if } i > j \end{cases}$$

Verify that the rows of M form a basis $\mathcal{B}$ of $\mathbb{R}^7$.
Further, let $T : \mathbb{R}^7 \to R^7$ map the vector $u \in \mathbb{R}^7$ to $[u]_{\mathcal{B}}$, its vector of coordinates relative to the basis $\mathcal{B}$. Prove that T is a linear mapping by showing that

$$T(u + v) = T(u) + T(v) \quad \text{and} \quad T(ru) = rT(u).$$

for any two symbolic vectors u and v in $\mathbb{R}^7$, and for any scalar $r \in \mathbb{R}$. Also find the matrix representation of T relative to the standard basis of $\mathbb{R}^7$.

11. Let the $n \times n$ matrix $A = E - \mathrm{Id}$ be given. Here E denotes the $n \times n$ matrix that is entirely filled with 1's. As usual Id is the $n \times n$ identity matrix.
    Find the characteristic polynomial of A, its eigenvalues and bases for the corresponding eigenspaces. You should do this for several small values of n. What is the general pattern?

12. Let $v \neq 0$ be a vector in $\mathbb{R}^n$. The $n \times n$ matrix H is given by

$$H := \mathrm{Id} - a\,vv^t \quad \text{with} \quad a := \frac{2}{v^t v}.$$

What are the eigenvalues and corresponding eigenvectors of H? Take $n = 5$ and choose for v a symbolic vector.

6.6   Survey of Used Maple Expressions

The list below contains a few important Maple expressions and commands used in this chapter. Other Maple expressions with relevance to the field of Linear Algebra can be found in an earlier chapter (see section 3.6).

expression		brief explanation
`eigenvects`	–	list of lists of eigenvalues, multiplicities and corresponding eigenspace bases
`nops(expr)`	–	number of first-level operands in `expr`
`sparsematrixplot`	–	2-dimensional plot of all non-zero matrix elements
`Svd(A,U,V)`	–	singular value decomposition of matrix A with orthogonal matrices U and V of left and right singular vectors respectively

The following Maple expressions and commands are used in this chapter for the first time. Most of them are part of the `linalg` package.
`companion`, `eigenvals`, `genmatrix`, `kernel`, `normalize`, `nullspace`, `orthogonal`, `polarplot`, `radical`, `round`, `singularvals`, `sort`, `Svd`.

Appendix A

Exercises in Experimentation

T he exercises of this appendix are meant to test your overall knowledge of the Maple system, or rather, your expertise in the way you employ Maple when dealing with non-trivial problems. So maybe we should speak of experiments rather than exercises. On the other hand, they clearly have the exercise format of step by step guidance through detailed instructions. To accommodate both elements, we have chosen the title: Exercises in Experimentation. These exercises cover many but certainly not all aspects of Maple that were exposed in the foregoing chapters.

A.1   Upper Bound for a Parameterized Function

In this exercise we are concerned with a polynomial function depending on a parameter, and we wish to express the maximum value this function attains on a given finite interval in terms of the parameter. This exercise was inspired by the main problem in [17].

The function we have chosen is the following polynomial of degree 6 in the variable x depending on the parameter p:

$$f(x,p) = (1 + px)^3(1 - px)(1 - x^2) \quad \text{with } 0 \le p \le 1.$$

We are interested in the global maximum of this function on the interval $[-1, 1]$, and because f is a continuous function of x, this maximum surely exists. Set

$$M(p) = \max\{f(x,p) \mid x \in [-1, 1]\}.$$

181

(a) To get some feeling for the problem, make a combined plot of $f(x,p)$ for $p = 0.1\,i$ $(i = 0,1,\ldots,10)$. You will notice that the global maximum is attained at a point in $[0,1]$.

It is easy to see, even without Maple's assistance, that $1 \le M(p) \le (1+p)^2$. Check this.

We would like to improve upon these obvious bounds, and we are especially interested to know the behaviour of $M(p)$ as p is close to 0.

From part (a) it follows that $\lim_{p\to 0} M(p) = 1$, but we would like to have a better approximation to $M(p)$ than this.

(b) The next step is to find the singular point(s) of f as a function of x. Solving the quintic equation $\frac{\partial}{\partial x} f(x,p) = 0$ with Maple's `solve`—use `factor` first and then apply `solve` to the cubic factor—gives very unwieldy formulas. So instead, use the `RootOf` function and get the taylor expansion of the root function $\alpha(p)$. Here one should be careful and not blindly accept Maple's output.

(c) Prove that $\frac{\partial}{\partial x} f(x,p) = 0$ has a unique solution $\alpha(p)$ in $[0,1]$ for every $p \in [0,1]$, and by considering the sign of $\frac{\partial}{\partial x} f(x,p)$, show that f's global maximum on $[-1,1]$ is indeed attained at $\alpha(p)$.

(d) The taylor expansion of $\alpha(p)$ suggests that $\alpha(p) \approx p - 3p^3$ for p close to 0. Show that f, as a function of x, is concave on the interval $[x_1, x_2]$, where $x_1 = p - 4p^3$ and $x_2 = p - 2p^3$ for $0 \le p \le p_0$. Find a suitable value for p_0. Also make sure that $[x_1, x_2]$ is contained in $[0,1]$. By checking signs again, show that $\alpha(p) \in [x_1, x_2]$.

(e) Since f is concave on $[x_1, x_2]$, the tangents to the graph of f at the points $(x_1, f(x_1,p))$ and $(x_2, f(x_2,p))$ meet at a point that lies above the graph of f. Use Maple's `solve` again to find this meeting point, and by direct substitution into $f(x,p)$, also the corresponding upper bound for $M(p)$. The rational expression so obtained is a guaranteed upper bound for $M(p)$, but the sizes of the polynomials (in p) involved are enormous! Get the taylor expansion of this new upper bound and check that it agrees very closely to that obtained from $f(\alpha(p), p)$.

(f) It would be a challenge to try and find positive constants c_1 and c_2 such that

$$1 + p^2 - c_1 p^4 \le M(p) \le 1 + p^2 - c_2 p^4$$

for all p with $0 \le p \le p_0 < 1$, and an explicit p_0.

A.2   Matrix Differentiation

The purpose of this exercise is to design a number of Maple procedures for differentiating scalars, vectors, and matrices with respect to a scalar variable, a vector of variables or a matrix of variables, preserving structure.

Basically, there are three different types of differentiation processes we would like to distinguish, namely

- **Matrix to scalar.** Differentiation of any matrix with respect to a scalar variable. All elements of the matrix are seen as functions of this variable. Included are the cases 'scalar to scalar' and '(row or column) vector to scalar'.

- **Vector to vector.** Differentiation of any vector with respect to any vector of scalar variables, including 'scalar to scalar', 'vector to scalar' and 'scalar to vector'. The first vector should be seen as a list of functions, each depending on the same scalar variables. The second vector is composed of these independent scalar variables.

- **Scalar to matrix.** Differentiation of any scalar with respect to a matrix of scalar variables, the independent variables. Special cases are: 'scalar to scalar' and 'scalar to (row or column) vector'.

In each of these three cases a Maple procedure should be developed that is generally applicable. We adopt the convention that a row or column vector is a matrix with a single row or a single column respectively (see worksheet MatrW3b.mws). An important Maple function to be used in all three procedures is `map`.

(a) Give a detailed description of the Maple command `map`. Use Maple's extensive help facility if you are not sure and choose suitable examples to illustrate the different ways `map` may be used.

(b) The following procedure could be used for the 'matrix to scalar' case. By definition, the derivative of a matrix or vector with respect to a scalar variable preserves its structure. Hence the result is again a matrix or vector of the same dimensions.

```
>   'diff/mat/sc' := proc(A,x)
>   map(Diff,args[1],args[2])
>   end;
```

Here A is a matrix, a vector or a scalar, and x is a scalar. Type-checking is omitted.

Observe that the Maple function `Diff` is written with a capital D. This is not accidental. Can you think of a plausible reason?

Check that the procedure 'diff/mat/sc' works on small symbolic input. For instance, choose a symbolic scalar, a symbolic 3-vector and a symbolic 3×5 matrix, and apply the Maple command `value` to the output returned by 'diff/mat/sc'. Explain the answers.

Also check the procedure on a 3×5 matrix the elements of which are functions of a single variable x. Take for instance the matrix $A = (a_{ij})$ with $a_{ij} = x^{i+j-2}$.

(c) This part is about the 'vector to vector' case. By definition, the derivative of a vector $v = [v_1, \ldots, v_m]$ with respect to a vector $w = [w_1, \ldots, w_n]$ is the $m \times n$ matrix $\left(\dfrac{\partial v_i}{\partial w_j} \right)$. Write a procedure

```
> 'diff/vec/vec' := proc(v,w) ...  end;
```

in which the procedure of part (b) is used to the extent that the vectors 'diff/mat/sc'(v,w[i]) are placed side by side to form the required matrix.

Test your procedure with two symbolic vectors v en w of dimensions 3 and 5 respectively.

This procedure can also be used to compute the Jacobi matrix of a differentiable function $F : \mathbb{R}^5 \to \mathbb{R}^3$. The Maple procedure `jacobian` does just that. Check that your procedure has the same effect as Maple's `jacobian`. Hint. Use the `alias` function to instruct Maple to view each component of the vector v as a function of the components of the vector w.

(d) Now a procedure of type 'scalar to matrix' is required. By definition, the (matrix) derivative of a scalar function a with respect to a $m \times n$ matrix X of scalar variables x_{ij} is the $n \times m$ matrix $\left(\dfrac{\partial a}{\partial x_{ji}} \right)$. In particular, the derivative of a scalar with respect to a (column) vector is a (row) vector. Now write a procedure

```
> 'diff/sc/mat' := proc(a,X) local f,Y; ...  end;
```

that returns the derivative of the scalar a with respect to the matrix (or vector or scalar) X. In this procedure f is the prescription of a function $f : t \mapsto \dfrac{\partial u}{\partial t}$, for fixed u. Now the `map` function can be applied to build up the matrix. Because, by definition, the derived matrix is the transpose of the input matrix, the transpose Y of X is required in the procedure. Furthermore, u should be replaced by the input x. This can be achieved by means of the `subs` function. Test your procedure with the same symbolic quantities used to check the procedure of part (b). Please do not forget to use the `evalm` command at the proper places.

(e) Apply the procedure of part (d) to solve the least squares problem (see page 65) for a 5×3 random matrix of coefficients A and a random 5×1 constant vector b in the following way:

```
>  'diff/sc/mat'(transpose(A&*x-b)&*(A&*x-b),x);
```

After that, apply the Maple function `solve` and check your answer with Maple's `leastsqrs` function.

(f) Finally, use the procedure of part (d) to verify the identity

$$\frac{\partial}{\partial A}(y^T A x) = x y^T + y x^T - \text{diag}(x y^T)$$

for any variable symmetric matrix A, and constant vectors x and y.

A.3   Chaotic Sequences

We shall call a sequence of numbers $(R(n))_{n \in \mathbb{N}}$ chaotic when there is an index k for which

$$R(k) < R(k+1) < R(k+2) \text{ and } R(k+3) < R(k)$$

or   (A.1)

$$R(k) > R(k+1) > R(k+2) \text{ and } R(k+3) > R(k).$$

(a) Write a Maple procedure that can be used for testing an arbitrary (finite) list of numbers for being chaotic. This should be done by counting the number of quadruples

$$R(k), R(k+1), R(k+2), R(k+3)$$

satisfying property (A.1). Your output should also contain a list of those k marking chaotic positions.

(b) Apply your procedure(s) to a list of 200 successive digits of the decimal expansion of the number π, starting at an arbitrary position.

Now consider the difference equation

$$x_{t+1} = 1 - |2x_t - 1|, \quad x_0 = \frac{1}{\sqrt{2}}.$$

(c) Generate a list $L = [x_1, x_2, \ldots, x_{200}]$ and show that L has the property (A.1). Be careful for loss of significance as a result of round-off. As a precaution against generating meaningless entries it might be a good idea to set the Maple constant **Digits** to a large value, say 100.
Now it is claimed that the elements of L are uniformly distributed over $[0, 1]$. This claim will be investigated in the remaining parts.

(d) Distribute L's entries over 10 classes of equal length 0.1 and construct a frequency diagram. Call f_i de (relative) frequency of class i ($i = 1, \ldots, 10$), and call F_i de cumulative frequency distribution, defined by $F_i = \sum_{k=1}^{i} f_k$. Further, put $\sigma(p) = \sqrt{p(1-p)/N}$, where N is the length of L, hence $N = 200$.

(e) Investigate the inequalities

$$\frac{i}{10} - 1.96\,\sigma(\frac{i}{10}) < F_i < \frac{i}{10} + 1.96\,\sigma(\frac{i}{10}) \quad \text{for } i = 1, \ldots, 10.$$

Suppose these inequalities are satisfied for all i. What does this mean for the class distribution?

The quantity

$$\chi_{10} = N \sum_{i=1}^{10} \frac{(f_i - \frac{1}{10})^2}{\frac{1}{10}}$$

is χ-squared distributed with 9 degrees of freedom.

(f) Compute χ_{10} for the list L. With a 5% level of significance, should the hypothesis be rejected that says the elements of L are uniformly distributed over $[1, 0]$?

Appendix B

Hints and Answers

In this appendix you will find hints for the exercises supplied with each chapter. Full answers are given in most cases, and often a complete solution is provided. For obvious reasons, hints and answers are neither supplied for the assignments nor for the exercises in experimentation.

B.1   Exercises 1.5

1. Type the following Maple lines

    ```
    >  history();
    >  x; y; z; %,%%,%%%; # Note the commas
    ```

    and consider the corresponding output. Apparently, the ditto's still work.

2. Use square brackets as in

    ```
    >  a := linalg[vector](3);
    ```

    This instruction defines a symbolic vector $a \in \mathbb{R}^3$.

3. Define the function $f : \mathbb{N} \to \mathbb{N}$ by

    ```
    >  f := n -> sum(floor(n/2^i),i=1..n);
    ```

    and verify that for (say) $n = 2, 3, \ldots, 25$ the integer $n!/2^{f(n)}$ is odd.
    Remark. There is no reason for letting the summation index i run all the way up to n, but this is not a problem either.

4. (a)   After evaluation, only one pair of right quotes remains.

(b) This combination is useful in case one wishes to use the variable name 'string' literally, so that unusual characters, such as spaces, can now be included.

(c) The inner right quotes have no function at all in this combination.

5. The following lines have the desired effect:

```
> p:=rand(1..1000)():
> if isprime(p) and isprime(p+2) then
> print(p,p+2,'is a prime pair')
> else print(p,p+2,'is not a prime pair')
> fi;
```

6. The argument (or input parameter) of the procedure is assigned to the local variable x. The procedure distinguishes between empty inputs, the input string 'Maple', and any other input string. In all three cases it takes care of producing informative output.
   Remark. Spaces and quotes have no effect unless they are placed somewhere in the middle of the input string.

7. The first decimal place of Maple's output to the following instruction gives the thousandth decimal place of π:

```
> frac(evalf(Pi*10^999,1002));
```

Removal of the decimal point and the last digit is easily achieved by multiplication by 10 and application of the floor function.

8. The instruction

```
> y := 5, p;
```

assigns the pair $5, p$ to y, thus causing an infinite loop, because p is a polynomial in the same variable y.

9. Working from 9999 backwards, the next lines of Maple code give the required prime pair:

```
> k := 9999:
> while not (isprime(k-2) and isprime(k)) do
> k := k-2 od:   [k-2,k];
```

B.2   Exercises 2.5

1. This is indeed a difficult exercise. Strictly speaking, the function $g(x,p)$ is not defined for numbers $x \in (0,1)$ that do not have a finite binary representation. But for any $x \in (0,1)$ with (infinite) binary expansion

$x = (0.b_1 b_2 \ldots)_2$ [1], a sequence $(x_n)_{n=1}^{\infty}$ exists that converges to x, namely the sequence with general term $x_n := (0.b_1 b_2 \ldots b_n)_2$. This is an immediate consequence of the inequality

$$|x - x_n| \leq 2^{-n-1}.$$

It now follows that for every pair $m, n \in \mathbb{N}$ with $m > n$ and for every $p \in (0, 1)$

$$|g(x_m, p) - g(x_n, p)| \leq \max\{p, 1 - p\}^n \longrightarrow 0 \quad (n \to \infty).$$

This is a sufficient condition (a so-called Cauchy condition) for the existence of $\lim_{n \to \infty} g(x_n, p)$. Assigning this limit to $g(x, p)$ produces a function $g(x, p)$ which is not only defined for all real $x \in [0, 1]$ but also continuous as a function of x on the whole of $[0, 1]$.

Let $0 \leq x < y \leq 1$ and suppose that the first $m \geq 1$ bits of the binary expansions of x and y coincide, then $y - x \leq 2^{-m-1} + 2^{-m-2} + \cdots = 2^{-m}$. This yields

$$\begin{aligned} g(y, p) - g(x, p) &= p^i (1 - p)^{m-i} (g((0.1 \ldots)_2, p) - g((0.0 \ldots)_2, p)) \\ &> p^i (1 - p)^{m-i} (p - p) = 0. \end{aligned}$$

In this formula i is the number of zeros occurring amongst the first m bits of the binary expansions of x and y. Hence $g(x, p)$ is strictly monotonically increasing as a function of x.

Finally we have

$$g((0.b_1 b_2 \ldots)_2, \tfrac{1}{2}) = \tfrac{1}{2} + \tfrac{1}{2} g((0.b_2 \ldots)_2, \tfrac{1}{2})).$$

A simple inductive argument now shows that for each $m \geq 1$

$$g(x, \tfrac{1}{2}) = x_m + 2^{-m} g((x - x_m) 2^m, \tfrac{1}{2}),$$

so that

$$|g(x, \tfrac{1}{2}) - x_m| \leq 2^{-m}.$$

Hence $x = \lim_{m \to \infty} x_m = g(x, \tfrac{1}{2})$.

2. Consider the cases $n = 4k + r$ for $r = 0, 1, 2, 3$ separately.

3. The Maple input line

```
>  limit(f(x),x=1,left) = limit(f(x),x=1,right)
```

gives an equation in a. Solve this equation using the command `solve`. Answer:

$$a = \tfrac{1}{3} - \alpha^{1/3} - \tfrac{1}{9}\alpha^{-1/3}, \quad \text{with } \alpha = \tfrac{1}{18}\left(\tfrac{25}{3} + \sqrt{69}\right) = -0.754877666\ldots$$

---

[1] Every real number has such a representation.

4. Maple immediately returns the limit value 1. In order to verify this answer, you could proceed as follows: define

$$h_n = n^{1/n} - 1$$

for each $n \in \mathbb{N}$. Then $n = (1 + h_n)^n$ or, equivalently, $\ln n = n \ln(1 + h_n)$. Applying Newton's binomium for $n \geq 2$ gives

$$n = (1 + h_n)^n = 1 + nh_n + \tfrac{1}{2}n^2 h_n^2 > \tfrac{1}{2}n^2 h_n^2,$$

and hence

$$0 < h_n < \sqrt{\frac{2}{n}}, \quad \text{for } n \geq 2.$$

From

$$\ln\left(\frac{(2n^{1/n} - 1)^n}{n^2}\right) = n \ln(1 + 2h_n) - 2n \ln(1 + h_n),$$

and the power series expansion of $\ln(1 + x)$ around $x = 0$, it follows that Maple indeed returned the correct limit value after all.

5. Let

$$a_n = \left(1 + \frac{1}{n}\right)^{n^2} n!\, n^{-(n+\frac{1}{2})}.$$

Applying Stirling's formula yields

$$\ln a_n = \ln\left(\sqrt{\frac{2\pi}{e}}\right) + \mathcal{O}(n^{-1}) \quad (n \to \infty).$$

Maple really finds that $\lim_{n \to \infty} a_n = \sqrt{\frac{2\pi}{e}}$.

It is far more difficult to show that the sequence $(a_n)_{n=1}^{\infty}$ is monotonically decreasing. On the other hand it is rather easy (with Maple's assistance) to make this plausible. Calculating the first 50 quotients a_{n+1}/a_n is very fast, and the Maple function `asympt` gives

$$\frac{a_{n+1}}{a_n} = 1 - \tfrac{5}{12}n^{-2} + \mathcal{O}(n^{-3}) \quad (n \to \infty).$$

In order to give a proper proof, first verify that $a_{n+1} < a_n$ is equivalent with the inequality

$$\left(1 + \frac{1}{n+1}\right)^{n^2+2n+1} < \left(1 + \frac{1}{n}\right)^{n^2+n+\frac{1}{2}}.$$

That $(a_n)_{n=1}^{\infty}$ is monotonically decreasing now follows from the same property shared by the sequence $(b_n)_{n=1}^{\infty}$, where

$$b_n := \left(1 + \frac{1}{n}\right)^{n+\frac{1}{2}}.$$

6. Consider $a_n^2 - a_{n-1}^2$. Further, $\lim_{n\to\infty} a_n = \frac{1}{2} + \frac{1}{2}\sqrt{5}$.

7. The function $\sin x - x$ is strictly monotonically decreasing on $[0, \infty)$. Maple finds

$$\lim_{x\downarrow 0} \left(\frac{1}{\sin^2 x} - \frac{1}{x^2}\right) = \frac{1}{3}.$$

8. Provided the `assume` function is used and only right limits are considered at 0, Maple finds the correct results:

$$\lim_{x\downarrow 0} x^a \log x = \begin{cases} 0 & \text{if } a > 0, \\ -\infty & \text{if } a \leq 0. \end{cases}$$

9. Straightforward code for the `Plus` procedure is:

```
>   Plus := proc(f,x) max(f(x),0) end;
```

Some type-checking could be added. The relation between `Plus`, `Minus` and `abs` is: `Plus − Minus = abs`.

10. Put

$$a_n := \left(1 - \frac{1}{n}\right)^n, \quad \text{for } n = 1, 2, \ldots.$$

Now use Maple to show that

$$\frac{a_{n+1}}{a_n} = \frac{n}{n+1}\left(1 + \frac{1}{n^2 - 1}\right)^n > \frac{n}{n+1}\left(1 + \frac{n}{n^2 - 1}\right) > 1.$$

Maple finds that $\lim_{x\to\infty} a_n = e^{-1}$.

11. Let

$$a_n := (2k^{\frac{1}{n}} - 1)^n.$$

Maple computes: $\lim_{n\to\infty} a_n = k^2$. Put $t_n := k^{\frac{1}{n}} - 1$. Then $\lim_{n\to\infty} t_n = 0$ and $\lim_{n\to\infty} n t_n = \log k$. The latter is a direct consequence of the standard limit

$$\lim_{x\to 0} \frac{\log(1+x)}{x} = 1.$$

Hence

$$\lim_{n\to\infty} \log a_n = 2 \log k.$$

12. It is rather straightforward to show with mathematical induction that the sequence (a_n) is monotonically increasing and that $0 < a_n < 1$ for all $n \in \mathbb{N}$. Hence (a_n) is convergent. Maple is of limited use here. The limit of (a_n) is $-\frac{1}{2} + \frac{1}{2}\sqrt{5}$, which is the unique solution to the equation

$$3x = 1 + x + x^3$$

in the range $(0, 1)$. Maple's solve has no problems finding this solution.

B.3   Exercises 3.5

1. To verify the associative property of matrix multiplication, the following Maple code can be used:

```
>   restart:   with(linalg):
>   A := matrix(3,3):   B := matrix(3,3):
>   C := matrix(3,3):
>   evalm((A&*B)&*C - A&*(B&*C));
```

Remark. If you need to check that two given expressions are equal, we advise you to evaluate the difference of these expressions rather than each individual expression separately.

2. Use randmatrix(5,5) to generate the random matrices. However, if you wish to work with random matrices with random elements in the interval $[0, 1]$, you can use the code:

```
>   N := 1000:
>   A := matrix(5,5,(i,j) -> rand(N)()/(N-1));
```

Generally, the matrix elements generated in this way will be random rational numbers with 3-digit numerators and denominator 999.

3. The first two arguments 10 give the number of rows and columns of the matrix respectively. The third and last 10 is the constant function that assigns the value 10 to each position (i, j).

4. Use

```
>   map(evalf,A);
```

Also

```
>   evalf(evalm(A));
```

gives the desired result.

5. Let

> ```
> A := (m,n) -> matrix(m,n,(i,j) -> 1/(i+j-1));
> ```

For each matrix $A(m,n)$ you should first calculate the rank, which is equal to $\min\{m,n\}$.

(a) The null space consist of the zero vector only, and the columns of $A(10,10)$ form a basis for the column space.

(b) The rank of $A(15,1)$ is 5. Therefore, the columns of this matrix are linearly independent.

(c) The rank of $A(12,20)$ is 12, and the dimension of the null space is 8. Here you can use the Maple functions `kernel` and `rowspace`. The latter should be applied to the transpose of the matrix.

6. It follows from the assumptions that $Ax = a^t x$ and

$$\mathrm{Ker}(A) = \{x \mid Ax = 0\} = a^\perp.$$

Thus, the null space of A and the orthogonal complement of a coincide. The following Maple input provides the desired parameter representation:

> ```
> a := vector(8,[1,-2,3,-4,5,-6,7,-8]):
> b := vector(8,0):    # null vector
> A := stackmatrix(a,b,b,b,b,b,b,b):
> rref(A); # returns A unaltered
> linsolve(A,b);
> ```

7. Let a_i be the i-th column (vector) of A. The projection of b onto the column space of A is the vector

$$u = Ac = \sum_{i=1}^{5} c_i a_i,$$

where the c_i are the components of the vector c, and $(b - u)$ is orthogonal to the vector a_i for each $i = 1, \ldots, 5$. Hence

$$A^t(b - u) = 0, \quad \text{and so } A^t Ac = A^t b.$$

This means that

> ```
> u := linsolve(transpose(A)&*A,transpose(A)&*b):
> ```

is the desired orthogonal projection. The exact answer takes up a lot of space. Therefore the following numerical approximation will have to do:

$$u := [315.98\ldots, -6436.46\ldots, 29757.95\ldots, -47606.41\ldots, 24427.64\ldots].$$

8. Solve the linear system in the unknowns c_0, c_1, and c_2, by taking first columns in the Cayley-Hamilton matrix relation. The following Maple code gives the result required:

```
>   A := matrix(3,3,[21,22,23,24,25,26,27,28,29]):
>   augment(vector([1,0,0]),col(A,1),col(A^2,1)):
>   c := linsolve(%,-col(A^3,1)):
>   for i from 0 to 2 do c.i := c[i+1] od:
>   p := x^3 + c.2*x^2 + c.1*x +c.0;
>   evalm(subs(x=A,p));
```

The final instruction checks the result.

9. The following simple Maple procedure returns the orthogonal projection of a given vector onto another given vector:

```
>   proj := proc(u::vector,v::vector)
>   innerprod(u,v)/innerprod(v,v)*v end;
```

Verification can be achieved by

```
>   n := 20:   u:=randvector(n):   v:=randvector(n):
>   innerprod(u - proj(u,v),v);
```

B.4   Exercises 4.5

1. The Maple code is rather obvious, and as Maple immediately returns correct answers in both cases, we shall merely reproduce these answers.

$$\text{(a)} \quad \binom{n+r+1}{n}, \quad \text{(b)} \quad \frac{n+1}{2}\binom{r}{n+1}.$$

Both identities can be proved by direct (manual) evaluation.

2. Application of the technique of generating functions to the identity

$$(1+x)^r(1-x)^r = (1-x^2)^r,$$

gives

$$\sum_{k=0}^{n} \binom{r}{k}\binom{r}{n-k}(-1)^k = c_n,$$

where c_n is the coefficient of x^n in the (formal) power series expansion of $(1-x^2)^r$. So

$$c_{2k} = (-1)^k\binom{r}{k} \quad \text{and} \quad c_{2k+1} = 0.$$

The first c_{2k}-values can be verified with the following Maple instructions:

```
> for n from 2 by 2 to 50 do if not
> normal(sum(binomial(r,k)*binomial(r,n-k)*(-1)^k,
> k=0..n)-(-1)^(n/2)*binomial(r,n/2),'expanded') = 0
> then print('For n = ',n,' the formula suggested
> is probably wrong.') fi od;
```

3. The Maple instructions printed below yield

$$f_n(1) - f_{n-1}(1) = \frac{1}{n},$$

and consequently

$$f_n = \sum_{k=1}^{n} \frac{1}{k} = \ln n + \gamma + \frac{1}{2n} + \mathcal{O}(n^{-2}) \quad (n \to \infty)$$

```
> a := (k,n,x) -> (-1)^(k+1)*binomial(n,k)*x^k/k:
> df := (n,x) -> sum(diff(a(k,n,x),x),k=1..n):
> assume(n>0):  int(df(n,x) - df(n-1,x),x=0..1);
```

4. For relatively small values of n, the given congruence can be easily tested using the Maple procedures mods and isprime. For large values of n, the binomial coefficient $\binom{2n}{n}$ gets very large which causes the run-time to grow exponentially. To keep the size down, it seems best to generate $\binom{2n}{n}$ modula $2n + 1$. This rather falls outside the scope of our book, so we shall not give any details.

Another method, less suitable than this, but at least faster than the direct one, is based on a recurrence relation which makes use of the specific way $\binom{2n}{n}$ depends on n.

```
> p := proc(n) option remember;
> if n=0 then 1 else (2/n-4)*p(n-1) fi end;
```

Here $p_n = (-1)^n \binom{2n}{n}$. A disadvantage of this method is that for large values of n a lot of memory space is required. The Maple code

```
> for n from 1 to 3000 do
> if not isprime(2*n+1) and mods(p(n),2*n+1)=1 then
> print(n) fi od;
```

finds $n = 2953$.

5. The estimated probability is 0.5. The Maple code is rather obvious:

```
> N := 10000:  c := 0:
> for i from 1 to 1000 do s := [seq(rand(N)()/(N-1),
> j=1..3)]:  if (s[1]+s[2]>s[3] and s[1]+s[3]>s[2]
```

```
> and s[2]+s[3]>s[1]) then
> c := c+1 fi od:
> evalf(c/1000);
```

6. The Maple procedure below follows a path of n steps, starting at $(0,0)$, and returns the squared Euclidean distance of its endpoint to the origin.

```
> path := proc(n) local i,x,y,r;
> x:=0; y:=0;
> for i from 1 to n do
> r := rand(4)():
> if r=0 then x := x+1
> elif r=1 then x := x-1
> elif r=2 then y := y+1
> elif r=3 then y := y-1
> fi od;
> x^2 + y^2
> end;
```

For given n, say $n = 20$, a list of squared distances for 1000 paths is generated by

```
> n :=20:  s := [seq(path(n),i=1..1000)]:
> evalf(convert(s,'+')/1000);
```

The final input line produces the mean of the squared distances to the origin. In theory, for arbitrary n, this should be equal to n.

7. The following instructions provide a candidate for the sought-after recurrence relation:

```
> f:=n -> sum(binomial(n+k,n-k),k=0..n);
> with(linalg):
> for n to 5 do A := matrix(3,3,(i,j) -> f(i+j+n)):
> linsolve(A,[0,0,0]):  print(%) od:
```

Now use Maple's rsolve function to solve the recurrence relation

$$c_n = 3c_{n-1} - c_{n-2} \text{ for } n \geq 2, c_0 = 1, c_1 = 2.$$

8. The next lines contain possible Maple code for this experiment.

```
> test := proc() local Rsq, counter, i;
> Rsq := [seq(rand(),i=1..200)]:
> counter := 0:  for i from 1 to (nops(Rsq)-2) do
> if (Rsq[i] > Rsq[i+1]) and (Rsq[i+1] > Rsq[i+2])
> then counter := counter + 1 fi od;
> counter/(nops(Rsq)-2) end:
> [seq(test(),j=1..20)]:
> m := evalf(convert(%,'+')/20,3);
```

$$m := .160$$

Here m denotes the mean, which is close enough to the expected value of $\frac{1}{6}$ to be acceptable.

9. Use the `seq` and `rand()` functions to generate a sequence of products of three random positive integers. Then apply Maple's `map` to reduce this sequence to a sequence of most significant digits.

```
>  triads := [seq((rand()+1)*(rand()+1)*(rand()+1),
>  i=1..1000)]:
>  SD := map(i -> floor(i/10^(length(i)-1)),triads):
```

Counting the digits 1 and 9 is easy. It turns out that the digit 1 generally occurs more frequently than the digit 9 by at least a factor 3.

10. First the `setseed` procedure chooses a position in the decimal expansion of π to start from. The next procedure `Pirand` checks the parity of each successive digit from the initial position in the decimal expansion of π onwards and generates a corresponding $(0, 1)$-sequence.

```
>  setseed := proc(n::integer) global seed;
>  seed := n end:

>  Pirand := proc() global seed; local t;
>  if not assigned(seed) then seed := 1 fi;
>  Digits := max(seed+10,20);
>  t := frac(evalf(10^(seed)*Pi));
>  seed := seed + 1;
>  irem(floor(10*t),2) end;
```

Applying the switch test to the bit-sequence so generated will generally not refute the hypothesis of a random bit-sequence.

B.5   Exercises 5.5

1. The Maple code

```
>  f := x -> ln(x^2+x+1):
>  df := n -> subs(x=-1/2,diff(f(x),x$n))/(n-1)!:
>  s := []:  for n from 1 to 20 do
>  s := [op(s),ifactor(df(n))] od:  s;
```

produces a list s of values $s_n = \dfrac{f^{(n)}\left(-\frac{1}{2}\right)}{(n-1)!}$ for $n = 1, \ldots, 20$. This suggests that

$$s_{2k-1} = 0 \text{ and } s_{2k} = (-1)^{k+1}\frac{2^{2k+1}}{3^k},$$

a suggestion supported by Maple's answer to

```
> taylor(f(x),x=-1/2,12);
```

2. Assigning the value 1 to $f(0)$ makes f continuous on the entire interval $[0, \infty)$. The function f has a global minimum 1 at $x = 1$, and its global maximum $1.61015987\ldots$ is attained at $x = 0.1179651892\ldots$.
   In order to obtain the global maximum, the following Maple code seems suitable:

```
> -minimize(-f(x),x,0..1);
```

   But Maple does not cooperate, as the system returns an incorrect answer.

3. Put

```
> R := x -> (x^2+6*x+6)/(x^12+1);
```

   The output of

```
> int(R(x),x);
```

   is not very transparent and of no use as a final result. But if a complete partial fraction decomposition of $R(x)$ is available before symbolic integration is attempted, then a much more readable (but still not very attractive) expression for the primitive function is obtained. Possible Maple instructions to serve this purpose are

```
> convert(factor(R(x),{sqrt(2),sqrt(6)}),parfrac,x);
> simplify(int(%,x));
```

   The primitive so obtained is too involved to be printed here.

4. Put

```
> f := x -> x^2+sin(x);
```

   The largest value of δ for which f is strictly increasing on $(-\delta, \infty)$ is given by $\delta = -0.4501836113\ldots$.
   You can get the taylor expansion of the inverse of f as follows:

```
> RootOf(f(x)=y,x):
> taylor(%,y=0);
```

   This produces the Maple output

$$y - y^2 + \frac{13}{6}y^3 - \frac{35}{6}y^4 + \frac{703}{40}y^5 + \mathcal{O}(y^6)$$

5. The Maple instruction

    ```
    >  J := m -> Int(tan(x)^m,x=0..Pi/4);
    ```

   defines J. The input lines

    ```
    >  combine(J(m+1)+J(m-1)):
    >  student[changevar](y=tan(x),%,y):
    >  value(%);
    ```

   now produce the following recurrence relation for $J(m)$:

   $$J(m+1) + J(m-1) = \frac{1}{m} \quad \text{for } m \geq 1.$$

   Starting from the initial values $J(0) = \pi/4$ and $J(1) = \ln \sqrt{2}$, $J(m)$ can now be calculated for every $m \in \mathbb{N}$. The Maple procedure rsolve will produce a general expression for $J(m)$. Though real, this expression utilizes complex number notation.

6. The double integral can be written as the repeated integral

   $$\int_0^1 \int_{x^2}^x \sqrt{|x^2 - y|} \, dx \, dy.$$

   Maple reduces the latter to a single integral, but then some assistance is required. First, the signum function has to be removed from the integrand, and then a simple substitution using student[changevar] will do the trick. The symbolic value of the double integral is expressed in terms of the complete elliptic integral of the first kind:

   $$\frac{3}{80} 3^{3/4} \, \text{EllipticK}(\frac{1}{4}\sqrt{6} - \frac{1}{4}\sqrt{2})$$

   It has the numerical value .1366115990 . . . .

7. The function f is a polynomial in x, and therefore, a necessary and sufficient condition for f to be strictly concave on $[p, \infty)$ is that the second derivative of f is negative on (p, ∞). This is all rather straightforward and checks out nicely. Further, Maple finds two solutions of the equation $f'(x) = 0$, and on substituting these x-values into $f''(x)$ reveals that $f''(x) < 0$ for exactly one of them, a singular point that also happens to be part of the interval $[p, p + 1]$. The point in question is

   $$x = \frac{1}{3}\left(2p + 1 + \sqrt{p^2 + p + 1}\right).$$

8. Use the Maple instruction

    ```
    >  value('D(f(g(t)))' = D(f@g)(t);
    ```

   Make sure that f and g are undetermined. Also note the right quotes.

9. The following lines of code enable you to compare the k-th order derivative at $x = 0$ with the k-th coefficient of the taylor expansion:

```
>  f := x -> exp(sin(ln(1+x))):
>  [seq((D@@k)(f)(0)/k!,k=0..10)];
>  taylor(f(x),x=0,11);
```

10. Try the following code for indeterminate c:

```
>  c := 'c'; F := x -> int(f(t),t=c..x);
```

11. The substitution $x = 2y + \frac{1}{2}\pi$ gives, after some manipulation, the primitive

$$\pm 2\sqrt{2}\sin y,$$

where the $\pm$ is the sign of $\cos y$. This is the outcome of the following Maple instructions:

```
>  student[changevar](x=2*y + Pi/2,
>  int(sqrt(1+sin(x)),x),y);
>  simplify(normal(expand(%)));
```

B.6   Exercises 6.5

1. The standard matrix of T for arbitrary $n = 2, 3, \ldots$ is the $(n-1) \times n$ matrix

$$A = (a_{ij}) \text{ with } a_{ij} = \begin{cases} 0 & \text{if } j - i > 1 \\ 1 & \text{if } j - i \le 1 \end{cases}$$

2. Introduce the polynomials p_n as follows:

```
>  p := (n,t) -> sum((n-i+1)*t^i,i=0..n);
```

Some experimentation suggests

$$t^k = p_k(t) - 2\,p_{k-1}(t) + p_{k-2}(t) \quad \text{for all } k \ge 2.$$

Verification by means of the Maple code

```
>  normal(p(k,t) - 2*p(k-1,t) + p(k-2,t),expanded);
```

confirms this. Since $1 = p_0(t)$ and $t = p_1(t) - 2\,p_0(t)$, every power t^k $(0 \le k \le n)$ can be written as a linear combination of the elements of $\mathcal{B}_n$. Also, since degree$(p_k) = k$, it follows that the elements of $\mathcal{B}_n$ are linearly independent. Hence $\mathcal{B}_n$ is a basis for $\mathbb{P}_n$.
The matrix of the linear mapping $T : \mathbb{P}_n \to \mathbb{R}^{n+1}$ relative to $\mathcal{B}_n$ and the standard basis of $\mathbb{R}^{n+1}$ is the identity matrix.

3. It is not difficult to generate a list with information on the determinant, the characteristic polynomial, the eigenvalues and eigenspaces (in this order) for $n = 3, 4, 5, 6$:

```
> restart:  with(linalg):
> f := (i,j) -> if i=j then 0 else 1 fi;
> A := n -> matrix(n,n,(i,j) -> f(i,j));
> listA := []:  for n from 3 to 6 do listA :=
> [op(listA),[n,det(A(n)),charpoly(A(n),x),
> eigenvects(A(n))]] od:
> listA;
```

From these data you should be able to infer without any difficulty what happens in the general situation.

4. The null space has dimension 1 and the multiplicity of the eigenvalue 0 (as a zero of the characteristic polynomial) is 2. Therefore, $\mathbb{R}^4$ cannot have a basis entirely made up of eigenvectors of A.

5. The matrix C is not diagonalizable, because the eigenspace associated with eigenvalue -5 is of dimension 1, whereas -5 has multiplicity 2 as a root of C's characteristic equation.

   Use `Svd(C,U,V)` to find the singular values and store the right and left singular vectors in U and V respectively. The largest singular value of C is

   $$\sigma = \sqrt{954506} + \sqrt{952581} = 1952.99079\ldots$$

   Finally

```
> u := col(U,1):  v := col(V,1):
> Capp := evalf(sigma*(u&*transpose(v)));
```

   completes the exercise. The resemblance between the matrix `Capp` and the original matrix C is really quite good.

6. The matrix A is not symmetric, but even so, the information Maple supplies about its eigenvalues and eigenspaces, shows that A is diagonalizable. Unfortunately, eigenvectors corresponding to different eigenvalues are not orthogonal. So, Q can not be chosen orthogonal.

   The eigenvalues are 0, 2 and 20 with corresponding eigenspace dimensions of 1, 3, and 1 respectively. A basis for the eigenspace `EigSp[2]` associated with eigenvalue 2 can be obtained with

```
> alias(Id=&*()):  EigSp[2] := nullspace(A - 2*Id);
```

   The other two eigenspaces can be calculated analogously. Use the Maple command **augment** to build the matrix Q from the eigenspace bases.

7. It is clear that $\text{rank}(A)$ can be at most 4. The determinant of the matrix $A^t A$ is a polynomial $p(x)$ of degree 6 in x. Maple's function `factor` will factorize this polynomial. The result is

$$p(x) := \det(A^t A) = (654623\, x^2 - 7190096\, x + 20354423)\, (x - 1)^4.$$

The quadratic factor in the decomposition of $p(x)$ is positive definite, which implies that A has maximal rank unless $x = 1$, in which case $\text{rank}(A) = 2$. For $x \neq 1$ the null space contains the zero vector and nothing else; for $x = 1$ a basis for the null space of A is given by

$$\{[3\ 19\ 17\ 0], [0\ 11\ 13\ 3]\}.$$

8. Use Maple's `randmatrix` to generate the random matrices. As the dimensions of $\text{Ker}(T)$ and $\text{Range}(T)$ are equal to the dimension of the kernel of A and the rank of A respectively, the Maple instruction

```
>   nops(kernel(A)) + rank(A);
```

should have the desired output of 13.

9. The matrix representation of the operator D relative to the standard basis of $\mathbb{P}_n$ is

```
>   matrix(n,n,(i,j) -> if j=i+1 then i else 0 fi);
```

10. By definition, $T(u) = [u]_\mathcal{B}$ and $u = M^t\, [u]_\mathcal{B}$. Hence the matrix representation of T relative to the standard basis is given by

```
>   inverse(transpose(M));
```

11. The characteristic polynomial of the $n \times n$ matrix A is

$$p(x) = (x - n + 1)(x + 1)^{n-1}.$$

Use Maple's `factor` to obtain the factorization of $p(x)$. Let e_j be the j-th element of the standard basis of $\mathbb{R}^n$. Then $e := E e_1$ is an eigenvector associated with the eigenvalue $n-1$ of A, and the eigenspace associated with the eigenvalue -1 is generated by the $n - 1$ vectors $e_j - e_1$ for $j = 2, \ldots, n$. All this is readily verified with suitably chosen Maple commands.

12. The characteristic polynomial of H is $(x+1)(x-1)^4$. Further, the nullspace of $\text{Id} + H$ is generated by v, and the nullspace of $\text{Id} - H$ is the orthogonal complement of v in $\mathbb{R}^5$.

Appendix C

Quick Guide to Selected Maple Commands

by Lennart Hoogerheide

F or the Maple novice it is often not so easy to quickly find suitable Maple commands for the mathematical task at hand. The purpose of this appendix is to give brief summaries of selected Maple commands that are likely to meet at least some of your needs when working in certain branches of mathematics. From the perspective of a particular mathematical setting, some Maple functions are more relevant and useful than others; our selections of useful commands are listed under a natural subject heading, followed by brief explanations and examples. Although far from exhaustive, we hope and expect that this summary will be helpful to many users and to the Maple novice in particular.

The branches of mathematics and the mathematical topics covered are:

- **Linear Algebra:** matrix and vector algebra, solving systems of linear equations, computing the eigenvalues and eigenvectors of a matrix.

- **Mathematical Analysis:** elementary mathematical functions, writing your own procedures, plotting the graph of a function, computing limits, derivatives and integrals, and solving non-linear equations.

- **Statistics:** computing probabilities, generating random numbers, and analyzing statistical data.

- **Linear Programming:** solving LP problems with the simplex method.

203

- **Mathematical Finance**: computing the value of a call option using the Black-Scholes formula, and computing the net present value of a financial asset.

C.1 Linear Algebra

In order to have at your immediate disposal all Maple procedures typical to the linear algebra environment, you need to load the `linalg` package; the instruction

> `with(linalg):`

will do just that.

C.1.1 Elementary Matrix Algebra

There are three ways of introducing a matrix: by giving a list of its rows, or by giving a list of its elements, or by using a function prescription. If you do not specify any elements, then a symbolic matrix is obtained.

command form	example
`matrix([rows])`	— `A := matrix([[2,3,4],[3,4,5]]);`
`matrix(m,n,[elements])`	— `A := matrix(2,3,[2,3,4,3,4,5]);`
`matrix(m,n,prescription)`	— `A := matrix(2,3,(i,j) -> i+j);`
`matrix(m,n)`	— `B := matrix(2,3);`

The first three examples yield the same matrix $A = \begin{bmatrix} 2 & 3 & 4 \\ 3 & 4 & 5 \end{bmatrix}$.

The command `evalm` is required to make Maple print the elements of a matrix on the screen; for instance, with

> `evalm(A);`

all elements of A will be displayed in the usual way.

A summary of useful matrix procedures is given next.

math concept		command form
determinant	–	`det(A)`
row dimension	–	`rowdim(A)`
column dimension	–	`coldim(A)`
inverse	–	`inverse(A)`
matrix multiplication	–	`evalm(A &* B)`
rank	–	`rank(A)`
trace	–	`trace(A)`
transpose	–	`transpose(A)`

C.1.2   Elementary Vector Algebra

There are two ways of introducing a vector: by listing its elements, or by using a function prescription. If you do not specify any elements, Maple produces a symbolic vector.

Vectors are one-dimensional arrays. Occasionally it may be necessary to distinguish *row* vectors from *column* vectors. This can be achieved by using the `matrix` command with first or second range parameter 1. However, this definition of 'vector' produces a two-dimensional array.

command form		example
`vector(n,[elements])`	–	`u := vector(5,[2,4,6,8,10]);`
`vector(n,prescription)`	–	`u := vector(5,i -> 2*i);`
`matrix(1,n,[elements])`	–	`u := matrix(1,5,[2,4,6,8,10]);`
`vector(n)`	–	`v := vector(5);`

The first two examples yield the same vector $u = [2, 4, 6, 8, 10]$, while v is the symbolic vector $[v_1, v_2, v_3, v_4, v_5]$.

To have the elements of a vector printed on the screen requires the command `evalm`, for instance

```
>  evalm(v);
```

A summary of vector procedures is given in the next table.

math concept		command form
angle between two vectors (in radians)	–	`angle(u,v)`
dimension	–	`vectdim(v)`
Euclidean norm	–	`norm(v,2)`
inner product	–	`innerprod(u,v)`
Gram-Schmidt orthogonalization	–	`GramSchmidt([vectors])` (yields a list of non-normalized orthogonal vectors)
normalization by the Euclidean norm	–	`map(normalize,list)` (`map` applies the `normalize` procedure to all vector elements of `list` simultaneously)

C.1.3   Solving a System of Linear Equations $Ax = b$

The following commands can be used in the process of solving a system of linear equations. For non-linear equations, see page 210.

math concept		command form
exact solution of $Ax = b$	–	`linsolve(A,b)`
least-squares solution to (infeasible) system $Ax = b$	–	`leastsqrs(A,b)`
matrix A augmented with vector b	–	`augment(A,b)`
row-echelon form of matrix A	–	`gausselim(A)`
back substitution (matrix R should be in row-echelon form)	–	`backsub(R)`
reduced row-echelon form of matrix A	–	`rref(A)`
LU-decomposition of matrix A	–	`LUdecomp(A,L=NameL,U=NameU)`

Elementary row operations are summarized in the next table. Each operation produces a new matrix.

math concept		command form
interchange rows i and j	–	`swaprow(A,i,j)`
multiply row i by a constant c	–	`mulrow(A,i,c)`
add a constant c times row i to row j	–	`addrow(A,i,j,c)`

C.1.4   Eigenvalues and Eigenvectors

The following table gives a few procedures that are useful for the computation of eigenvalues and eigenvectors of a square matrix.

math concept	command form
characteristic polynomial of the matrix A in the variable λ	– charpoly(A,lambda)
eigenvalues of the matrix A	– eigenvals(A)
eigenvectors of the matrix A	– eigenvects(A) (yields a list of lists of type [eigenvalue, algebraic multiplicity, {basis of the eigenspace}])

C.2   Mathematical Analysis

Maple commands for some elementary mathematical functions are listed in the table below.

math function	command form
$|x|$	– abs(x)
$\binom{n}{k}$	– binomial(n,k)
$e^x,\ \ln(x)$	– exp(x), ln(x)
$\sqrt{x}$	– sqrt(x)
$n!$	– n!
$\sin(x),\ \cos(x),\ \tan(x)$	– sin(x), cos(x), tan(x)

The evalf command can be used to convert an exact (symbolic) value like $\sqrt{2}$ into a numerical approximation. For instance, the instruction:

```
>  evalf(sqrt(2),7);
```

rounds $\sqrt{2}$ to seven significant digits.

C.2.1 Writing Your Own Procedures

There are essentially two different ways of creating functions of one or several variables: by giving a function prescription in arrow notation, or by writing a procedure.

math notation	example
$x \mapsto f(x)$	– f := x -> 2*x + 1;
	f := proc(x) 2*x + 1 end;
$(x, y, z) \mapsto g(x, y, z)$	– g := (x,y,z) -> x + y*z;
	g := proc(x,y,z) x + y*z end;

C.2.2 Plotting the Graph of a Function

Plotting the graph of a function $f(x)$, restricted to a given range, can be achieved with the `plot` command. It is possible to plot the graphs of several functions together in a single picture.

command form	example
plot(expression,range)	– plot(sin(x),x=0..Pi);
plot({expressions},range)	– plot({sin(x),cos(x)},x=0..Pi);

C.2.3 Computing Limits

The following table gives the command form for limits of functions.

math notation	command form
$\lim\limits_{x \to a} f(x)$	– limit(f(x),x=a)
$\lim\limits_{x \downarrow a} f(x)$	– limit(f(x),x=a,right)
$\lim\limits_{x \to \infty} f(x)$	– limit(f(x),x=infinity)

C.2.4   Differential Calculus

Some basic elements of differential calculus are gathered in the table below.

math concept		command form
derivative of $f(x)$	–	`D(f)(x)`
partial derivative of $g(x,y,z)$ with respect to its (second) argument y	–	`D[2](g)(x,y,z)`
gradient (vector of derivatives) of $g(x,y,z)$	–	`linalg[grad](g(x,y,z),[x,y,z])`
hessian (matrix of second order derivatives) of $g(x,y,z)$	–	`linalg[hessian](g(x,y,z),[x,y,z])`
k-th order derivative of $f(x)$	–	`(D@@k)(f)(x)`
taylor series expansion (up to order n) of $f(x)$ about the point $x = a$	–	`taylor(f(x),x=a,n)`
taylor series expansion (up to order n) of $g(x,y,z)$ about the point $(x,y,z) = (a,b,c)$	–	`mtaylor(g(x,y,z),[x=a,y=b,z=c],n)` (the function `mtaylor` is not available by default, but must be loaded with the `readlib` command)

C.2.5   Integration

Some tools for the integration of functions of a single variable that Maple offers are listed in the table below.

math concept		command form
$\int f(x)dx$ (indefinite integration)	–	`int(f(x),x)`
$\int_a^b f(x)dx$ (definite integration)	–	`int(f(x),x=a..b)`
change of variables (substitute $g(u)$ for the integration variable x)	–	`student[changevar](x=g(u),Int(f(x),x))`

math concept		command form
integration by parts ($g(x)$ is the factor of the integrand $f(x)$ to be differentiated)	–	`student[intparts](Int(f(x),x),g(x))`
partial fraction decomposition (applied to the rational function $f(x)$)	–	`convert(f(x),parfrac,x)`

C.2.6   Solving Equations

For the solution of systems of linear equations, see page 206.

There are essentially two commands for solving an equation: `solve` for the symbolic or exact solution process, and `fsolve` for its numerical counterpart.

math concept		command form
exact (or symbolic) solution of any equation $f(x) = 0$	–	`solve(f(x))`
numerical approximation of a (usually one) solution x of any equation $f(x) = 0$ in the range $[a, b]$	–	`fsolve(f(x),x=a..b)`
numerical approximation of all (complex) solutions of the polynomial equation $p(x) = 0$	–	`fsolve(p(x),x,complex)`
exact (or symbolic) solution of any equation $f(x, y) = 0$ with respect to the variable x	–	`solve(f(x,y),x)`
exact (or symbolic) solution of the system of equations $f(x, y, z) = 0$, $g(x, y, z) = 0$	–	`solve({f(x,y,z),g(x,y,z)},{x,y,z})`

C.2.7   Solving Differential/Difference Equations

The `dsolve` command can be used to solve an ordinary differential equation.

math concept	**command form**
solution to the ordinary differential equation DE with initial conditions IC	– `dsolve({DE,IC},function)`
	example
$y'' - 3y' + 2y = e^x$	– `DE := (D@@2)(y)(x)-3*D(y)(x)+ 2*y(x) = exp(x);`
$y(0) = y'(0) = 1$	`IC := y(0)=1,D(y)(0)=1; dsolve({DE,IC},y(x));`

Similarly, the `rsolve` command can be used to solve the discrete counterpart of the ordinary differential equation, the recurrence relation.

math concept	**command form**
solution to the recurrence relation RR with initial conditions IC	– `rsolve({RR,IC},function)`
	example
$y(k + 2) - y(k + 1) - y(k) = 0$ $y(0) = 0,\ y(1) = 1$	– `RR := y(k+2)-y(k+1)-y(k) = 0;` `IC := y(0)=0,y(1)=1;` `rsolve({RR,IC},y(k));`

C.3   Statistics

The subpackage `statevalf` of the `stats` package is required to get access to Maple's probability functions. This specific package is loaded with the instruction

```
> with(stats[statevalf]):
```

C.3.1   Probabilities

Use Maple's help facility (`?distributions`) to get information on the available probability distributions. Most names speak for themselves, except `fratio` which is Maple's name for the F-distribution, and `studentst` by which the t-distribution is known.

Functions available for the discrete distributions are given in the following table.

description		command form
cumulative distribution function (yields $P(X \le x)$)	–	`dcdf[distribution](x)`
inverse cumulative distribution function (yields the largest integer x for which $P(X \le x) \le y$)	–	`idcdf[distribution](y)`
probability function (yields the probability $P(X = x)$)	–	`pf[distribution](x)`

For continuous distributions Maple has the functions as listed in the next table.

description		command form
cumulative distribution function (yields $P(X \le x)$)	–	`cdf[distribution](x)`
inverse cumulative distribution function (yields x for which $P(X \le x) = y$)	–	`icdf[distribution](y)`
probability density function (yields the value of the density function at the point x)	–	`pdf[distribution](x)`

C.3.2   Generating Random Numbers

The subpackage `random` of the `stats` package is required for the generation of random numbers for various distributions. It can be loaded with the instruction

```
> with(stats[random]):
```

The function `distr(n)` then produces a sequence of n randomly distributed numbers consistent with the distribution `distr`. For instance, the Maple command

```
> normald[0,1](100);
```

generates a sequence of 100 random numbers with a standard normal distribution.

C.3.3   Analysis of Statistical Data

First we need to load the `describe` subpackage of the `stats` package with the instruction

> `with(stats[describe]):`

Below we give a list of some of the available functions with their calling convention.

math concept		command form
covariance	–	`covariance(list1,list2)`
mean	–	`mean(list)`
median	–	`median(list)`
sum of n-th powers of data in `list`	–	`sumdata(list,n)`
standard deviation	–	`standarddeviation(list)`
variance	–	`variance(list)`

C.4   Linear Programming

Maple's LP functions are gathered in the `simplex` package that can be loaded in the usual way by

> `with(simplex):`

This package contains procedures for solving LP problems using the simplex method. Some important functions are given below.

description		command form
maximizes the objective function `obj`, subject to the constraints `constr` (the parameter `ranges` restricts the variables)	–	`maximize(obj,constr,ranges)`
minimizes the objective function `obj`, subject to the constraints `constr` (the parameter `ranges` restricts the variables)	–	`minimize(obj,constr,ranges)`

description		command form
the dual of an LP problem (the third argument y is used to tell Maple which name the dual variables should have)	–	`dual(obj,constr,y)`

math concept		example

maximize $8x_1 + 6x_2 + 10x_3$
 subject to $3x_1 + x_2 + 3x_3 \leq 30$
 $2x_1 + 2x_2 + 3x_3 \leq 40$
 $x_1, x_2, x_3 \geq 0$
	–	`with(simplex):`
		 `obj := 8*x1+6*x2+10*x3;`
		 `constr := {3*x1+x2+3*x3<=30,`
		 `2*x1+2*x2+3*x3 <= 40};`
		 `x_values := maximize(obj,`
		 `constr,NONNEGATIVE);`

The `maximize` procedure of the example in the preceding table yields the optimal x-values: $x_1 = 5$, $x_2 = 15$, $x_3 = 0$. In case of an infeasible problem, Maple returns empty braces {}, and for unbounded problems Maple does not give any output. The `subs` procedure can be used to determine the optimal objective value (here 130) by substituting the optimal x-values into the objective function, as in

> `obj_value := subs(x_values,obj);`

C.5   Mathematical Finance

Maple's `finance` package contains procedures for computing the value of a call option and for computing net present values. After the instruction

> `with(finance):`

these and all other procedures contained in this package are immediately available.

The value of a European call option can be computed using the Black-Scholes formula. The Maple instruction is

> `evalf(blackscholes(S,X,r,T,sigma));`

The next table lists the arguments of this Black-Scholes formula with a brief description for each.

description

B-S argument

(see `blackscholes` on page 214)

description		B-S argument
current stock price	–	`S`
exercise price of the call option	–	`X`
risk-free interest rate per period (continuously compounded)	–	`r`
number of periods	–	`T`
standard deviation per period of the continuous return on the stock	–	`sigma`

Some functions for computing the net present value (NPV) of financial assets (when the interest rate is `r`) are listed in the table below.

description

command form

description		command form
NPV of an annuity which yields the fixed cash flow `CF` for `T` periods	–	`annuity(CF,r,T)`
NPV of a growing perpetuity with growth rate `g` which pays the cash flow `CF1` after one period	–	`growingperpetuity(CF1,r,g)`
NPV of a level coupon bond with face value `face`, coupon rate `cr` and maturity after `T` periods	–	`levelcoupon(face,r,cr,T)`
NPV of a perpetuity which pays a fixed cash flow `CF` forever	–	`perpetuity(CF,r)`

Bibliography

[1] Nancy R. Blachman and Michael J. Mossinghoff, *Maple© V Quick Reference*. Brooks/Cole Publ. Co., Pacific Grove CA, 1994.

[2] Bruce W. Char et al, *First Leaves: A Tutorial Introduction to Maple V*. Springer-Verlag, New York etc., 1992.

[3] Bruce W. Char et al, *Maple V Language Reference Manual*. Springer-Verlag, New York etc., 1991.

[4] Bruce W. Char et al, *Maple V Library Reference Manual*. Springer-Verlag, New York etc., 1991.

[5] A.M. Cohen, H. Cuypers and H. Sterk (eds.), *Some Tapas of Computer Algebra*. Springer-Verlag, Berlin-Heidelberg, 1998.

[6] Robert M. Corless, *Essential Maple™, An Introduction for Scientific Programmers*. Springer-Verlag, New York etc., 1995.

[7] Arthur Engel, *Exploring Mathematics with your Computer*. Math. Ass. of America, New Math. Library **35**, 1993.

[8] Walter Gander and Jiří Hřebíček, *Solving Problems in Scientific Computing Using Maple and MATLAB*. Springer-Verlag, Berlin-Heidelberg, third ed. 1997 (first ed. 1993, second ed. 1995).

[9] Ronald L. Graham, Donald E. Knuth and Oren Patashnik, *Concrete Mathematics*. Addison-Wesley Publ. Co., Reading, 1989.

[10] K.M. Heal, M.L. Hansen, and K.M. Rickard, *Maple V, Learning Guide*. Waterloo Maple Inc., Springer-Verlag, New York etc., 1996.

[11] André Heck, *Introduction to Maple*. Springer-Verlag, New York etc., second ed. 1996 (first ed. 1993).

[12] Eugene Johnson, *Linear Algebra with Maple V*. Brooks/Cole Publ. Co., Pacific Grove CA, 1993.

[13] Donald E. Knuth, *The Art of Computer programming Vol. 2: Seminumerical Algorithms.* Addison-Wesley Publ. Co., Reading, third ed. 1998 (first ed. 1969, second ed. 1981).

[14] Michael Kofler, *Maple. An Introduction and Reference.* Addison-Wesley Longman Ltd., Harlow, 1997.

[15] M.B. Monagan, K.O. Geddes, G. Labahn, and S. Vorkoetter, *Maple V, Programming Guide.* Waterloo Maple Inc., Springer-Verlag, New York etc., 1996.

[16] Darren Redfern, *Maple™ Handbook, Maple V Release 4.* Springer-Verlag, New-York etc., 1996.

[17] R.J. Stroeker, Improvement of Nakamula's Upper Bound for the Absolute Discriminant of a Sextic Number Field with Two Real Conjugates. *Math. Comp.* **59** (1992), p. 203–211.

[18] Martin Streng, Stephan van Gils, Adri van der Meer, *Maple, Wiskunde in berekenbaar perspectief* (Dutch). Addison-Wesley Longman Nederland BV, Amsterdam, second ed. 1998 (first ed. 1994).

Index